W9-BXL-478

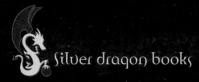

Silver dragon books

Top 10 Deadliest Sharks, December 2010. First Printing. Published by Silver Dragon Books, Inc., 501 Office Center Drive, Ste. 8, Fort Washington, Pennsylvania 19034. Silver Dragon Books and its logos are ® and © 2010 Silver Dragon Books, Inc. All Rights Reserved.

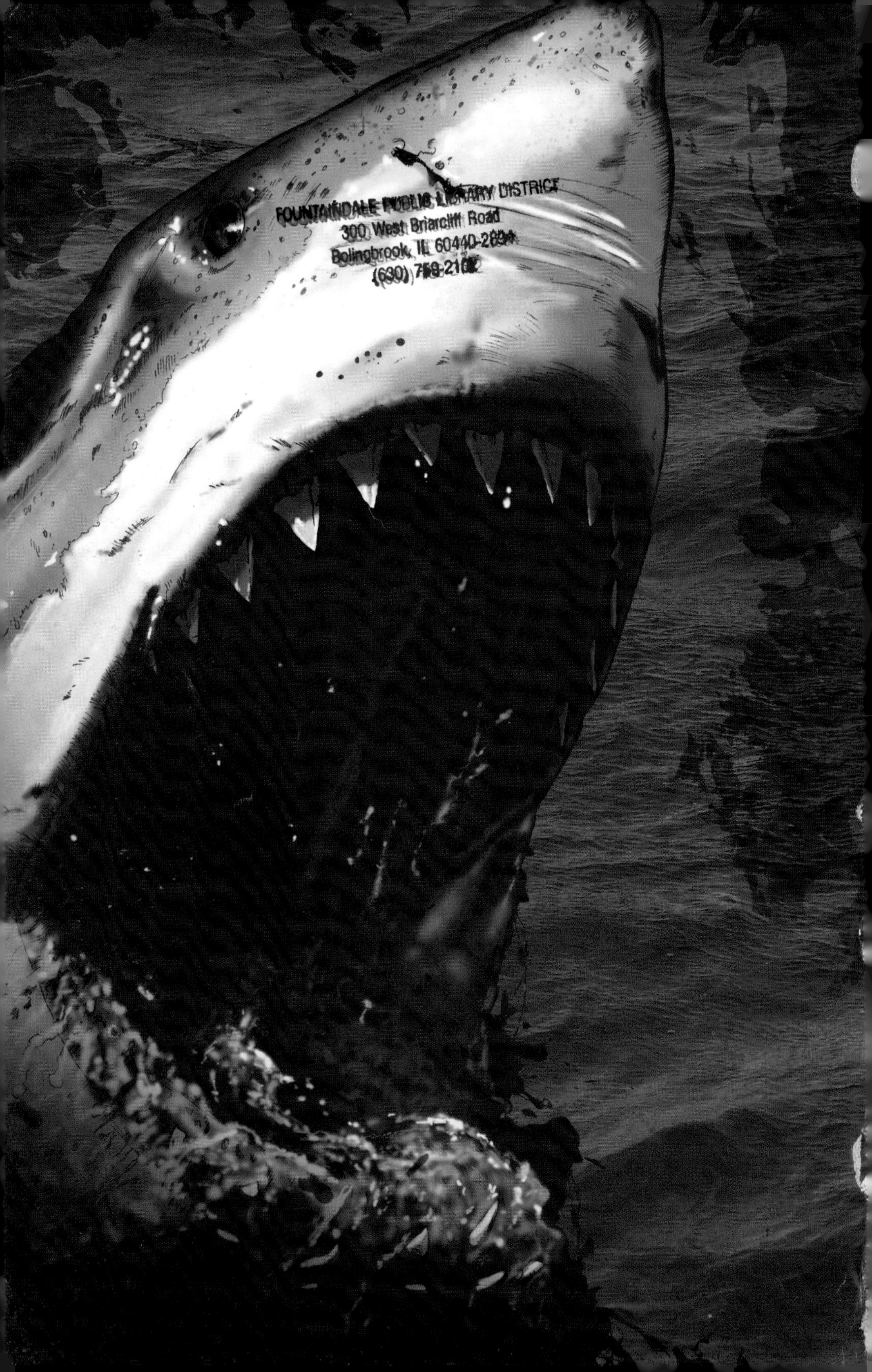

WRITTEN BY
JOE BRUSHA

ARTWORK BY
ANTHONY SPAY
SHAWN MCCAULEY
MARCIO ABREU
AGUSTIN ALESSIO
GERMAN NOBILE
HG YOUNG
GABRIEL REARTE
SHAWN VAN BRIESEN

COLORS BY
ANDREW ELDER
JOHN HUNT

LETTERS BY
JIM CAMPBELL

PRODUCTION AND DESIGN BY
DAVID SEIDMAN
CHRISTOPHER COTE

PUBLISHER
JOE BRUSHA

MANAGING EDITOR
JENNIFER BERMEL

CONTRIBUTING EDITOR
ANDY DEHART

EDITORIAL ASSISTANT
RALPH TEDESCO

SPECIAL THANKS TO THE TEAM AT DISCOVERY
GRANT MCALLISTER, SARA SHAFFER
BETSY FERG, HEIDI SCHADLER
AND ELIZABETH BAKACS

PUBLISHED BY
SILVER DRAGON BOOKS
501 OFFICE CENTER DRIVE, STE. 8
FORT WASHINGTON, PA 19034
WWW.SILVERDRAGONBOOKS.COM

FIRST PRINTING
ISBN: 978-0-9827507-2-8

Discovery CHANNEL

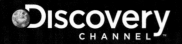

TOP 10 DEADLIEST

SHARKS

INTRODUCTION
BY ANDY DEHART

I have been fascinated by sharks since my first time swimming with them at the age of 5. I turned that fascination into a career, having worked with sharks for the last 20 years.

Sharks have always been a part of mankind's fear of the ocean. Over millions of years sharks have evolved into perfect predators. On very rare occasions humans have been bitten by these top predators, sometimes with tragic results. Coupled with the ocean not being our natural element this has heightened human fears about sharks.

Through my work at public aquariums and in shows for Discovery Channel's Shark Week, I have had numerous face to face encounters with many species of sharks, including some of the sharks known to be most dangerous. Through all of these experiences, one thing is clear: sharks are not the mindless eating machines they are often portrayed as.

There are over 400 species of sharks and not a single one has humans as part of its diet. Less than 100 attacks happen worldwide each year, and many of these are cases of mistaken identity. Each shark species has very specialized prey items.

And sharks are certainly not mindless. In fact, they are far smarter than most people realize. In the aquarium setting, we have trained sharks to do fairly complex behaviors. In fact, being able to work with the same sharks year after year and learning about their unique behaviors has been the best part of my career.

Unfortunately, sharks do have a good reason to fear humans. Not all species of sharks are threatened with extinction, but many of the larger sharks are, due to people fishing them for their fins to be used in shark fin soup. Sharks also often end up as bycatch, caught unintentionally by those intending to catch other fish.

It is not too late for the sharks, but it will take all of us working together to save them.

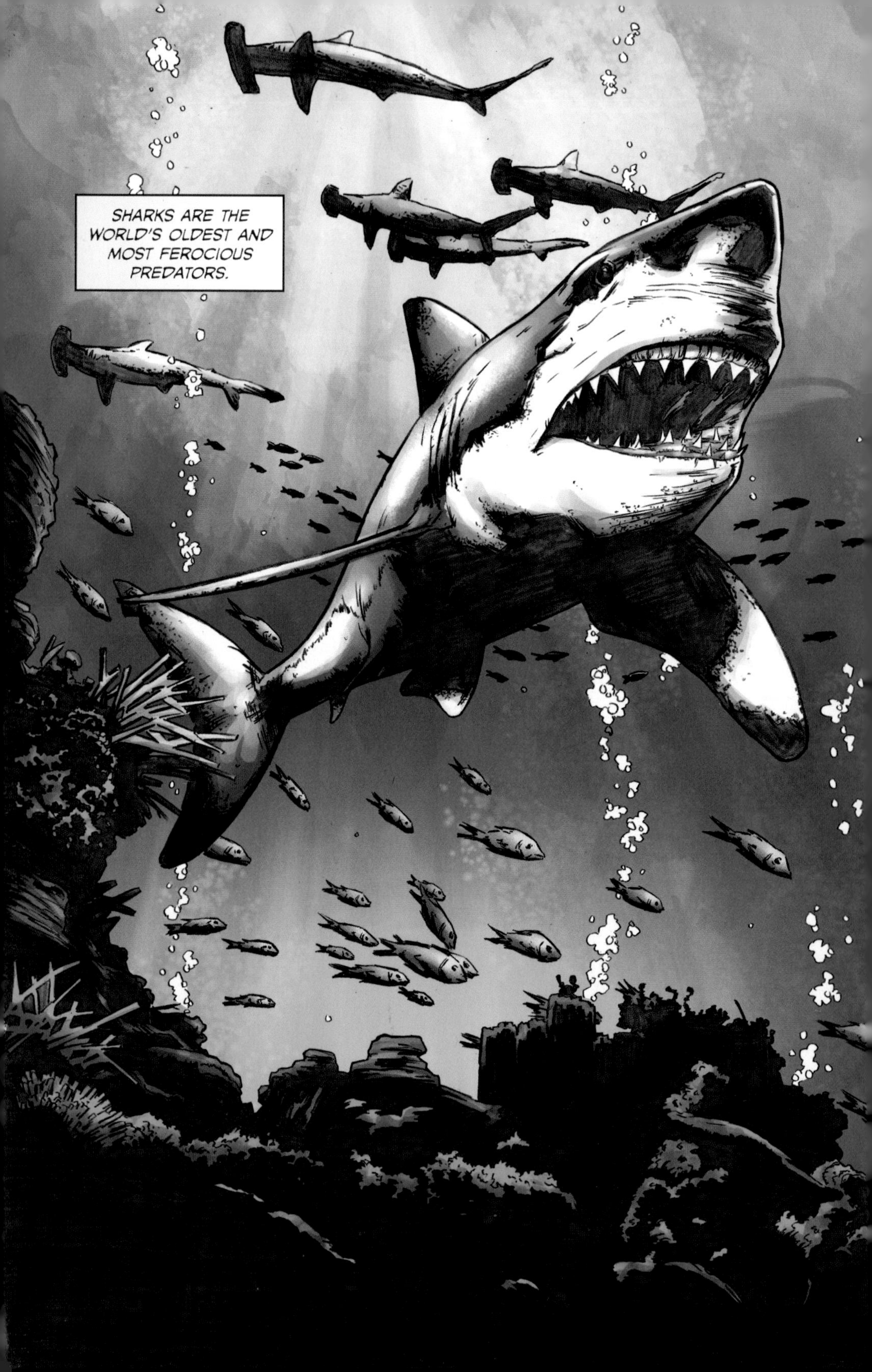
SHARKS ARE THE WORLD'S OLDEST AND MOST FEROCIOUS PREDATORS.

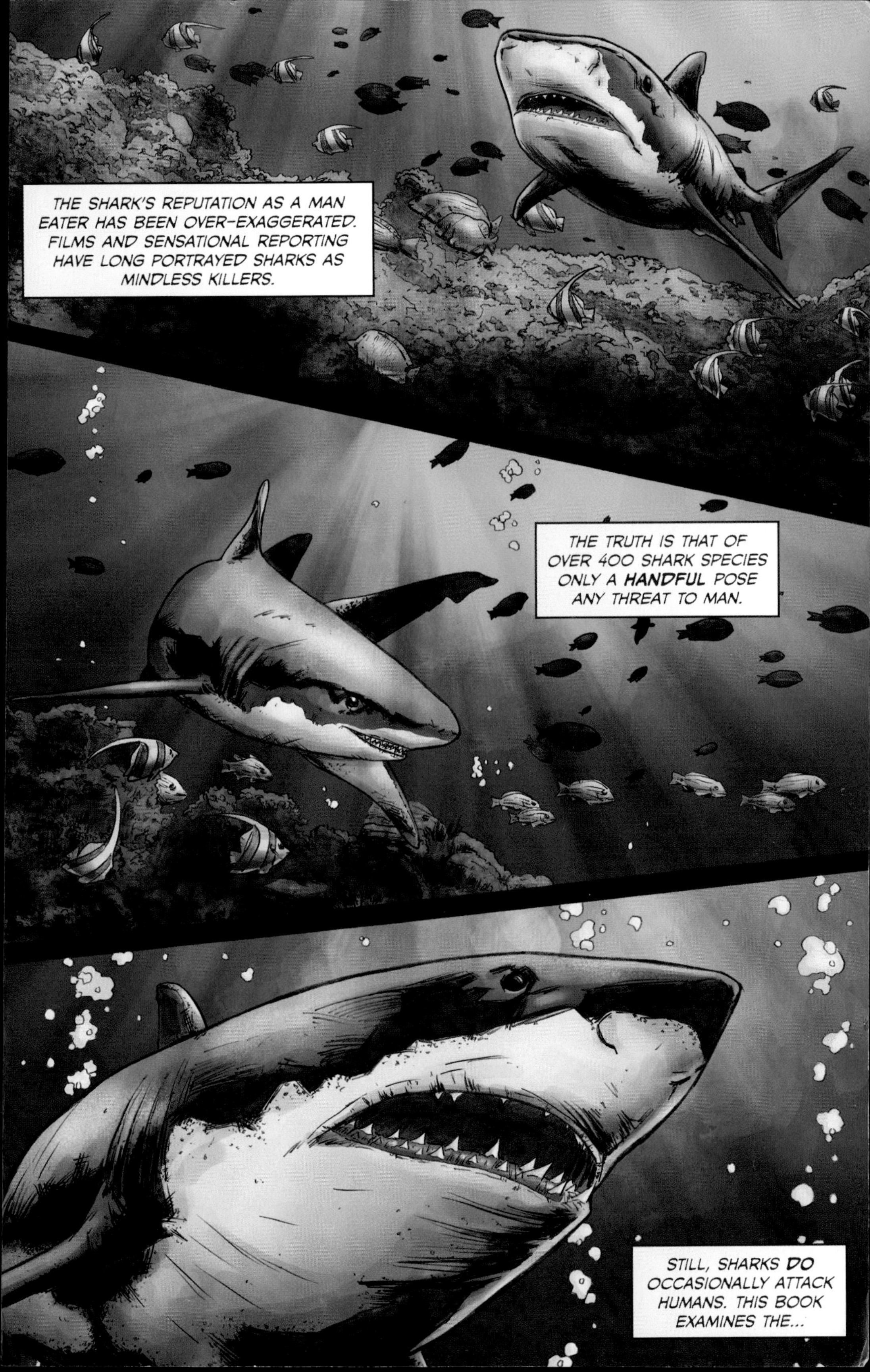
THE SHARK'S REPUTATION AS A MAN EATER HAS BEEN OVER-EXAGGERATED. FILMS AND SENSATIONAL REPORTING HAVE LONG PORTRAYED SHARKS AS MINDLESS KILLERS.
THE TRUTH IS THAT OF OVER 400 SHARK SPECIES ONLY A HANDFUL POSE ANY THREAT TO MAN.
STILL, SHARKS DO OCCASIONALLY ATTACK HUMANS. THIS BOOK EXAMINES THE...

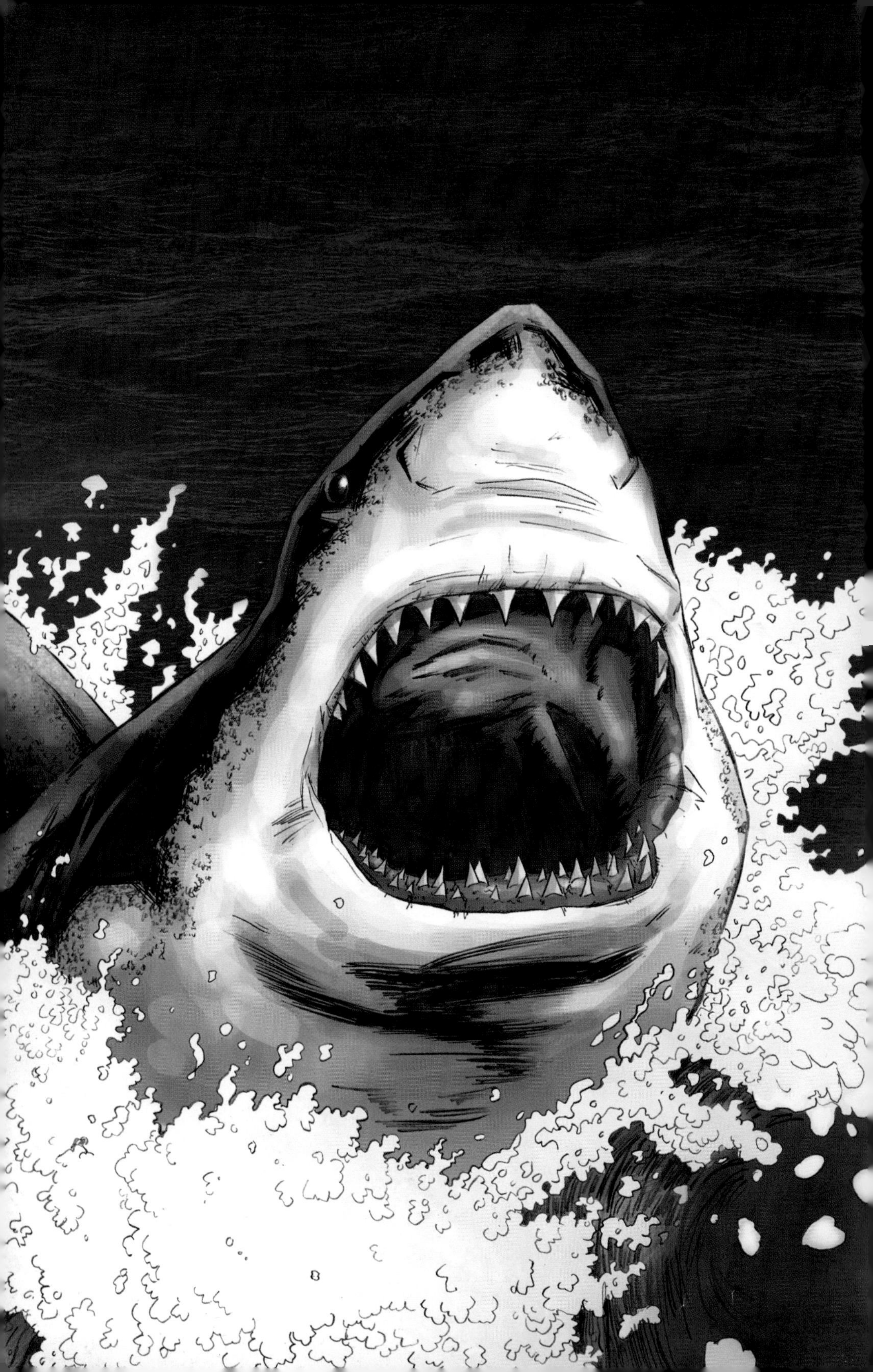

TOP 10 DEADLIEST SHARKS

#10 THE LEMON SHARK

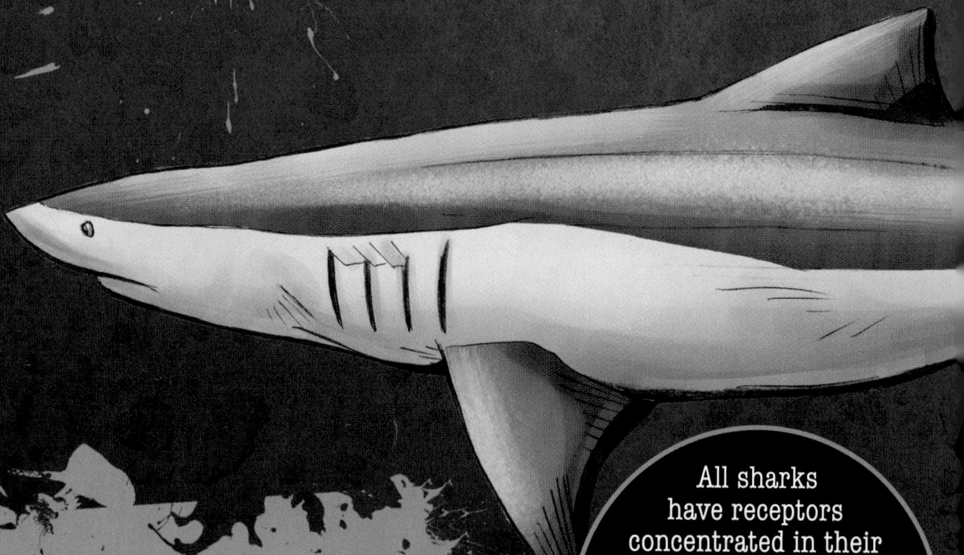

All sharks have receptors concentrated in their head that detect electrical pulses emitted by other animals. These sensors are called the ampulla of Lorenzini and they help sharks find their prey.

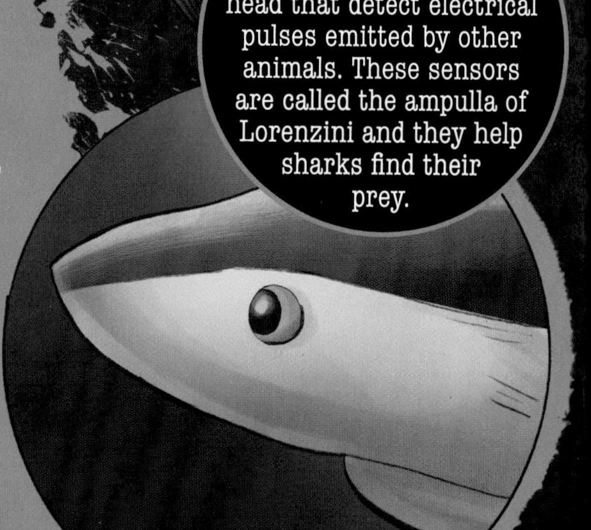

LEMON SHARK FACTS:

Average Size: 8-10 feet

Largest Recorded: 11.8 feet

Habitat: Shallow Coastal Waters

Preferred Prey: Small fish, crabs, stingrays and occasionally sea birds.

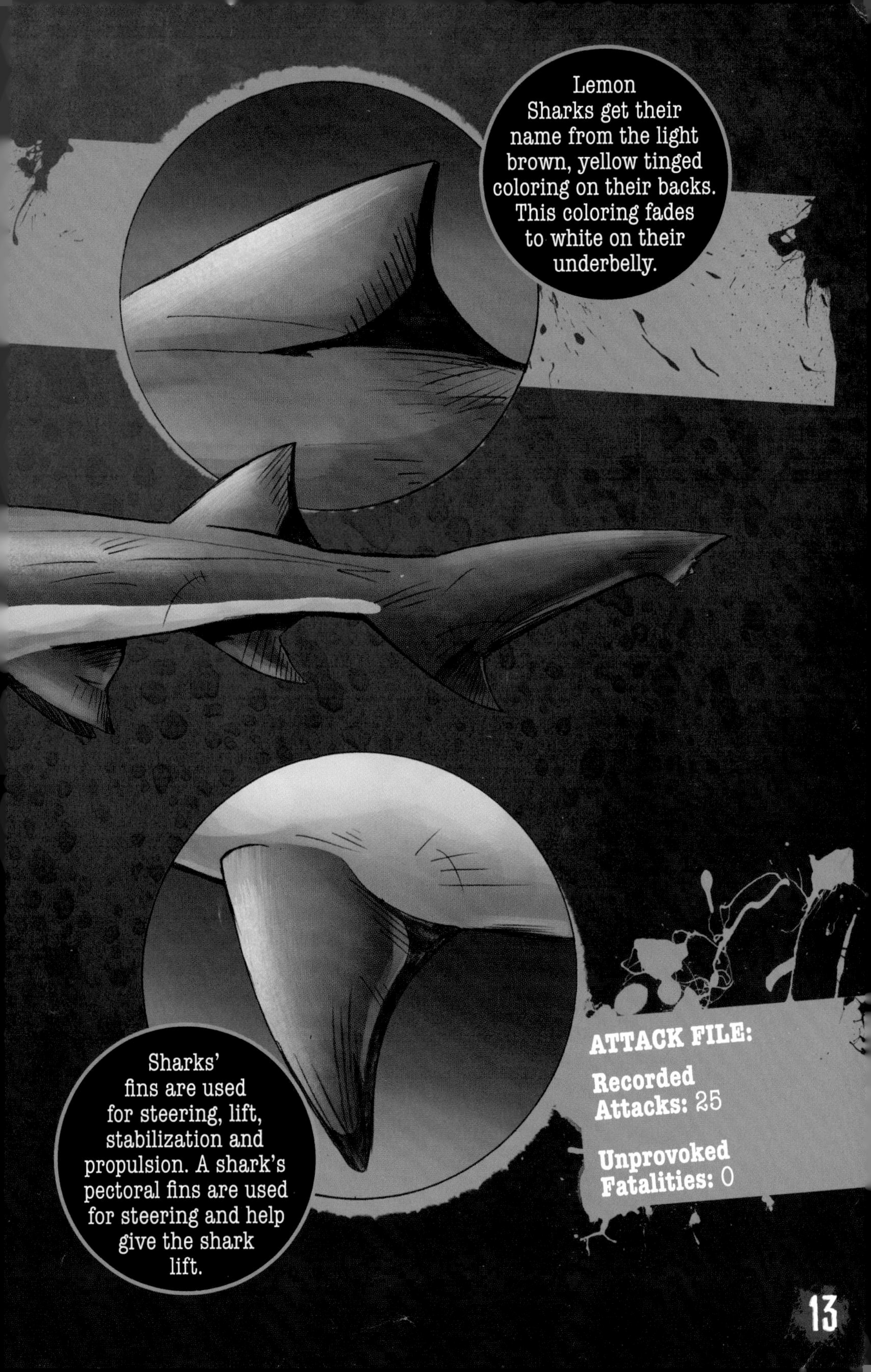

Lemon Sharks get their name from the light brown, yellow tinged coloring on their backs. This coloring fades to white on their underbelly.

Sharks' fins are used for steering, lift, stabilization and propulsion. A shark's pectoral fins are used for steering and help give the shark lift.

ATTACK FILE:

Recorded Attacks: 25

Unprovoked Fatalities: 0

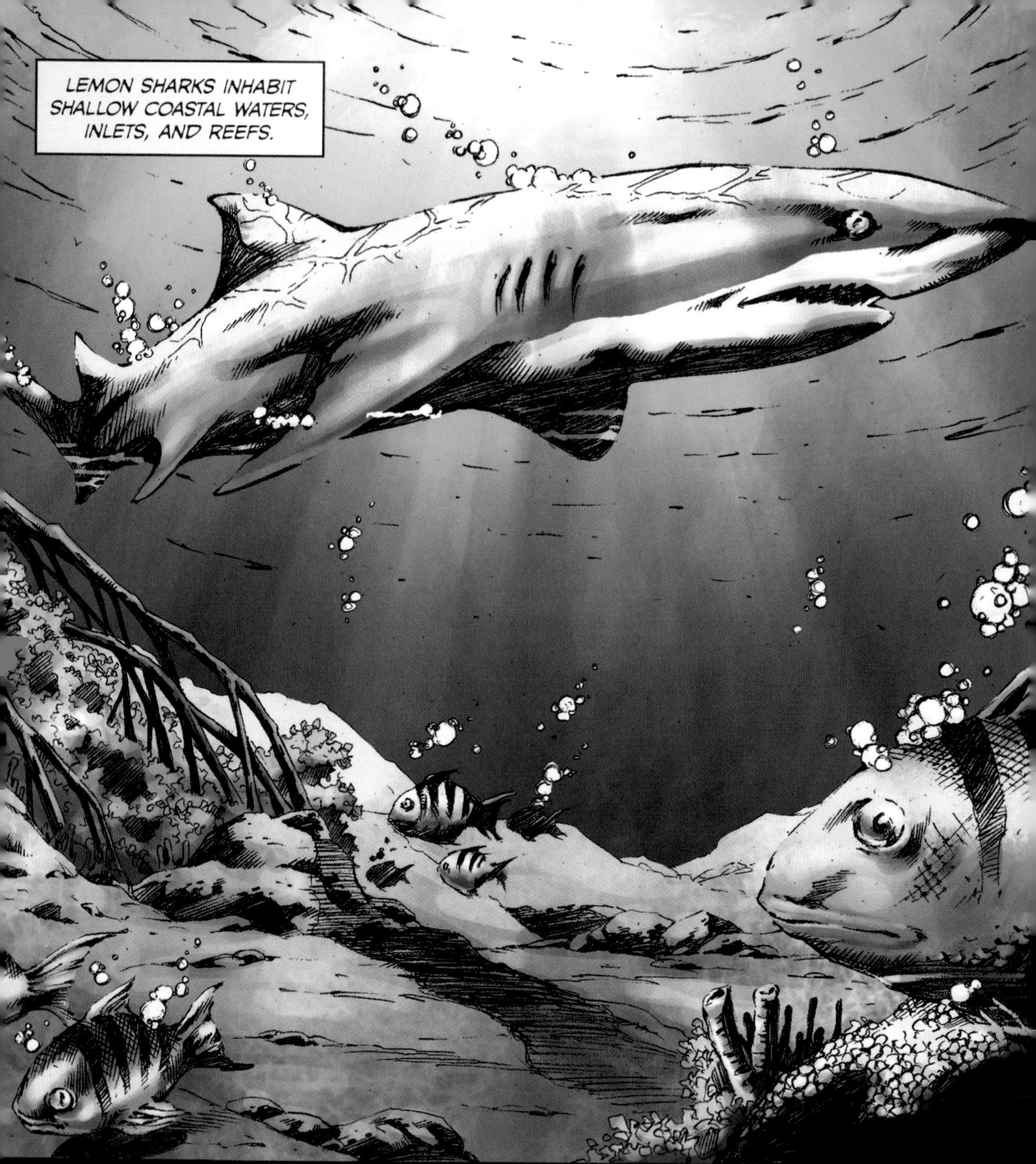
LEMON SHARKS INHABIT SHALLOW COASTAL WATERS, INLETS, AND REEFS.

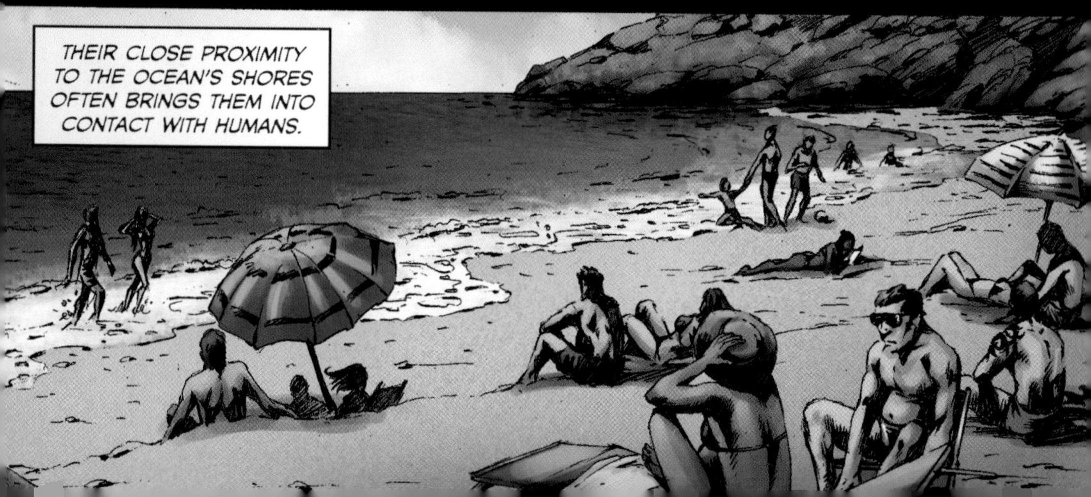
THEIR CLOSE PROXIMITY TO THE OCEAN'S SHORES OFTEN BRINGS THEM INTO CONTACT WITH HUMANS.

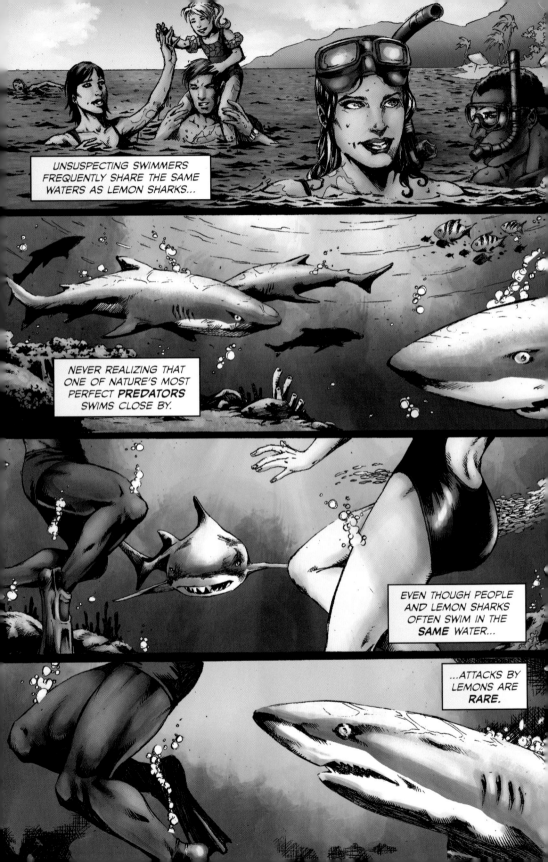

UNSUSPECTING SWIMMERS FREQUENTLY SHARE THE SAME WATERS AS LEMON SHARKS...

NEVER REALIZING THAT ONE OF NATURE'S MOST **PREDATORS** SWIMS CLOSE BY.

EVEN THOUGH PEOPLE AND LEMON SHARKS OFTEN SWIM IN THE **SAME** WATER...

...ATTACKS BY LEMONS ARE **RARE.**

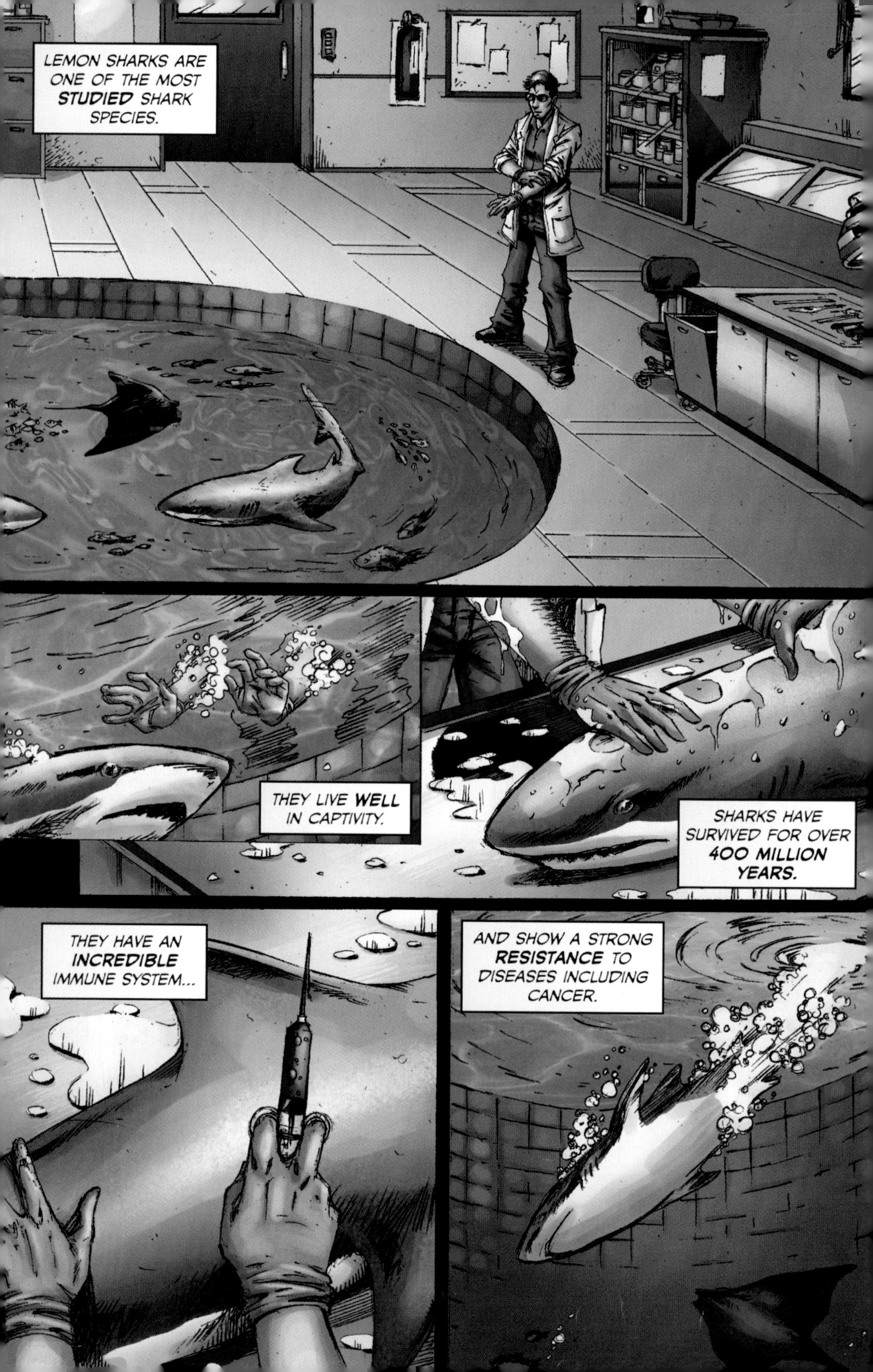
LEMON SHARKS ARE ONE OF THE MOST **STUDIED** SHARK SPECIES.
THEY LIVE **WELL** IN CAPTIVITY.
SHARKS HAVE SURVIVED FOR OVER **400 MILLION YEARS.**
THEY HAVE AN **INCREDIBLE** IMMUNE SYSTEM...
AND SHOW A STRONG **RESISTANCE** TO DISEASES INCLUDING CANCER.

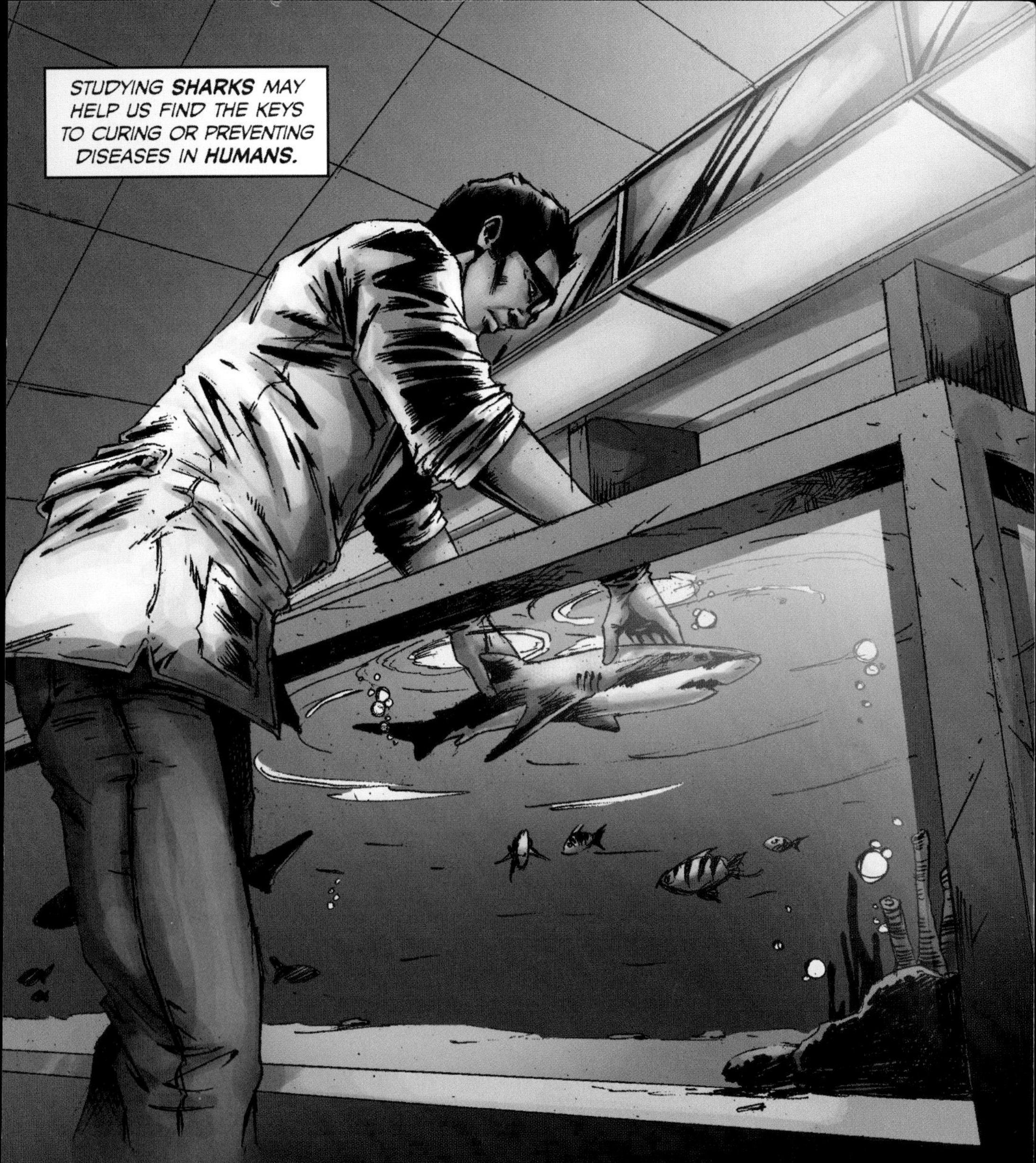
STUDYING **SHARKS** MAY HELP US FIND THE KEYS TO CURING OR PREVENTING DISEASES IN **HUMANS.**

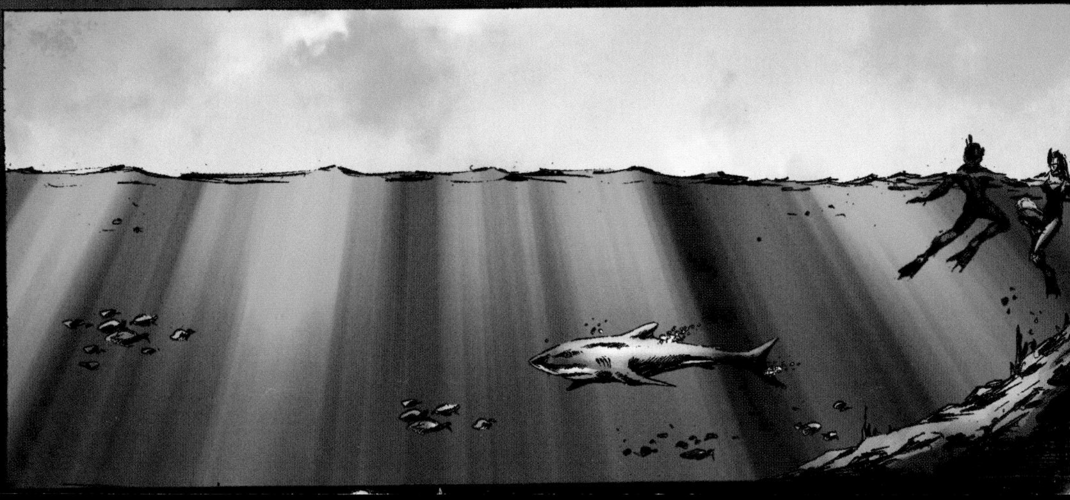

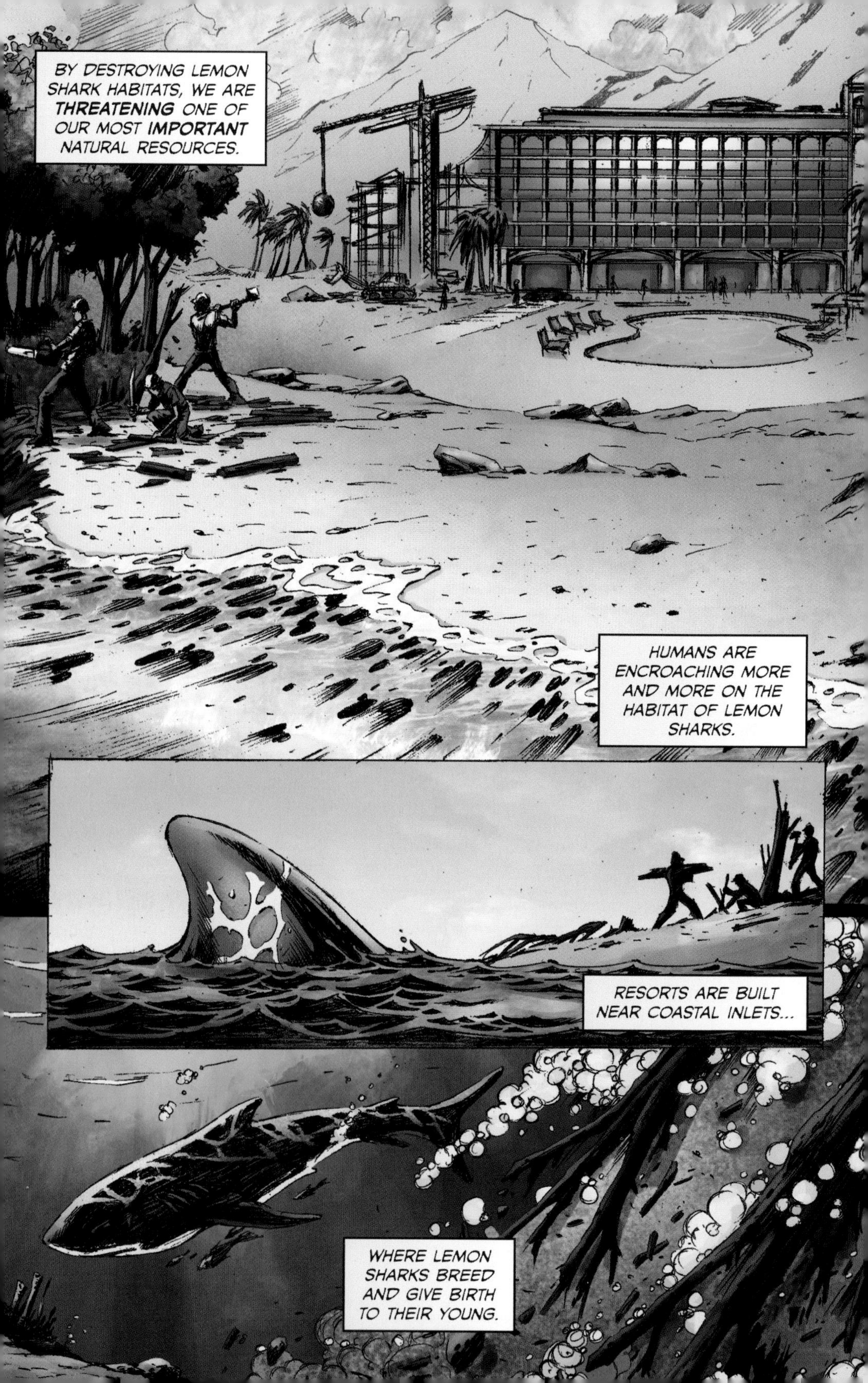
BY DESTROYING LEMON SHARK HABITATS, WE ARE **THREATENING** ONE OF OUR MOST **IMPORTANT** NATURAL RESOURCES.
HUMANS ARE ENCROACHING MORE AND MORE ON THE HABITAT OF LEMON SHARKS.
RESORTS ARE BUILT NEAR COASTAL INLETS...
WHERE LEMON SHARKS BREED AND GIVE BIRTH TO THEIR YOUNG.

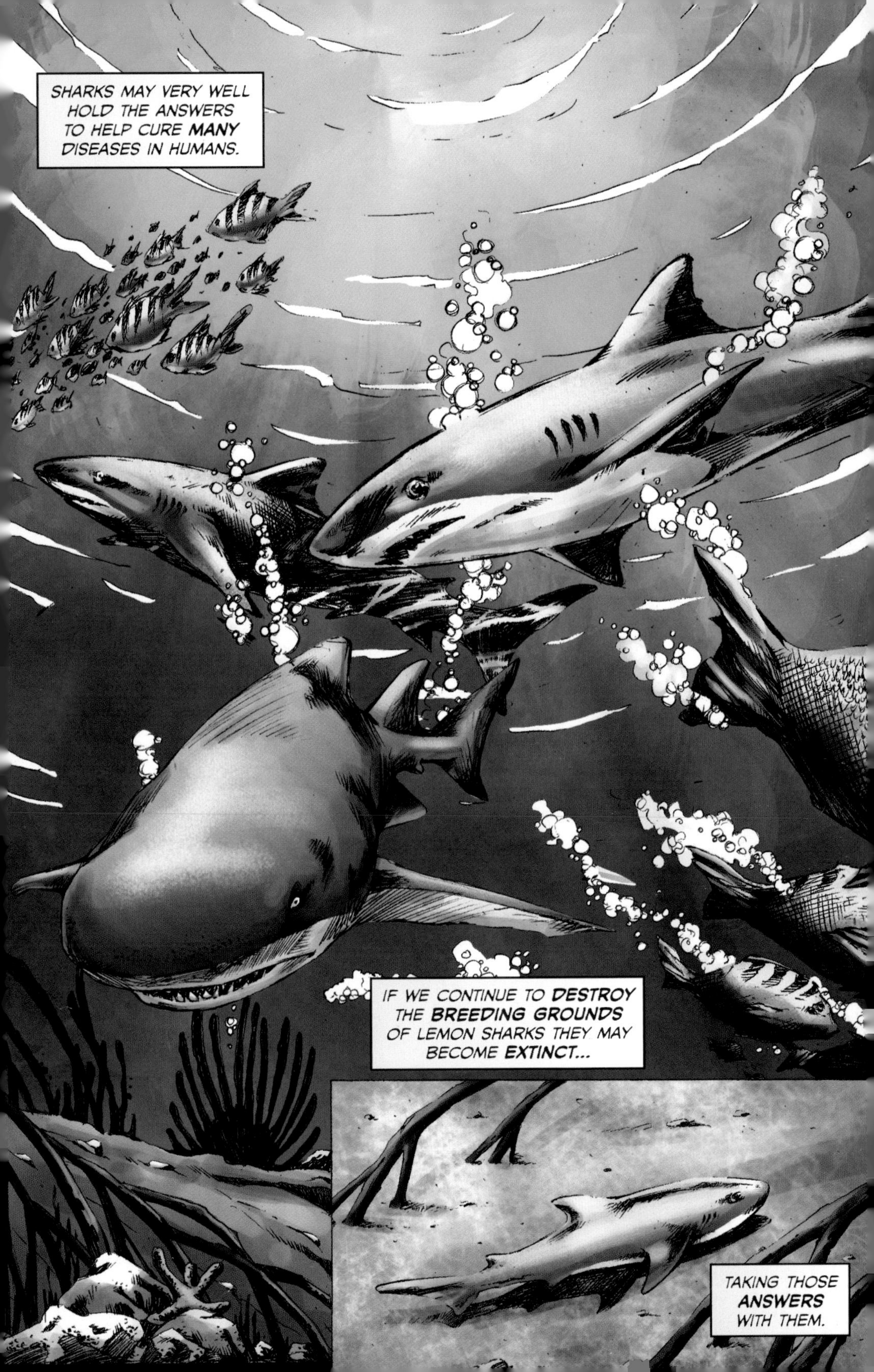
SHARKS MAY VERY WELL HOLD THE ANSWERS TO HELP CURE MANY DISEASES IN HUMANS.
IF WE CONTINUE TO DESTROY THE BREEDING GROUNDS OF LEMON SHARKS THEY MAY BECOME EXTINCT...
TAKING THOSE ANSWERS WITH THEM.

#9 THE BLUE SHARK

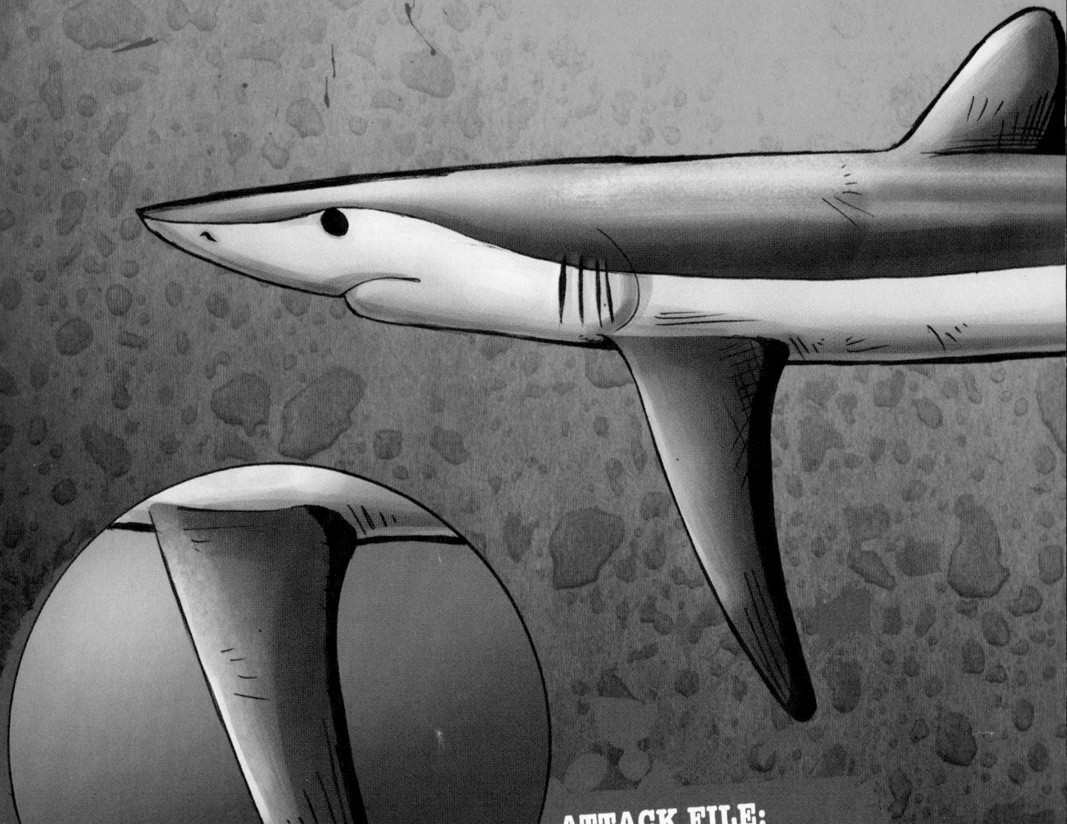

ATTACK FILE:

Recorded Attacks: 37

Unprovoked Fatalities: 4

Blue Sharks have extremely long, pointed pectoral fins. The shape and length enhances the sharks' ability to smoothly and quickly swim through the water.

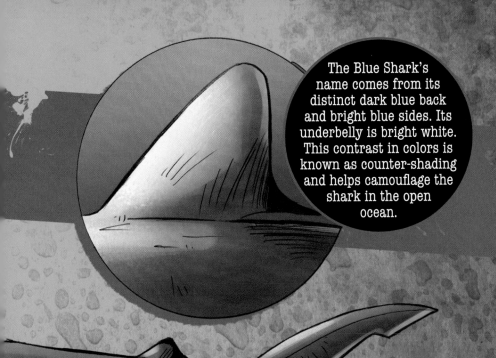

The Blue Shark's name comes from its distinct dark blue back and bright blue sides. Its underbelly is bright white. This contrast in colors is known as counter-shading and helps camouflage the shark in the open ocean.

The Blue Shark is one of the fastest swimming sharks and is known to jump out of the water. The elongated tail fin, called the caudal fin, provides plenty of power to propel the Blue Shark's torpedo shaped body.

BLUE SHARK FACTS:

Average Size: 12.6 feet

Largest Recorded: 13 feet

Habitat: Open ocean areas from the surface to 1,148 feet in depth. They prefer cooler water and rarely come near shore.

Preferred Prey: Herring, mackerel, cod, sardines and squid.

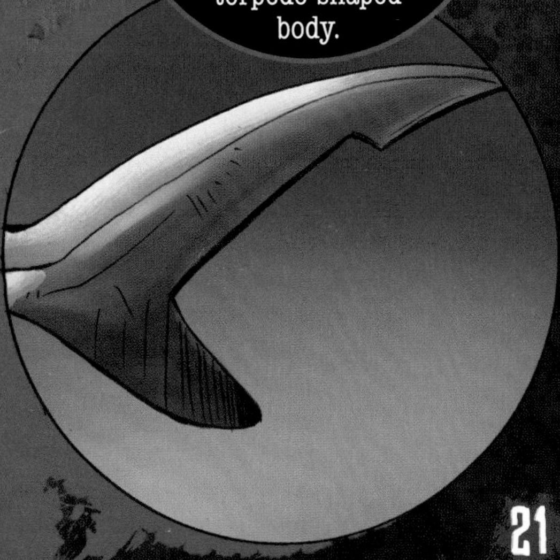

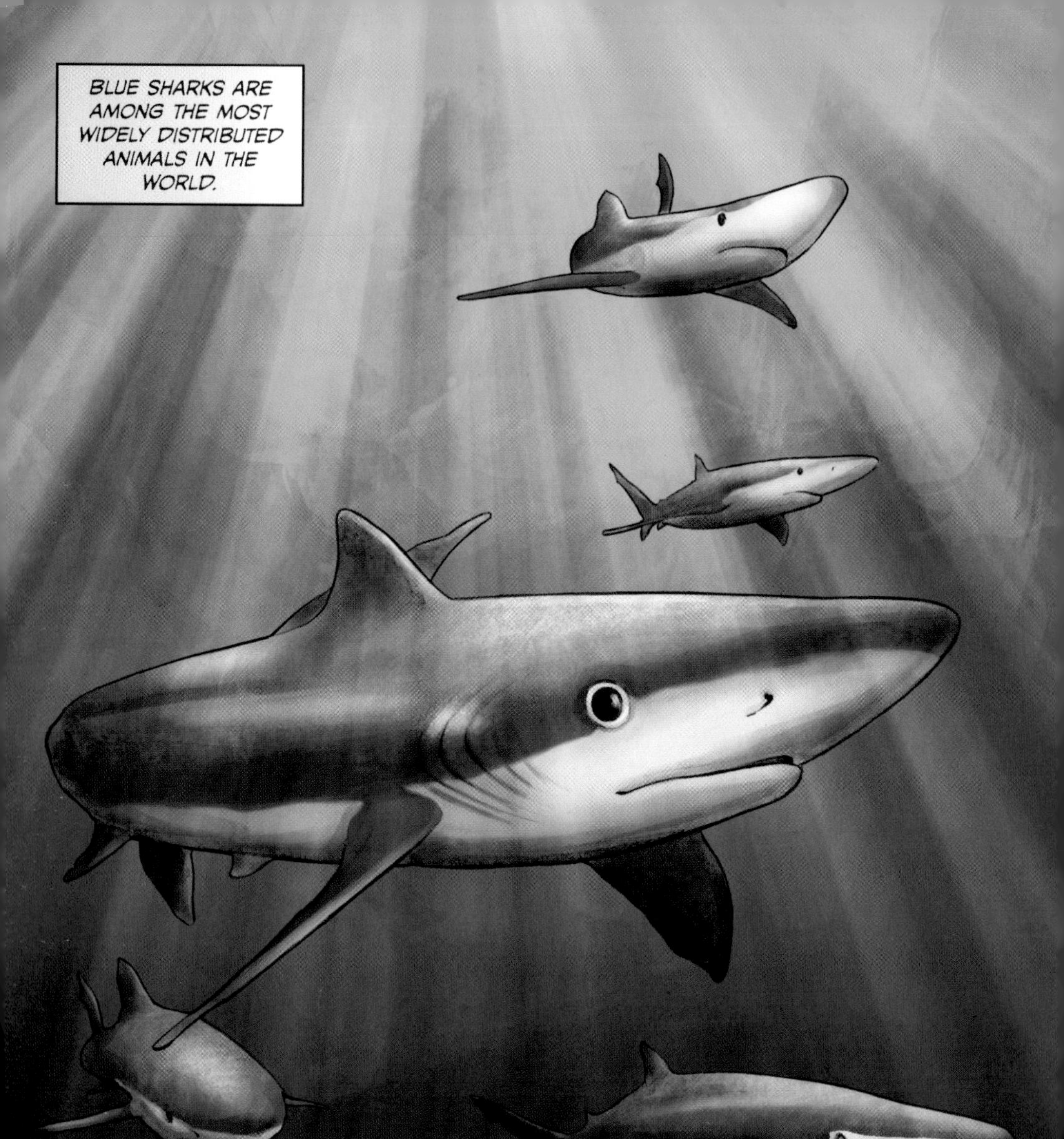
BLUE SHARKS ARE AMONG THE MOST WIDELY DISTRIBUTED ANIMALS IN THE WORLD.
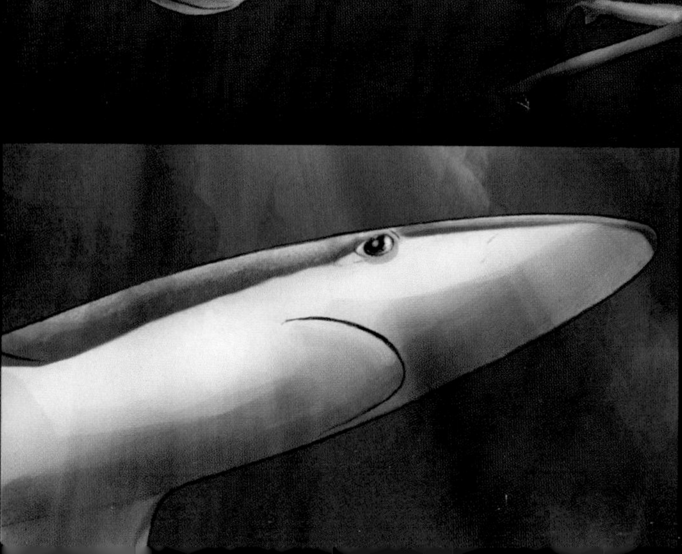

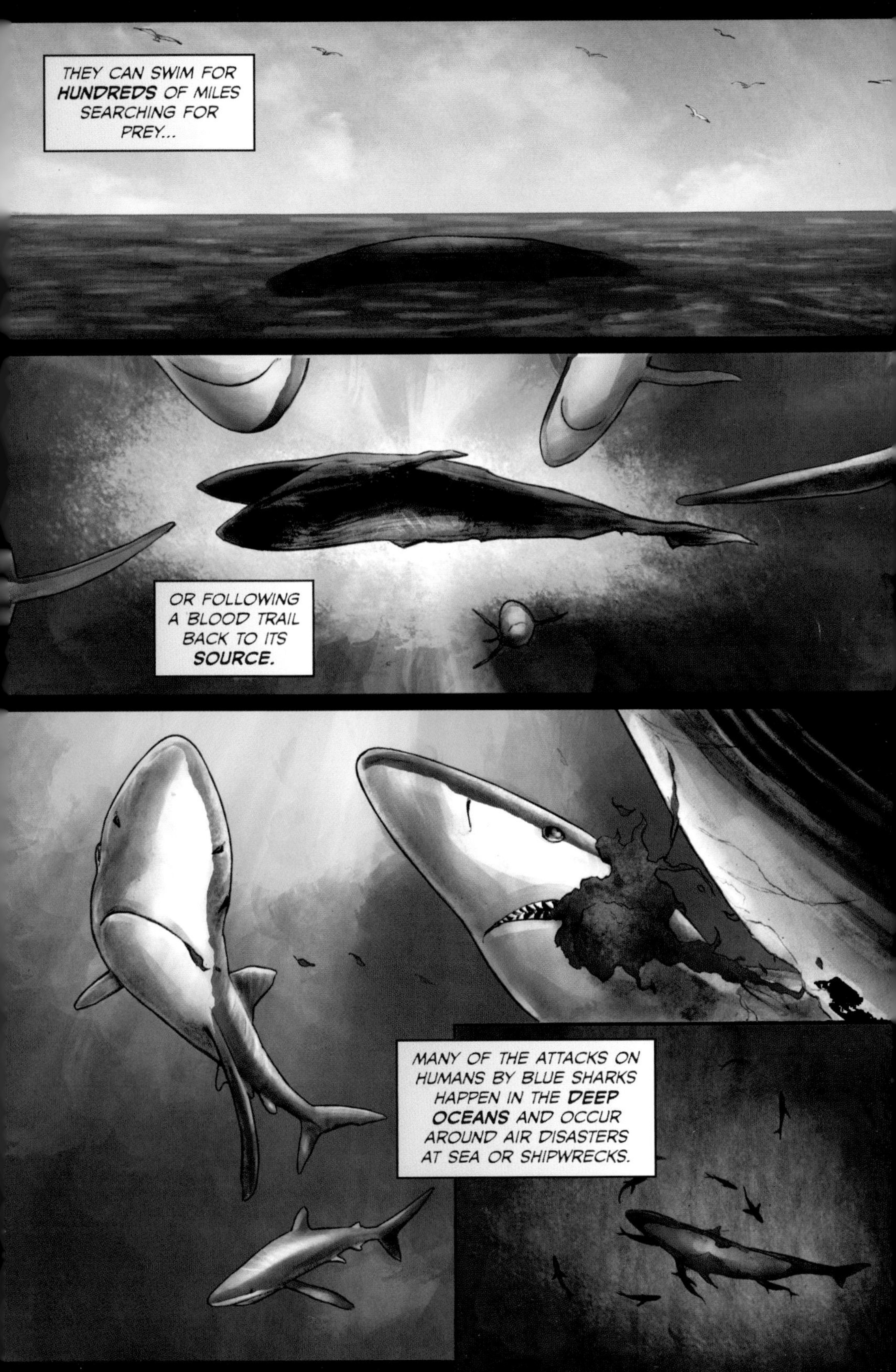
THEY CAN SWIM FOR HUNDREDS OF MILES SEARCHING FOR PREY...
OR FOLLOWING A BLOOD TRAIL BACK TO ITS SOURCE.
MANY OF THE ATTACKS ON HUMANS BY BLUE SHARKS HAPPEN IN THE DEEP OCEANS AND OCCUR AROUND AIR DISASTERS AT SEA OR SHIPWRECKS.

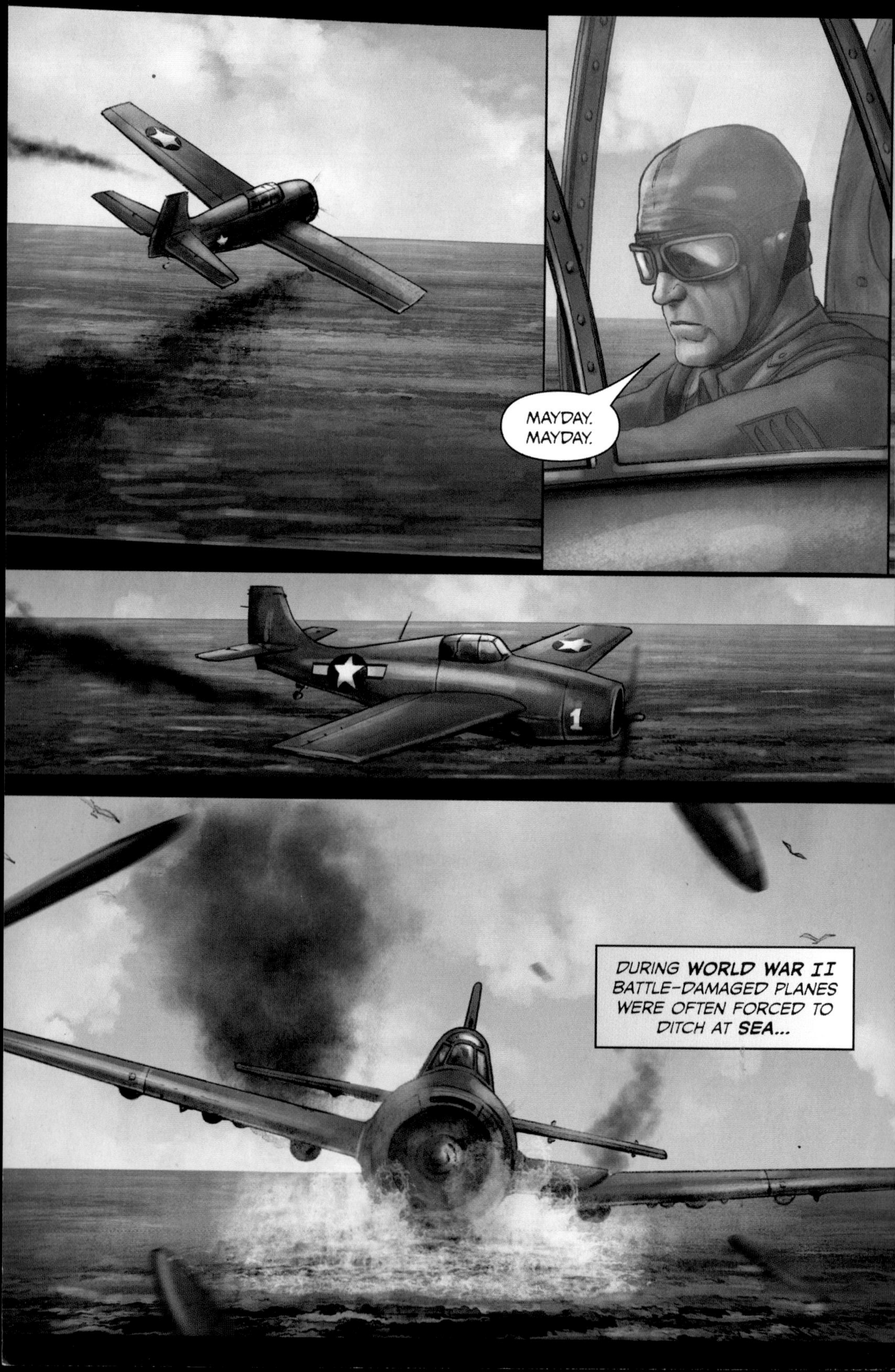
MAYDAY.
MAYDAY.
DURING WORLD WAR II BATTLE-DAMAGED PLANES WERE OFTEN FORCED TO DITCH AT SEA...

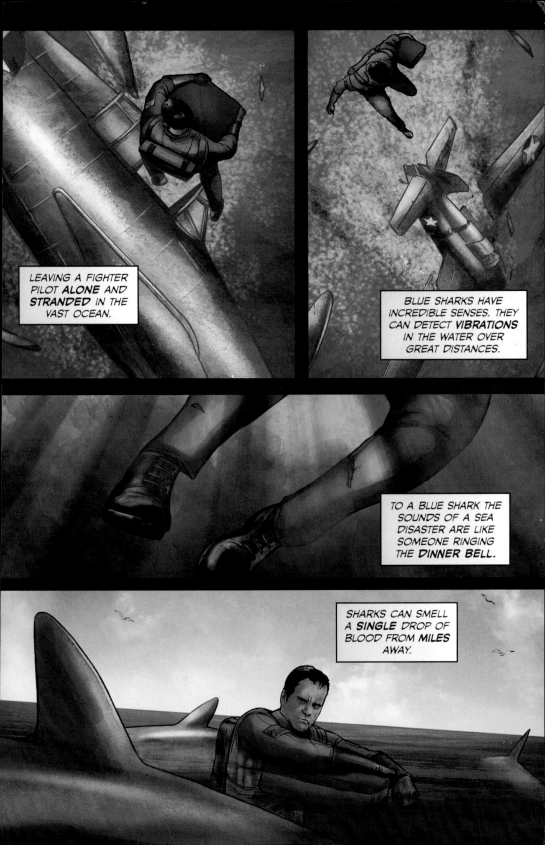

LEAVING A FIGHTER PILOT **ALONE** AND **STRANDED** IN THE VAST OCEAN.

BLUE SHARKS HAVE INCREDIBLE SENSES. THEY CAN DETECT **VIBRATIONS** IN THE WATER OVER GREAT DISTANCES.

TO A BLUE SHARK THE SOUNDS OF A SEA DISASTER ARE LIKE SOMEONE RINGING THE **DINNER BELL**.

SHARKS CAN SMELL A **SINGLE** DROP OF BLOOD FROM **MILES** AWAY.

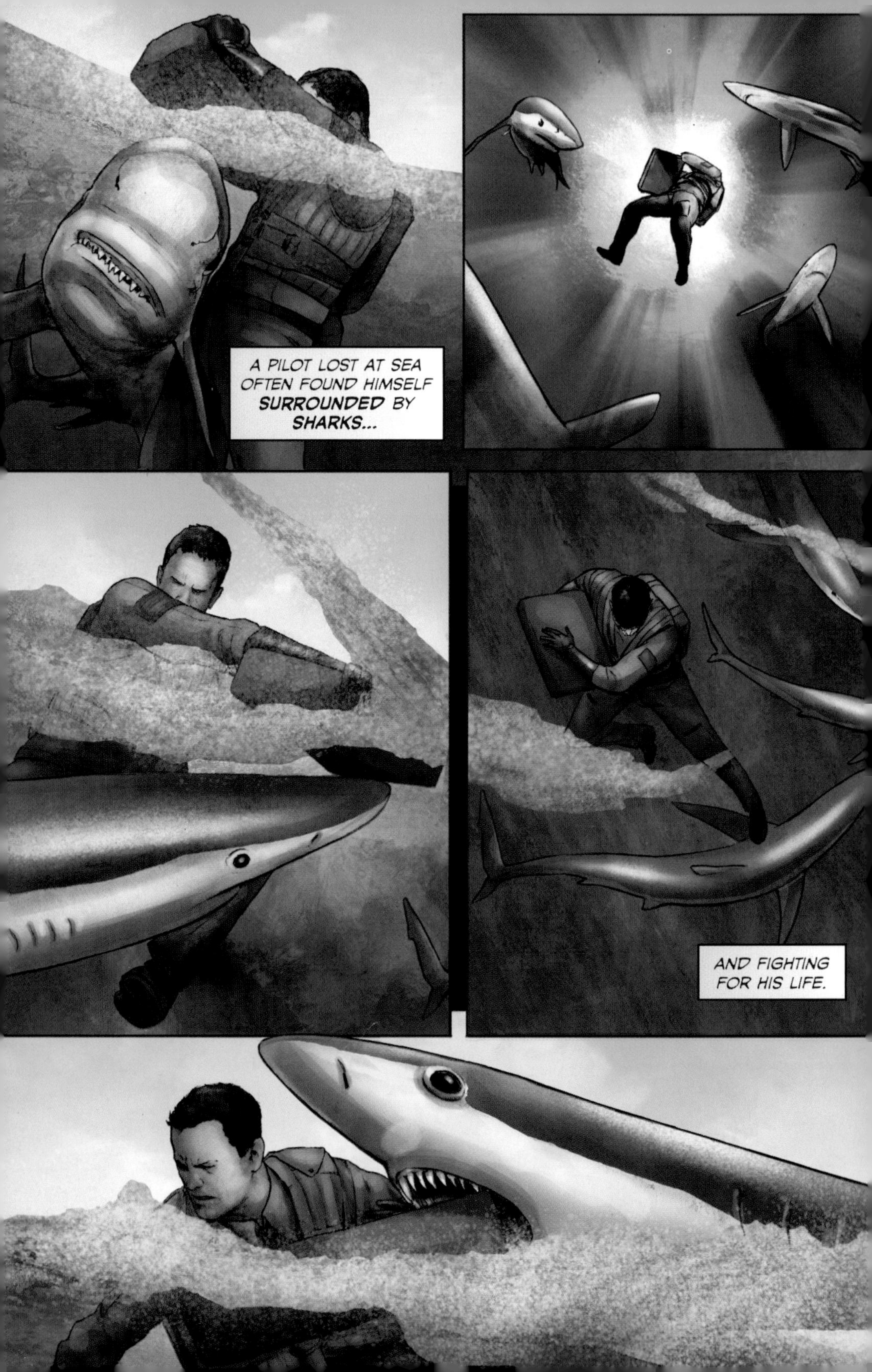
A PILOT LOST AT SEA OFTEN FOUND HIMSELF SURROUNDED BY SHARKS...
AND FIGHTING FOR HIS LIFE.

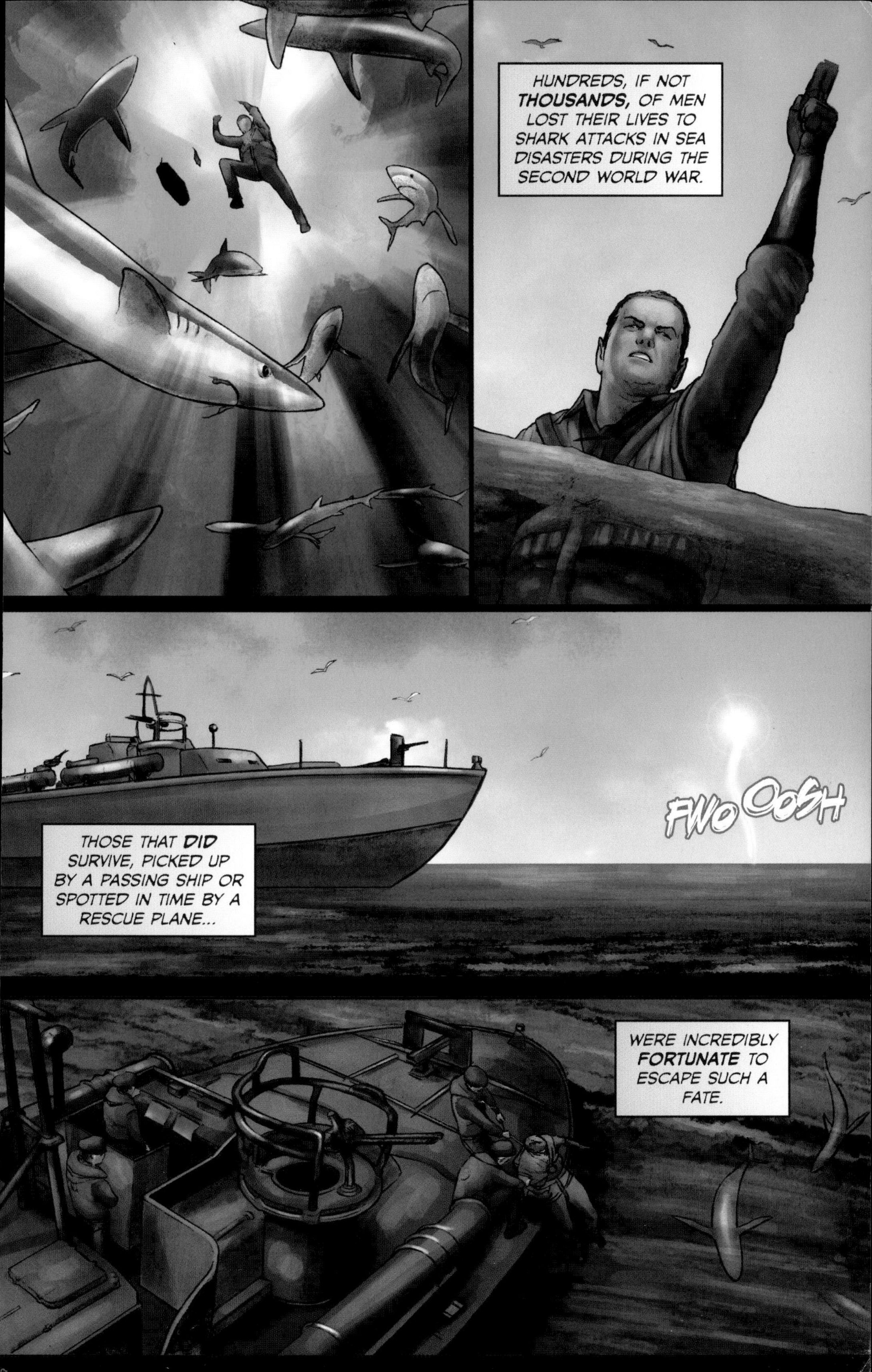
HUNDREDS, IF NOT **THOUSANDS,** OF MEN LOST THEIR LIVES TO SHARK ATTACKS IN SEA DISASTERS DURING THE SECOND WORLD WAR.
THOSE THAT **DID** SURVIVE, PICKED UP BY A PASSING SHIP OR SPOTTED IN TIME BY A RESCUE PLANE...
FWOOOSH
WERE INCREDIBLY **FORTUNATE** TO ESCAPE SUCH A FATE.

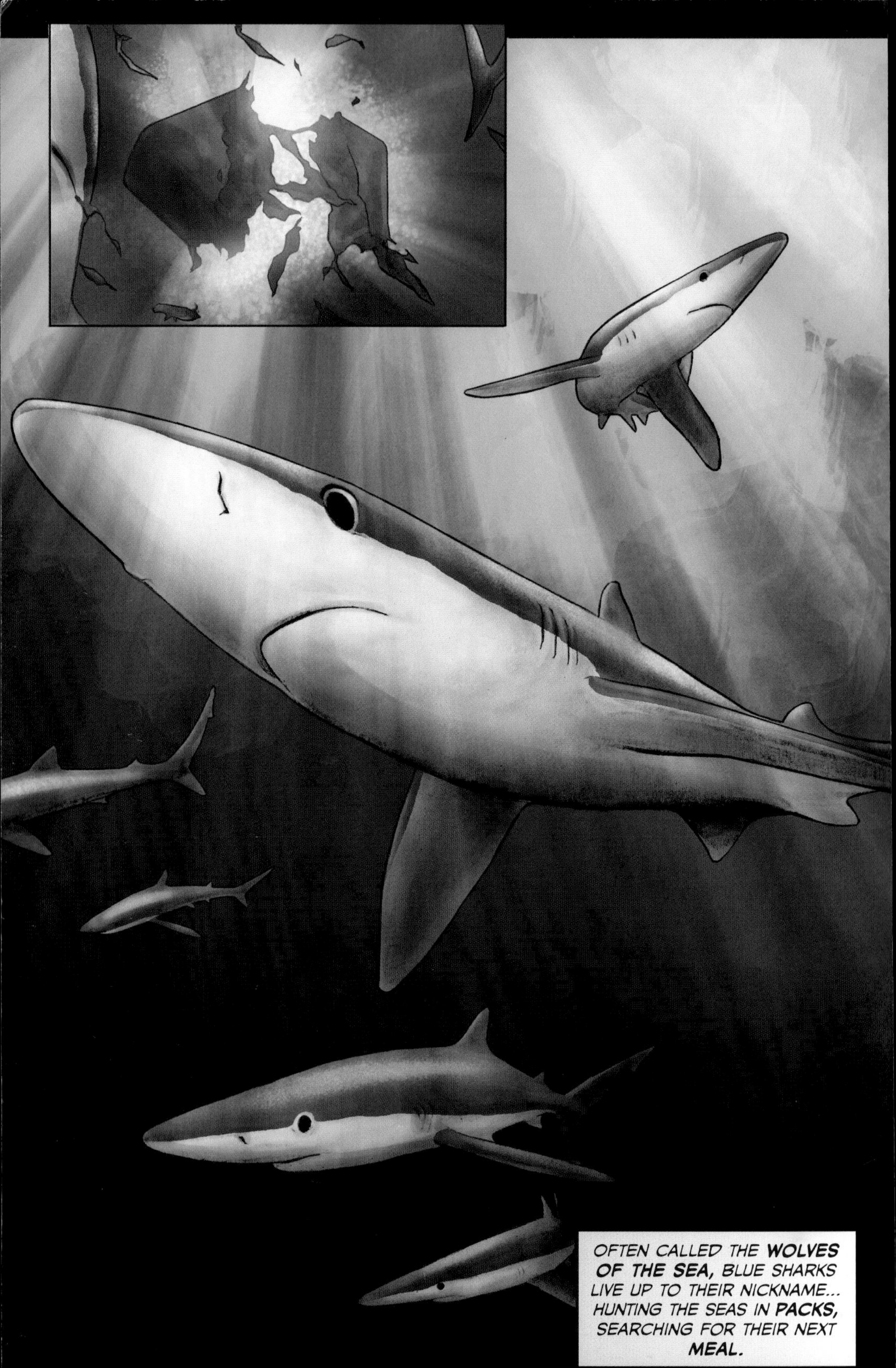
OFTEN CALLED THE WOLVES OF THE SEA, BLUE SHARKS LIVE UP TO THEIR NICKNAME... HUNTING THE SEAS IN PACKS, SEARCHING FOR THEIR NEXT MEAL.

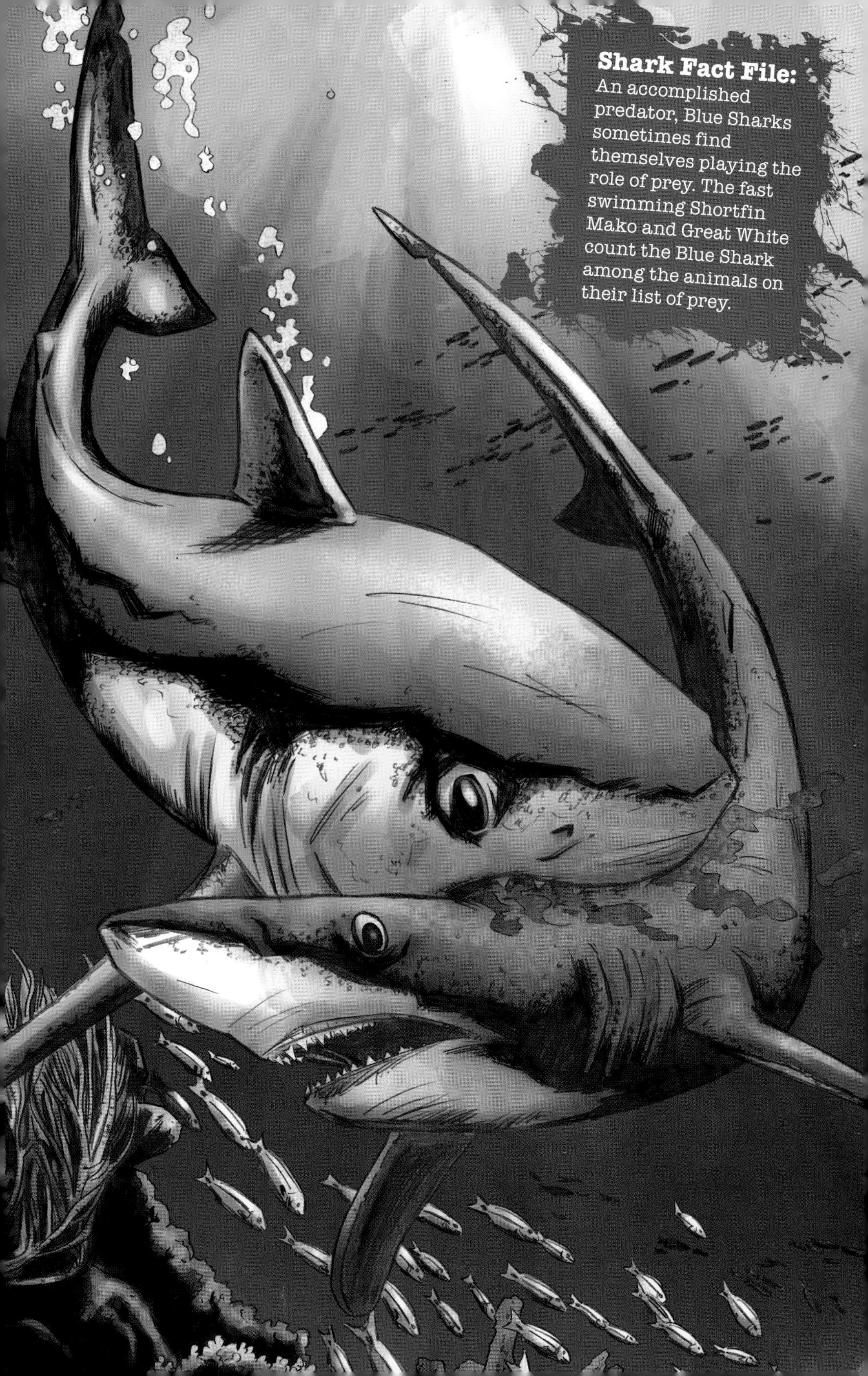

Shark Fact File:
An accomplished predator, Blue Sharks sometimes find themselves playing the role of prey. The fast swimming Shortfin Mako and Great White count the Blue Shark among the animals on their list of prey.

#8 THE HAMMERHEAD SHARK

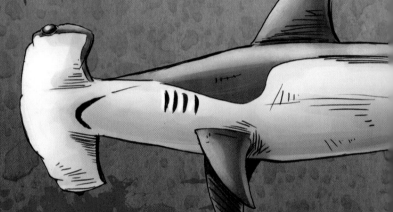

HAMMERHEAD FACTS:

Average Size: 11.5 feet

Largest Recorded: 20 feet

Habitat: Shallow coastal areas, such as over continental shelves and lagoons, as well as far offshore to depths of 300 feet.

Preferred Prey: Fish, other sharks, squid, stingrays, octopus and crustaceans.

The dorsal side of a Hammerhead is dark brown to light gray in color fading to white on the underside. Hammerheads have a tall, pointed first dorsal fin.

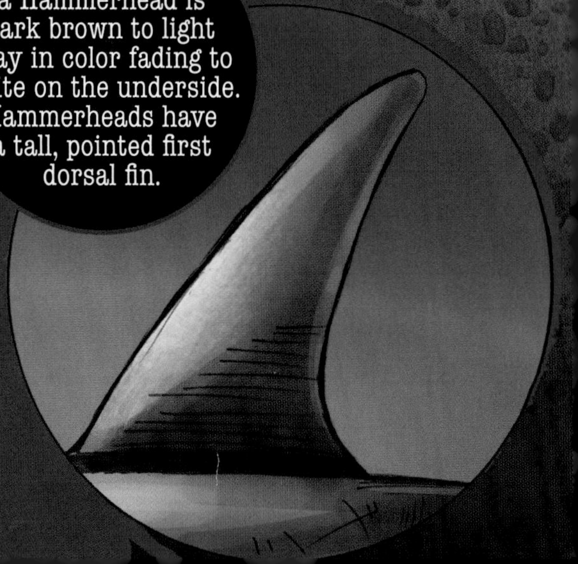

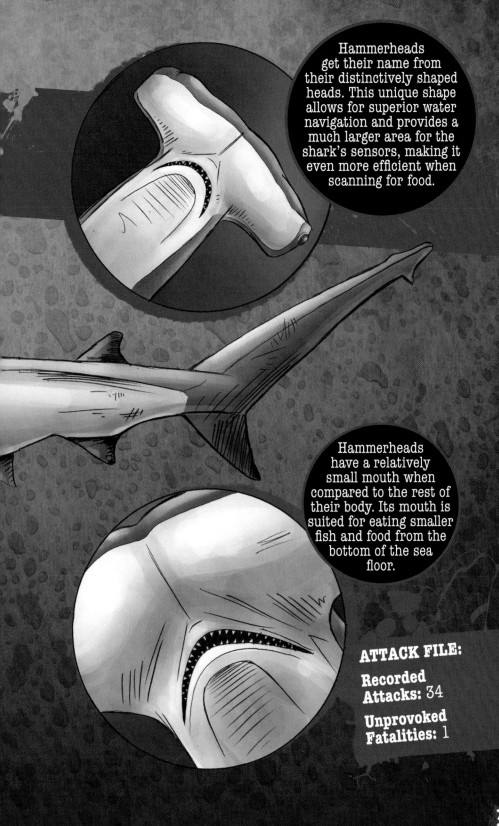

Hammerheads get their name from their distinctively shaped heads. This unique shape allows for superior water navigation and provides a much larger area for the shark's sensors, making it even more efficient when scanning for food.

Hammerheads have a relatively small mouth when compared to the rest of their body. Its mouth is suited for eating smaller fish and food from the bottom of the sea floor.

ATTACK FILE:

Recorded Attacks: 34

Unprovoked Fatalities: 1

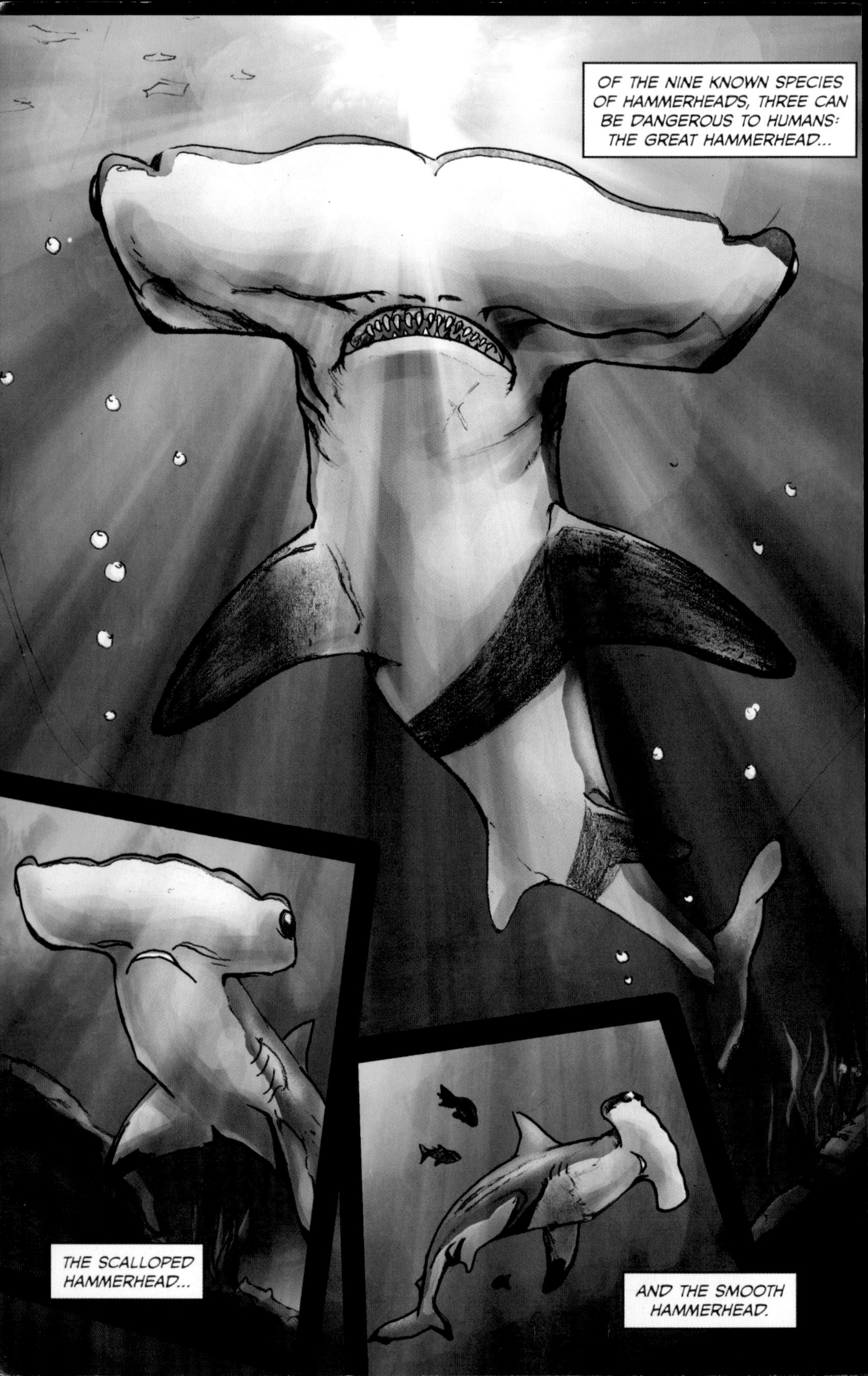
OF THE NINE KNOWN SPECIES OF HAMMERHEADS, THREE CAN BE DANGEROUS TO HUMANS: THE GREAT HAMMERHEAD...
THE SCALLOPED HAMMERHEAD...
AND THE SMOOTH HAMMERHEAD.

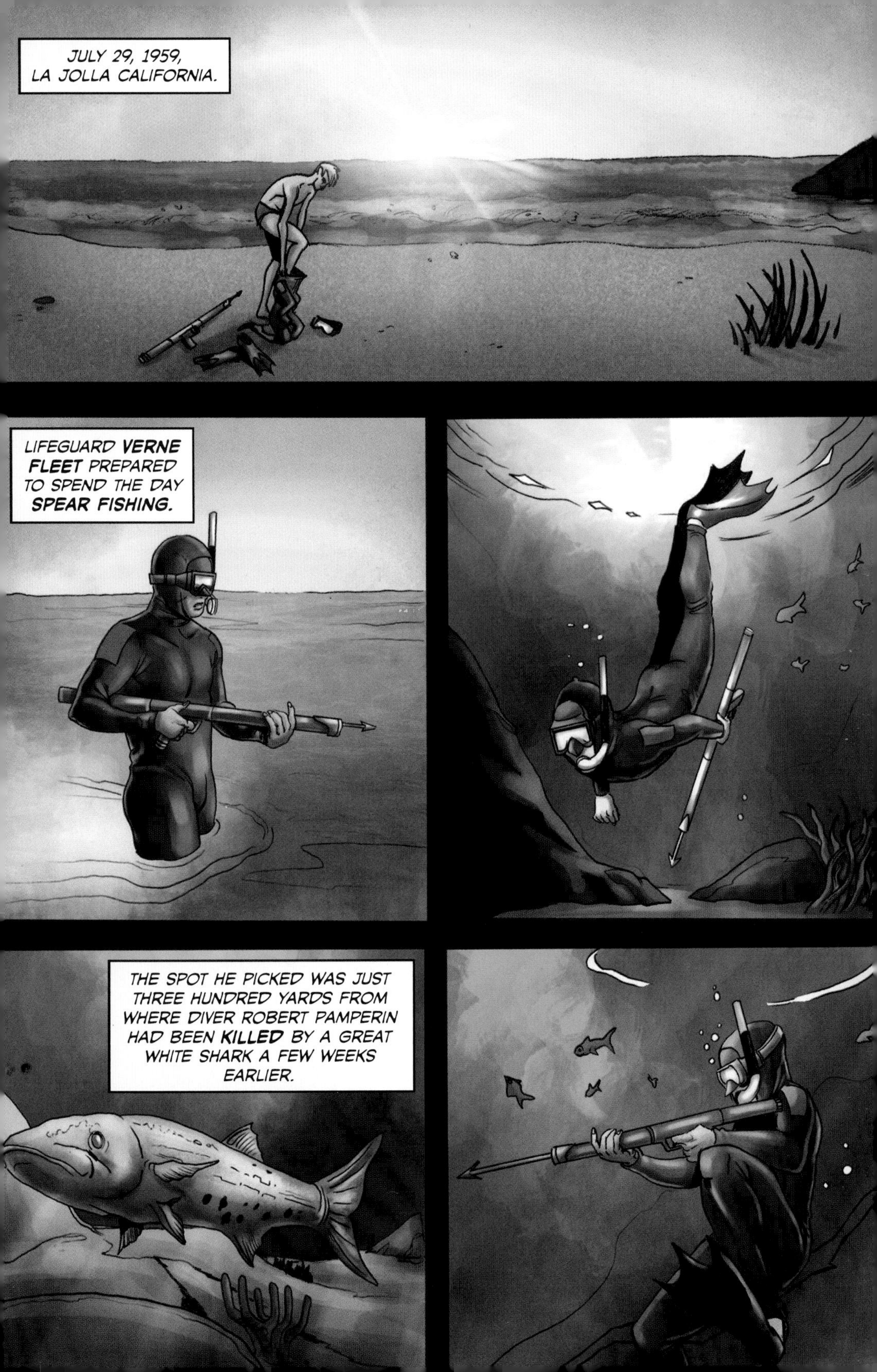
JULY 29, 1959, LA JOLLA CALIFORNIA.
LIFEGUARD **VERNE FLEET** PREPARED TO SPEND THE DAY **SPEAR FISHING.**
THE SPOT HE PICKED WAS JUST THREE HUNDRED YARDS FROM WHERE DIVER ROBERT PAMPERIN HAD BEEN **KILLED** BY A GREAT WHITE SHARK A FEW WEEKS EARLIER.

DIVING BELOW THE SURFACE OF THE WATER, FLEET **SPEARED** A FISH.

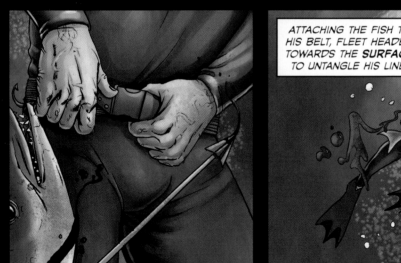

AS HE PULLED IN HIS CATCH, HIS LINE BECAME **TANGLED.**

ATTACHING THE FISH TO HIS BELT, FLEET HEADED TOWARDS THE **SURFACE** TO UNTANGLE HIS LINE.

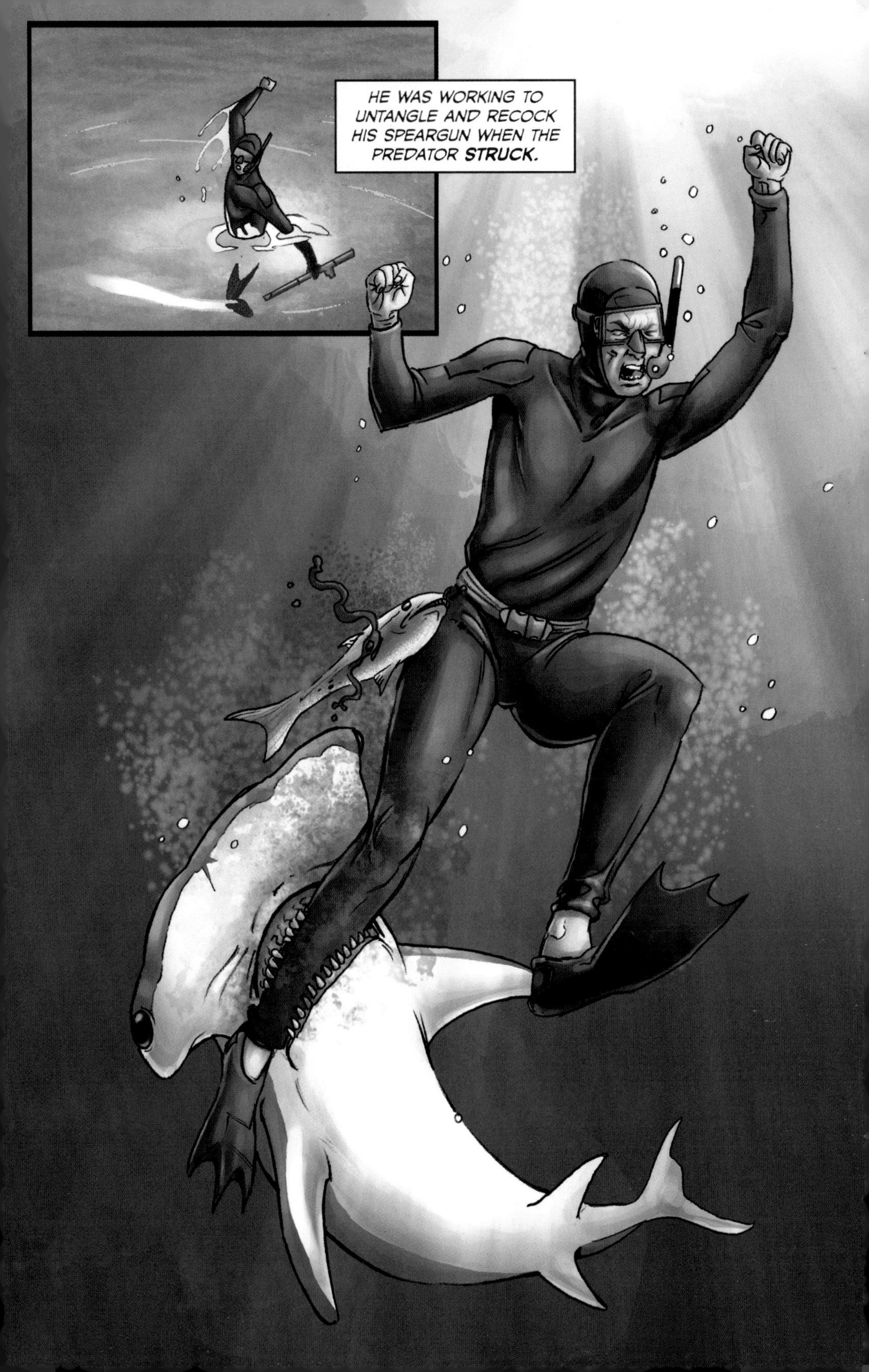
HE WAS WORKING TO UNTANGLE AND RECOCK HIS SPEARGUN WHEN THE PREDATOR STRUCK.

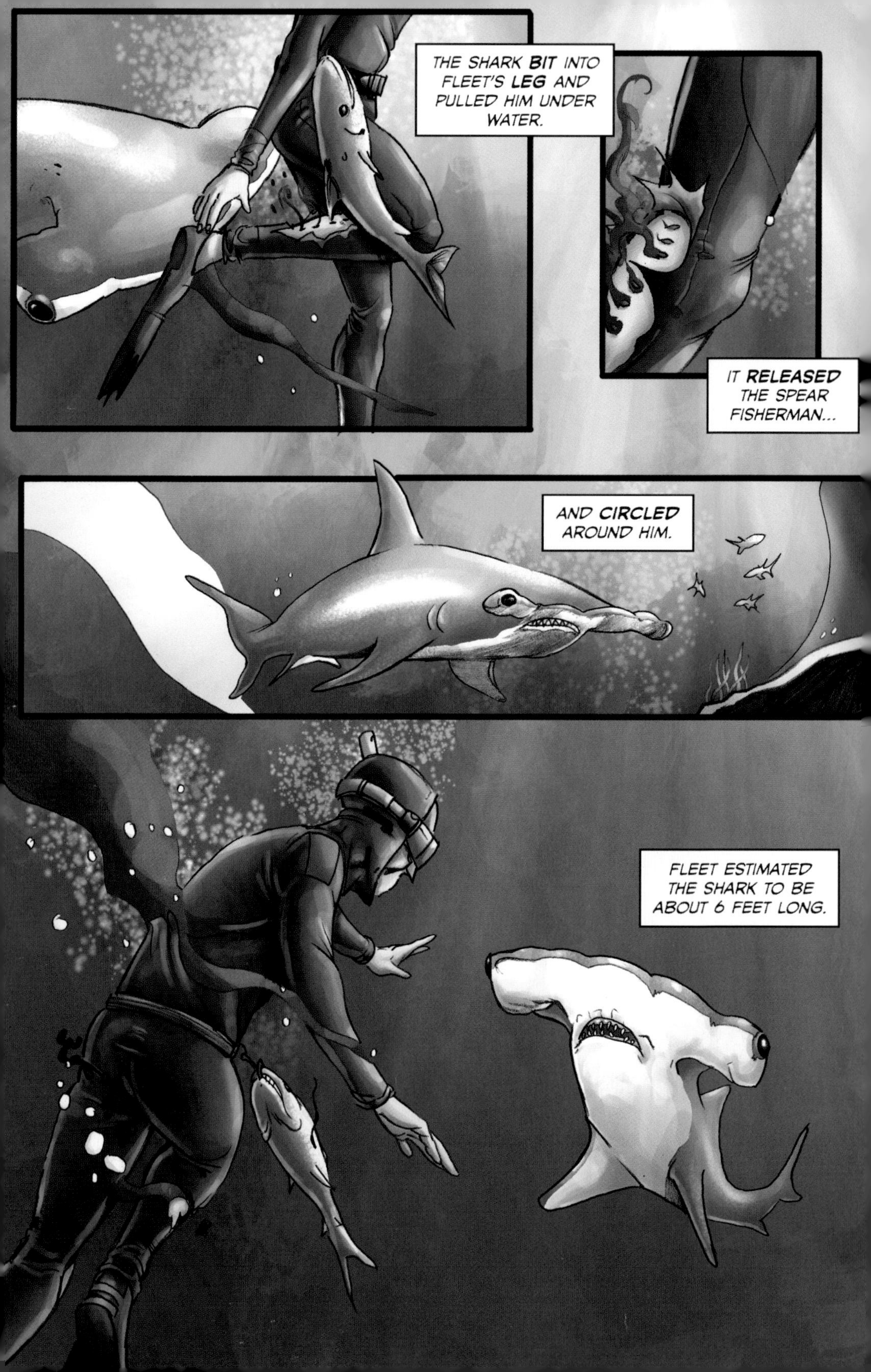
THE SHARK BIT INTO FLEET'S LEG AND PULLED HIM UNDER WATER.
IT RELEASED THE SPEAR FISHERMAN...
AND CIRCLED AROUND HIM.
FLEET ESTIMATED THE SHARK TO BE ABOUT 6 FEET LONG.

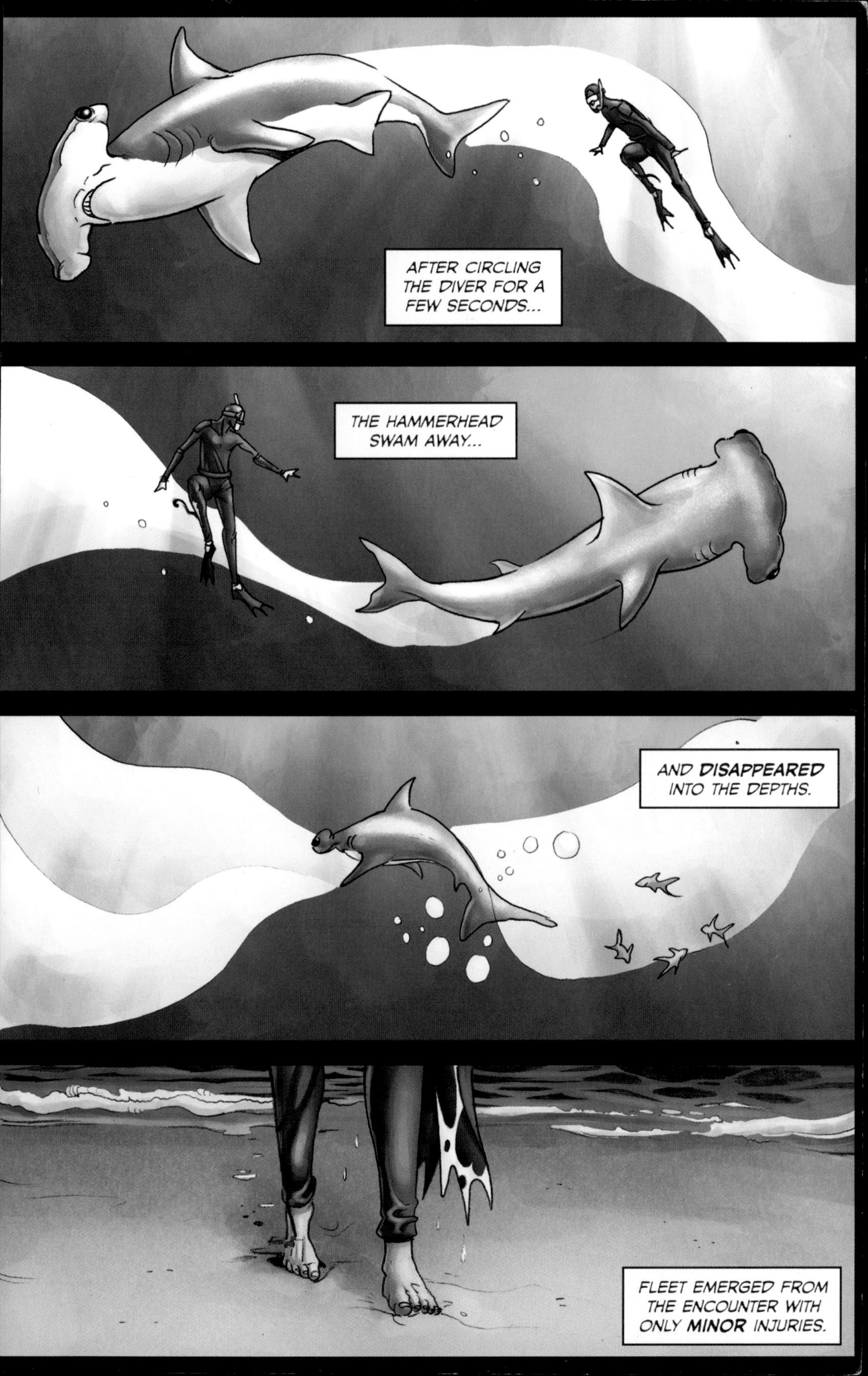
AFTER CIRCLING THE DIVER FOR A FEW SECONDS...
THE HAMMERHEAD SWAM AWAY...
AND DISAPPEARED INTO THE DEPTHS.
FLEET EMERGED FROM THE ENCOUNTER WITH ONLY MINOR INJURIES.

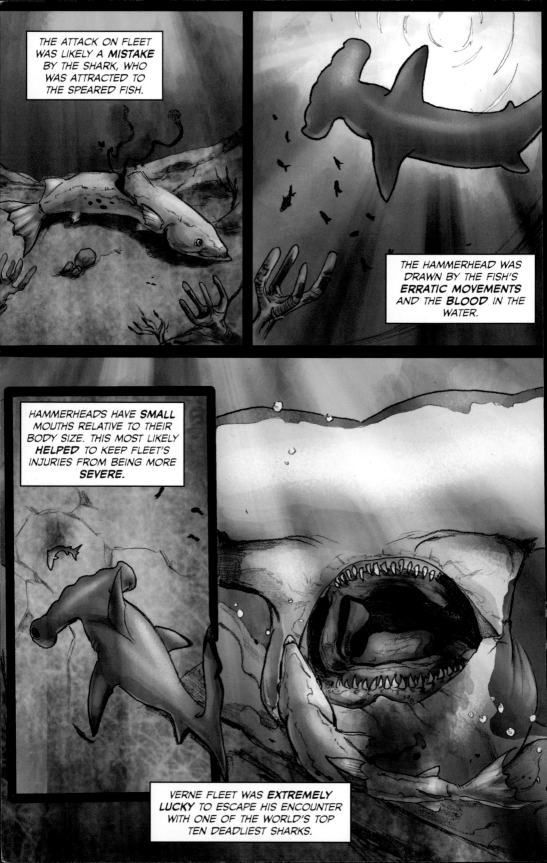

THE ATTACK ON FLEET WAS LIKELY A **MISTAKE** BY THE SHARK, WHO WAS ATTRACTED TO THE SPEARED FISH.

THE HAMMERHEAD WAS DRAWN BY THE FISH'S **ERRATIC MOVEMENTS** AND THE **BLOOD** IN THE WATER.

HAMMERHEADS HAVE **SMALL** MOUTHS RELATIVE TO THEIR BODY SIZE. THIS MOST LIKELY **HELPED** TO KEEP FLEET'S INJURIES FROM BEING MORE **SEVERE.**

VERNE FLEET WAS **EXTREMELY LUCKY** TO ESCAPE HIS ENCOUNTER WITH ONE OF THE WORLD'S TOP TEN DEADLIEST SHARKS.

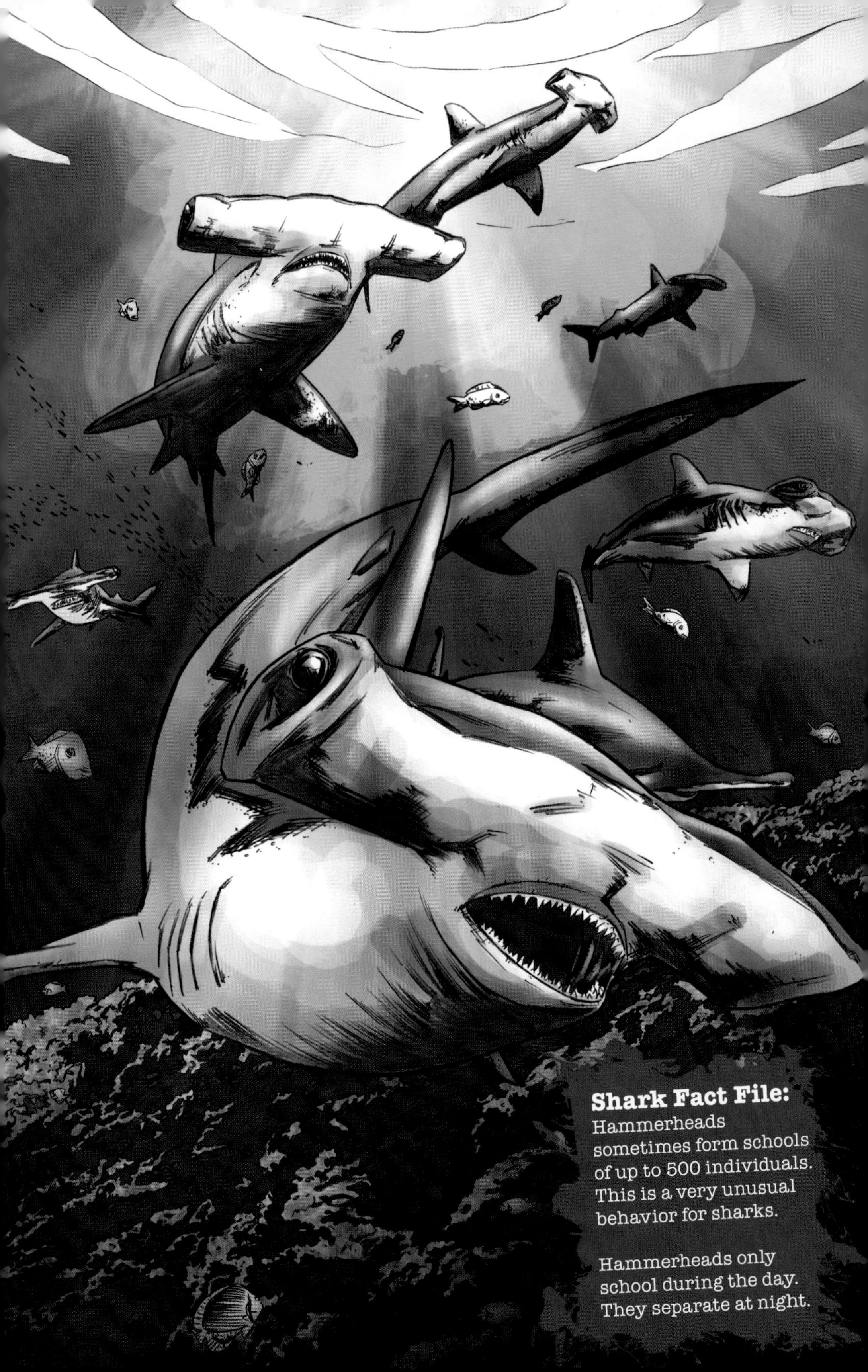

Shark Fact File:
Hammerheads sometimes form schools of up to 500 individuals. This is a very unusual behavior for sharks.

Hammerheads only school during the day. They separate at night.

#7 THE SAND TIGER SHARK

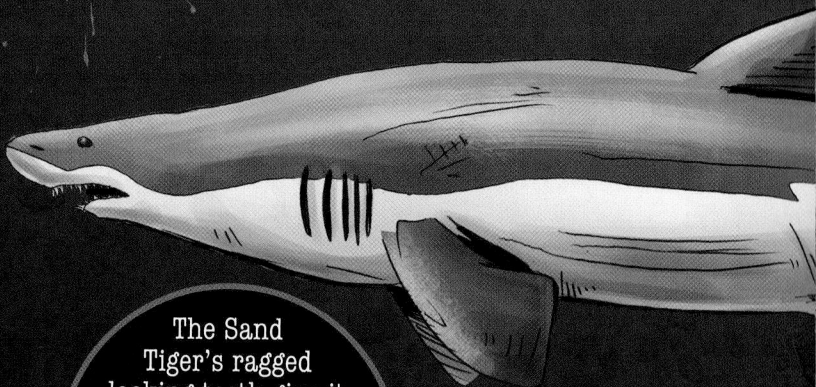

The Sand Tiger's ragged looking teeth give it a menacing look. The shark often swims with its mouth open making them one of the fiercest-looking fish in the world.

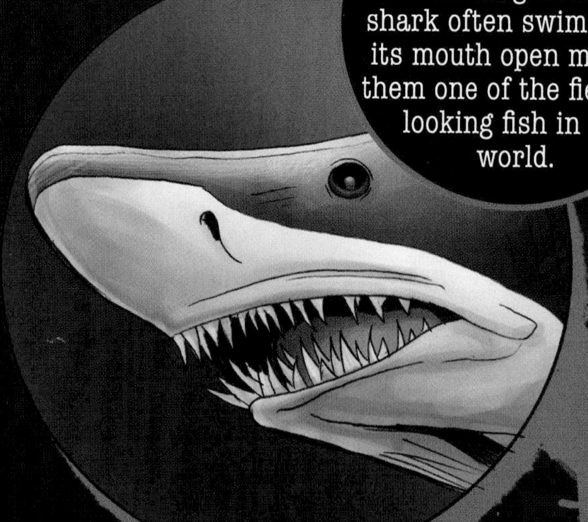

ATTACK FILE:

Recorded Attacks: 69

Unprovoked Fatalities: 3

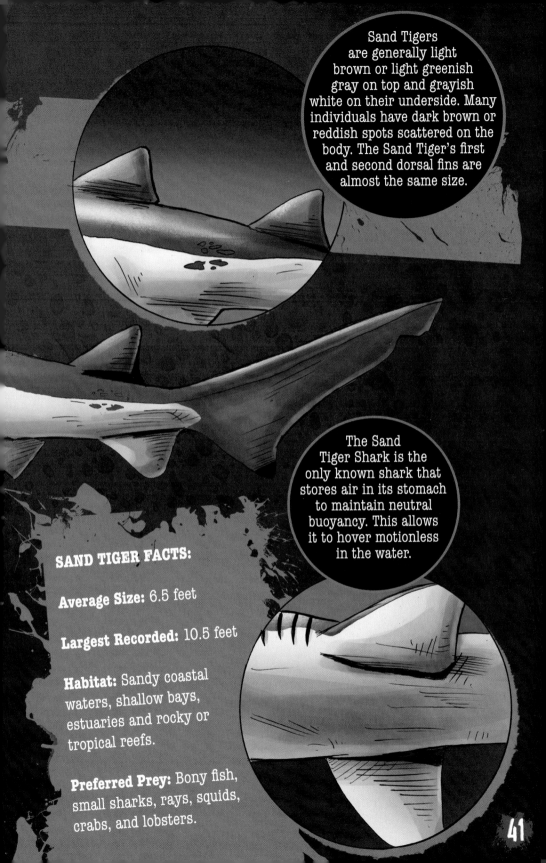

Sand Tigers are generally light brown or light greenish gray on top and grayish white on their underside. Many individuals have dark brown or reddish spots scattered on the body. The Sand Tiger's first and second dorsal fins are almost the same size.

The Sand Tiger Shark is the only known shark that stores air in its stomach to maintain neutral buoyancy. This allows it to hover motionless in the water.

SAND TIGER FACTS:

Average Size: 6.5 feet

Largest Recorded: 10.5 feet

Habitat: Sandy coastal waters, shallow bays, estuaries and rocky or tropical reefs.

Preferred Prey: Bony fish, small sharks, rays, squids, crabs, and lobsters.

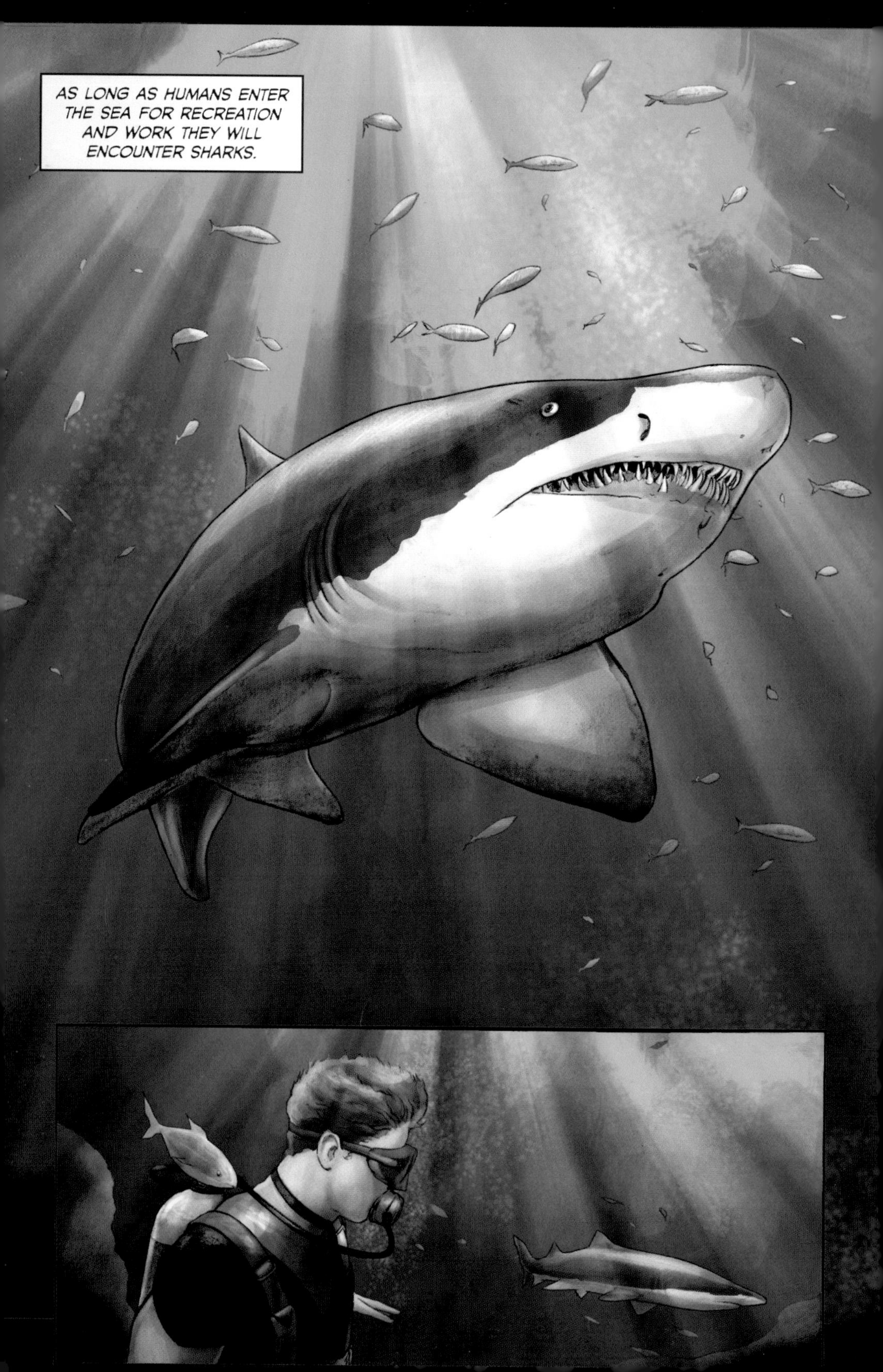
AS LONG AS HUMANS ENTER THE SEA FOR RECREATION AND WORK THEY WILL ENCOUNTER SHARKS.

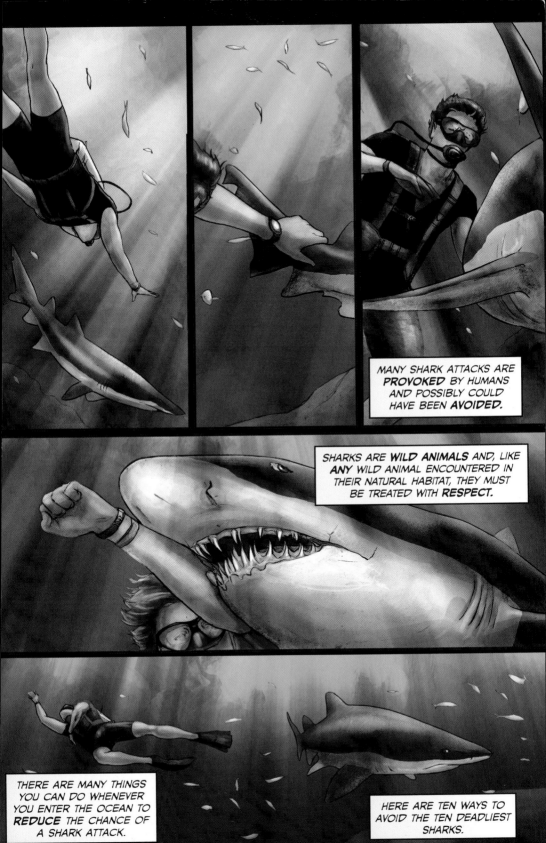

MANY SHARK ATTACKS ARE **PROVOKED** BY HUMANS AND POSSIBLY COULD HAVE BEEN **AVOIDED**.

SHARKS ARE **WILD ANIMALS** AND, LIKE **ANY** WILD ANIMAL ENCOUNTERED IN THEIR NATURAL HABITAT, THEY MUST BE TREATED WITH **RESPECT**.

THERE ARE MANY THINGS YOU CAN DO WHENEVER YOU ENTER THE OCEAN TO **REDUCE** THE CHANCE OF A SHARK ATTACK.

HERE ARE TEN WAYS TO AVOID THE TEN DEADLIEST SHARKS.

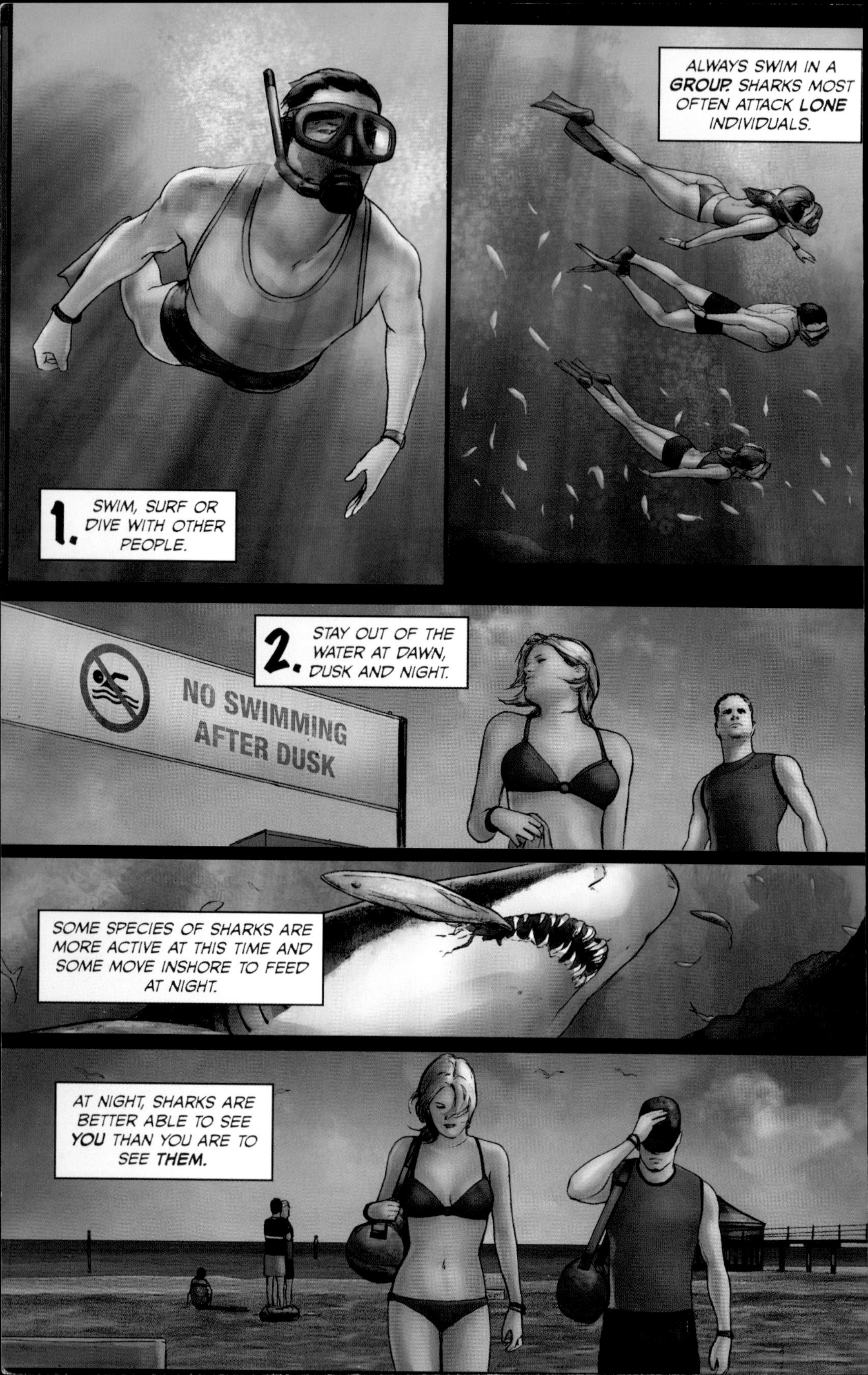
1. SWIM, SURF OR DIVE WITH OTHER PEOPLE.
ALWAYS SWIM IN A **GROUP**. SHARKS MOST OFTEN ATTACK **LONE** INDIVIDUALS.
2. STAY OUT OF THE WATER AT DAWN, DUSK AND NIGHT.
NO SWIMMING AFTER DUSK
SOME SPECIES OF SHARKS ARE MORE ACTIVE AT THIS TIME AND SOME MOVE INSHORE TO FEED AT NIGHT.
AT NIGHT, SHARKS ARE BETTER ABLE TO SEE **YOU** THAN YOU ARE TO SEE **THEM**.

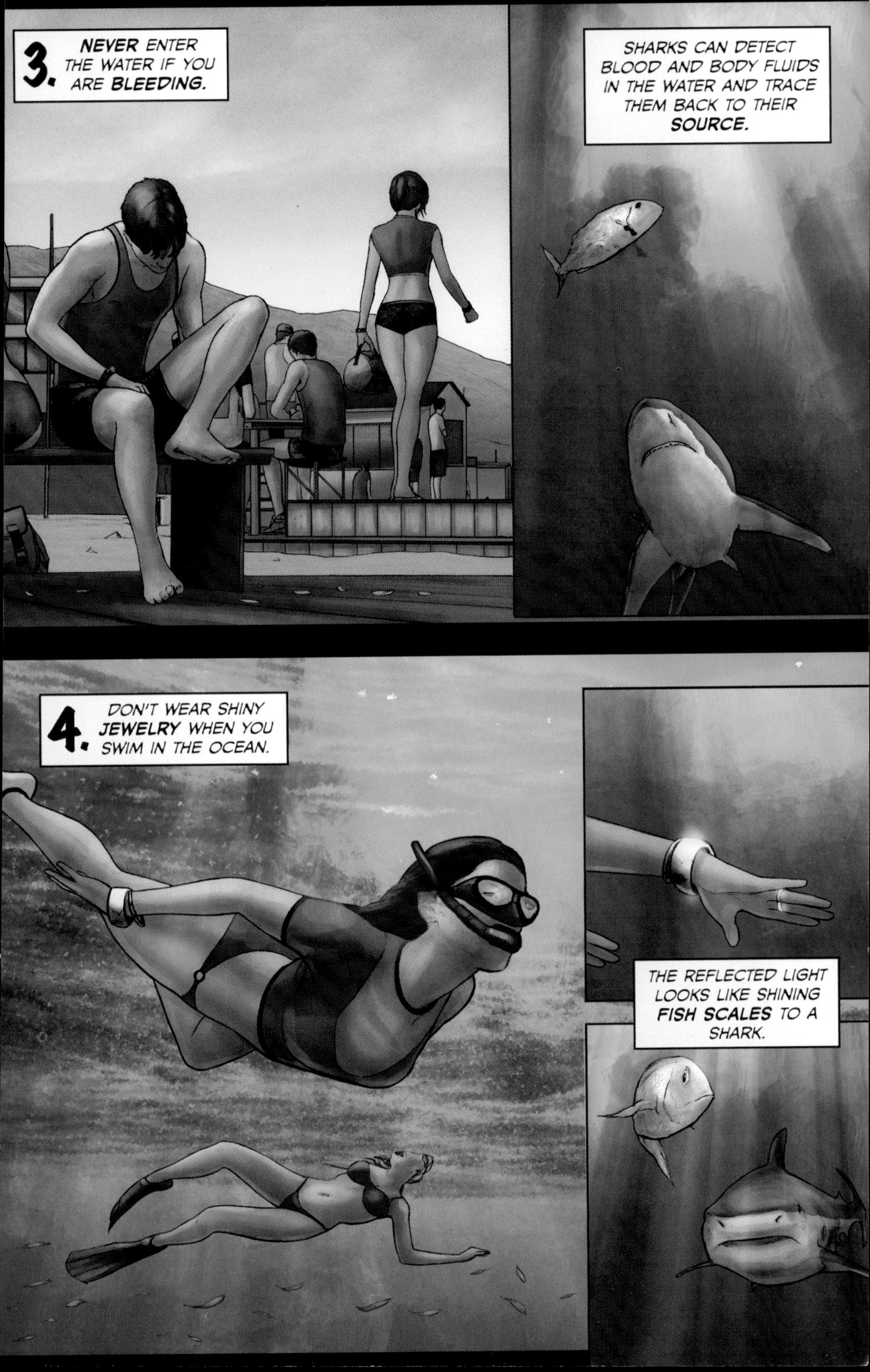
3. NEVER ENTER THE WATER IF YOU ARE BLEEDING.
SHARKS CAN DETECT BLOOD AND BODY FLUIDS IN THE WATER AND TRACE THEM BACK TO THEIR SOURCE.
4. DON'T WEAR SHINY JEWELRY WHEN YOU SWIM IN THE OCEAN.
THE REFLECTED LIGHT LOOKS LIKE SHINING FISH SCALES TO A SHARK.

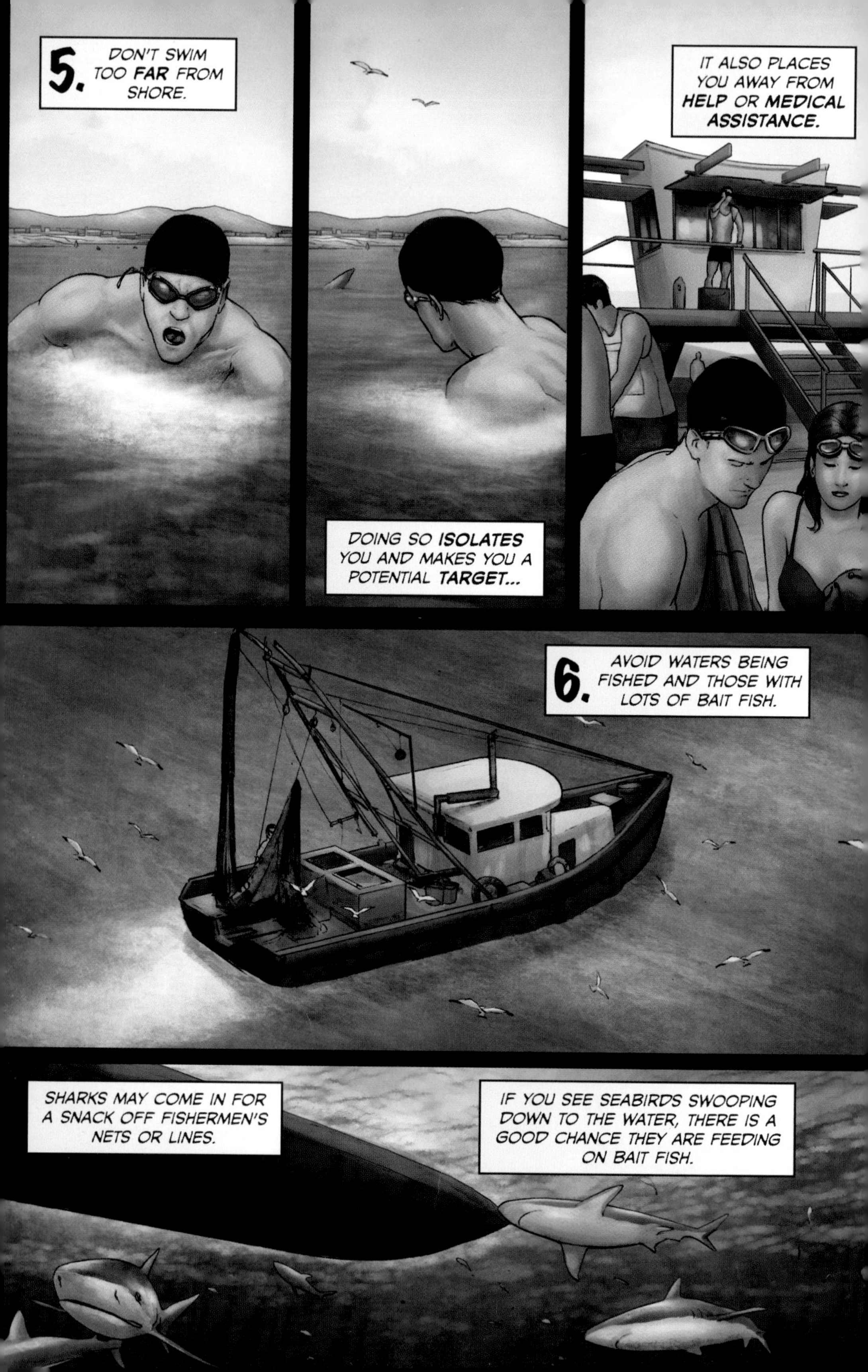
5. DON'T SWIM TOO FAR FROM SHORE.
DOING SO ISOLATES YOU AND MAKES YOU A POTENTIAL TARGET...
IT ALSO PLACES YOU AWAY FROM HELP OR MEDICAL ASSISTANCE.
6. AVOID WATERS BEING FISHED AND THOSE WITH LOTS OF BAIT FISH.
SHARKS MAY COME IN FOR A SNACK OFF FISHERMEN'S NETS OR LINES.
IF YOU SEE SEABIRDS SWOOPING DOWN TO THE WATER, THERE IS A GOOD CHANCE THEY ARE FEEDING ON BAIT FISH.

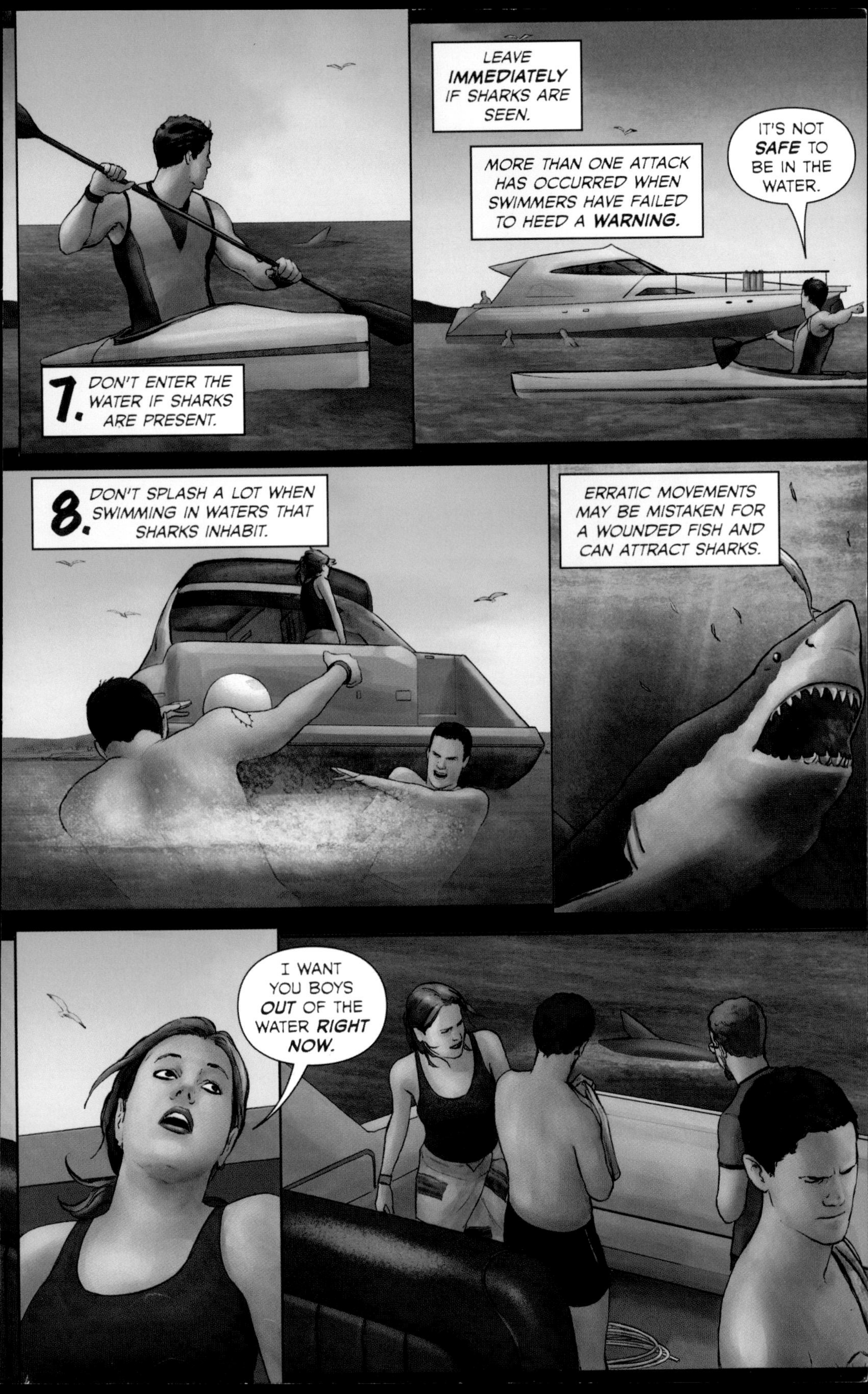
7. DON'T ENTER THE WATER IF SHARKS ARE PRESENT.
LEAVE IMMEDIATELY IF SHARKS ARE SEEN.
MORE THAN ONE ATTACK HAS OCCURRED WHEN SWIMMERS HAVE FAILED TO HEED A WARNING.
IT'S NOT SAFE TO BE IN THE WATER.
8. DON'T SPLASH A LOT WHEN SWIMMING IN WATERS THAT SHARKS INHABIT.
ERRATIC MOVEMENTS MAY BE MISTAKEN FOR A WOUNDED FISH AND CAN ATTRACT SHARKS.
I WANT YOU BOYS OUT OF THE WATER RIGHT NOW.

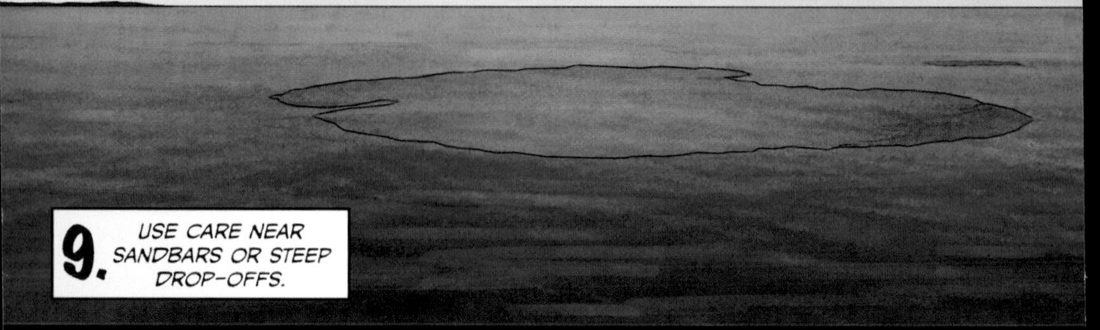
9. USE CARE NEAR SANDBARS OR STEEP DROP-OFFS.

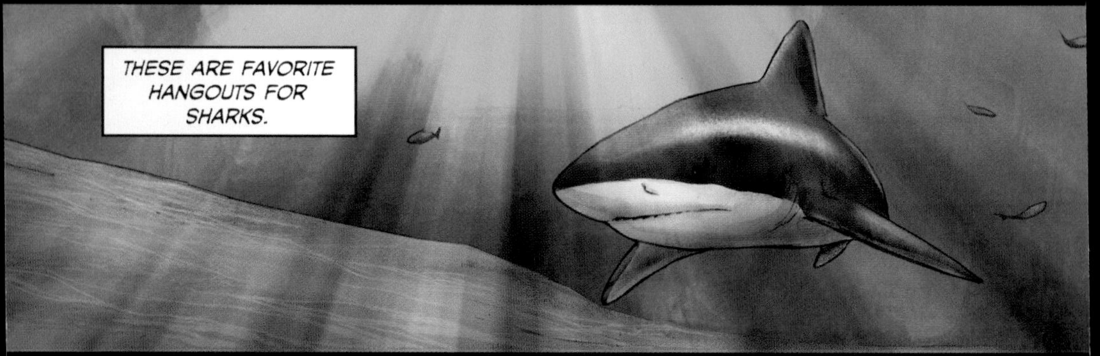
THESE ARE FAVORITE HANGOUTS FOR SHARKS.

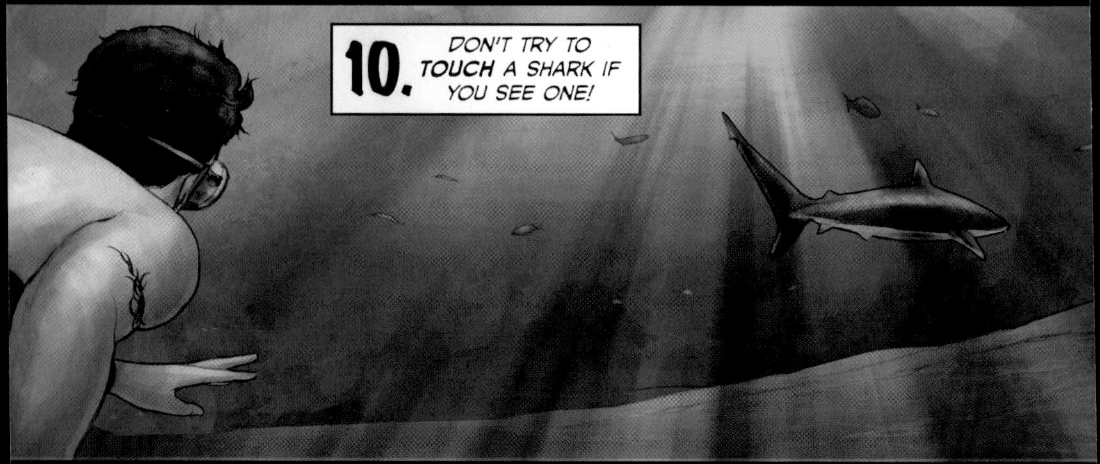
10. DON'T TRY TO **TOUCH** A SHARK IF YOU SEE ONE!

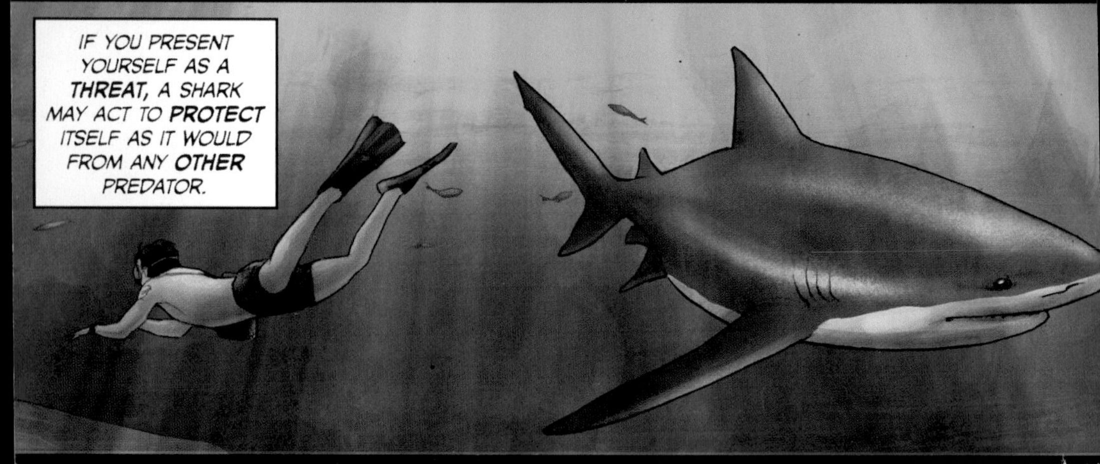
IF YOU PRESENT YOURSELF AS A **THREAT,** A SHARK MAY ACT TO **PROTECT** ITSELF AS IT WOULD FROM ANY **OTHER** PREDATOR.

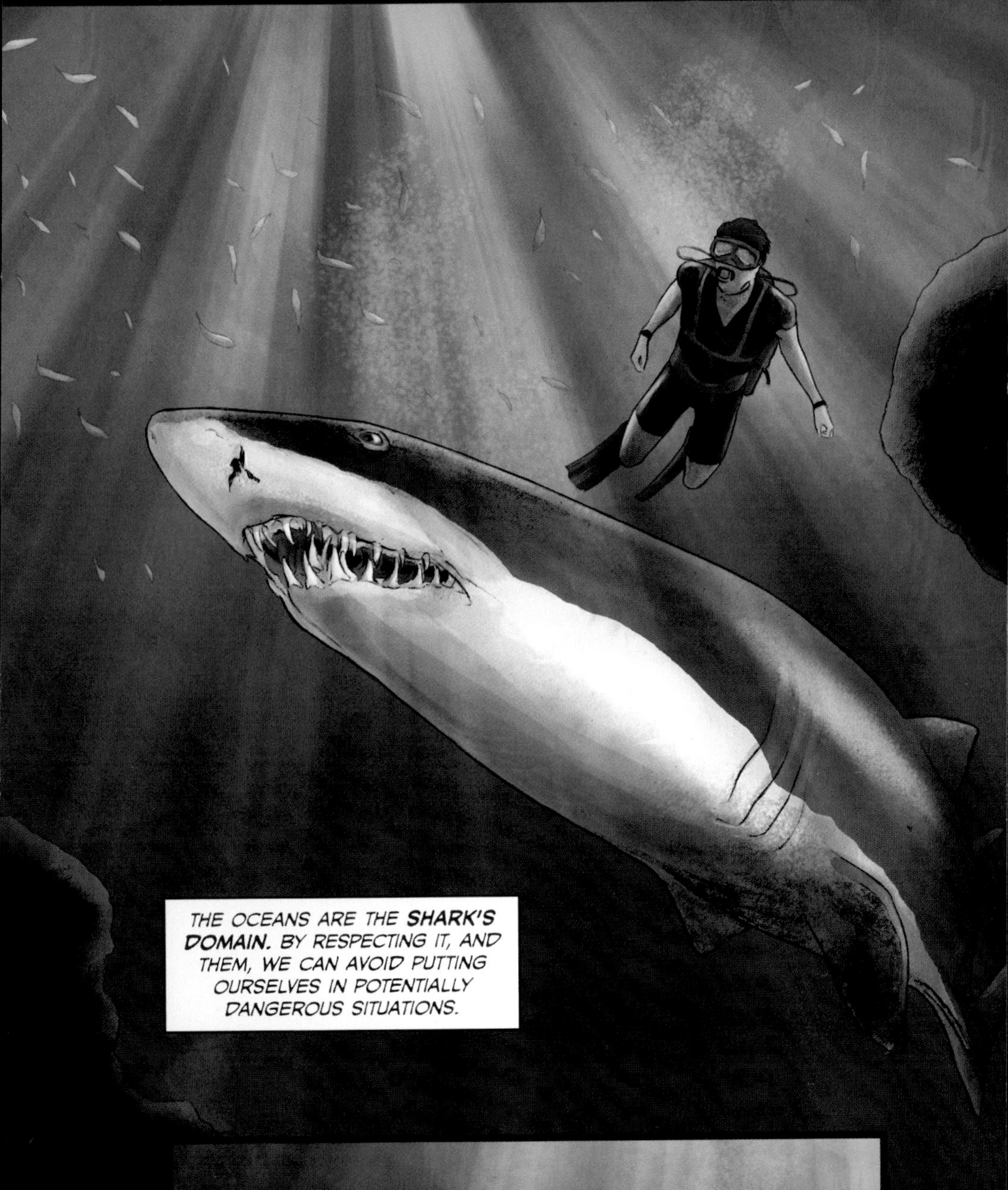
THE OCEANS ARE THE SHARK'S DOMAIN. BY RESPECTING IT, AND THEM, WE CAN AVOID PUTTING OURSELVES IN POTENTIALLY DANGEROUS SITUATIONS.

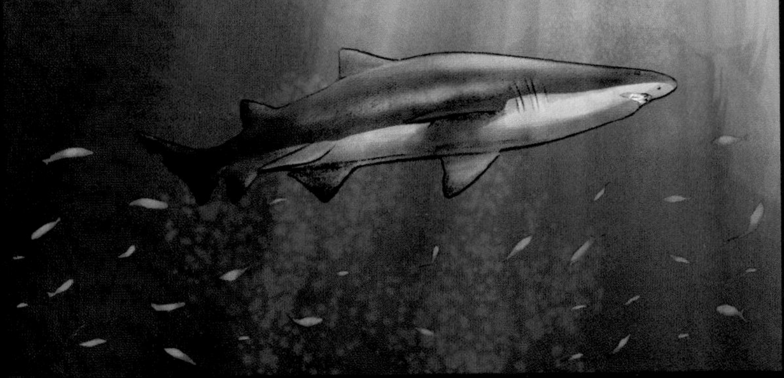

#6 THE GREY REEF SHARK

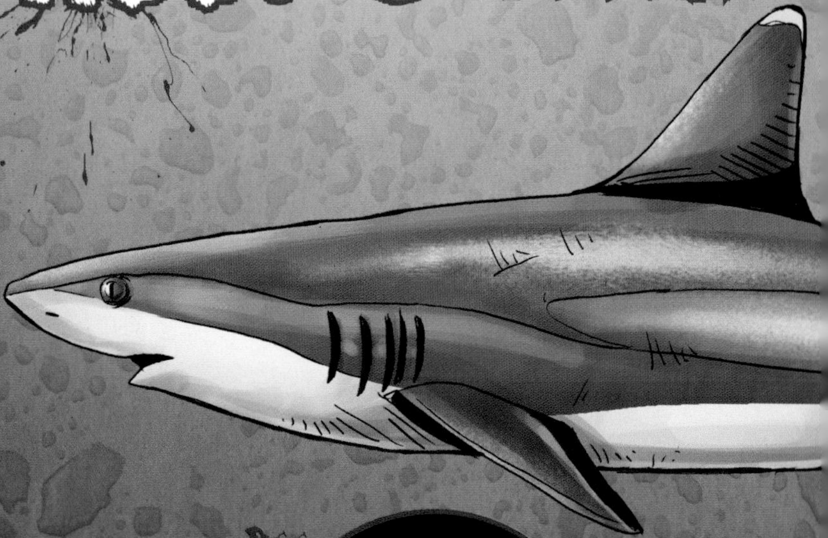

A shark's skin is covered with tough scales called Dermal denticles. These small scales are covered with hard enamel and rough skin that help protect them against predators.

GREY REEF SHARK FACTS:

Average Size: 6 feet

Largest Recorded: 8.4 feet

Habitat: Shallow tropical and subtropical waters, near coral reefs, atolls and lagoons adjacent to reef habitats.

Preferred Prey: Bony fish, cephalopods such as squid and octopus, crustaceans such as crabs and lobsters.

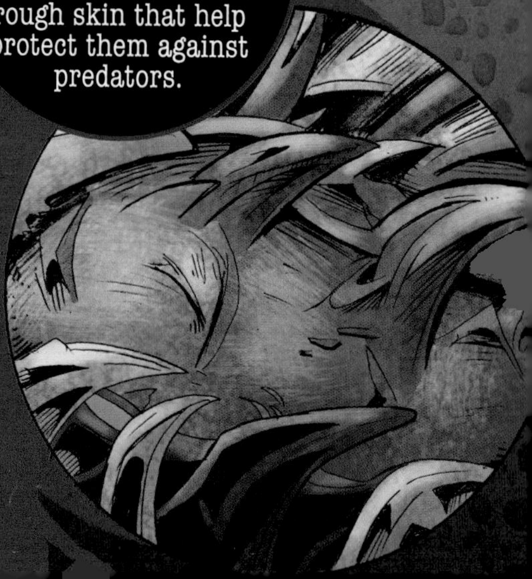

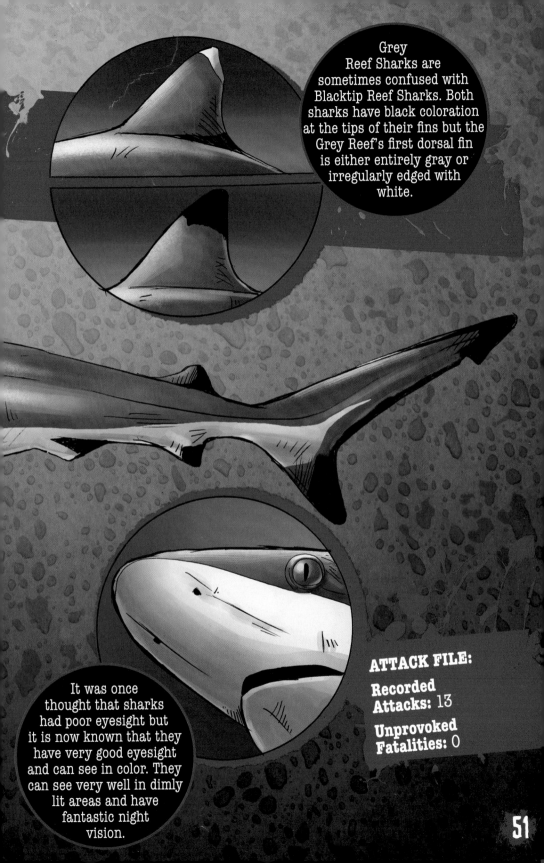

Grey Reef Sharks are sometimes confused with Blacktip Reef Sharks. Both sharks have black coloration at the tips of their fins but the Grey Reef's first dorsal fin is either entirely gray or irregularly edged with white.

It was once thought that sharks had poor eyesight but it is now known that they have very good eyesight and can see in color. They can see very well in dimly lit areas and have fantastic night vision.

ATTACK FILE:

Recorded Attacks: 13

Unprovoked Fatalities: 0

51

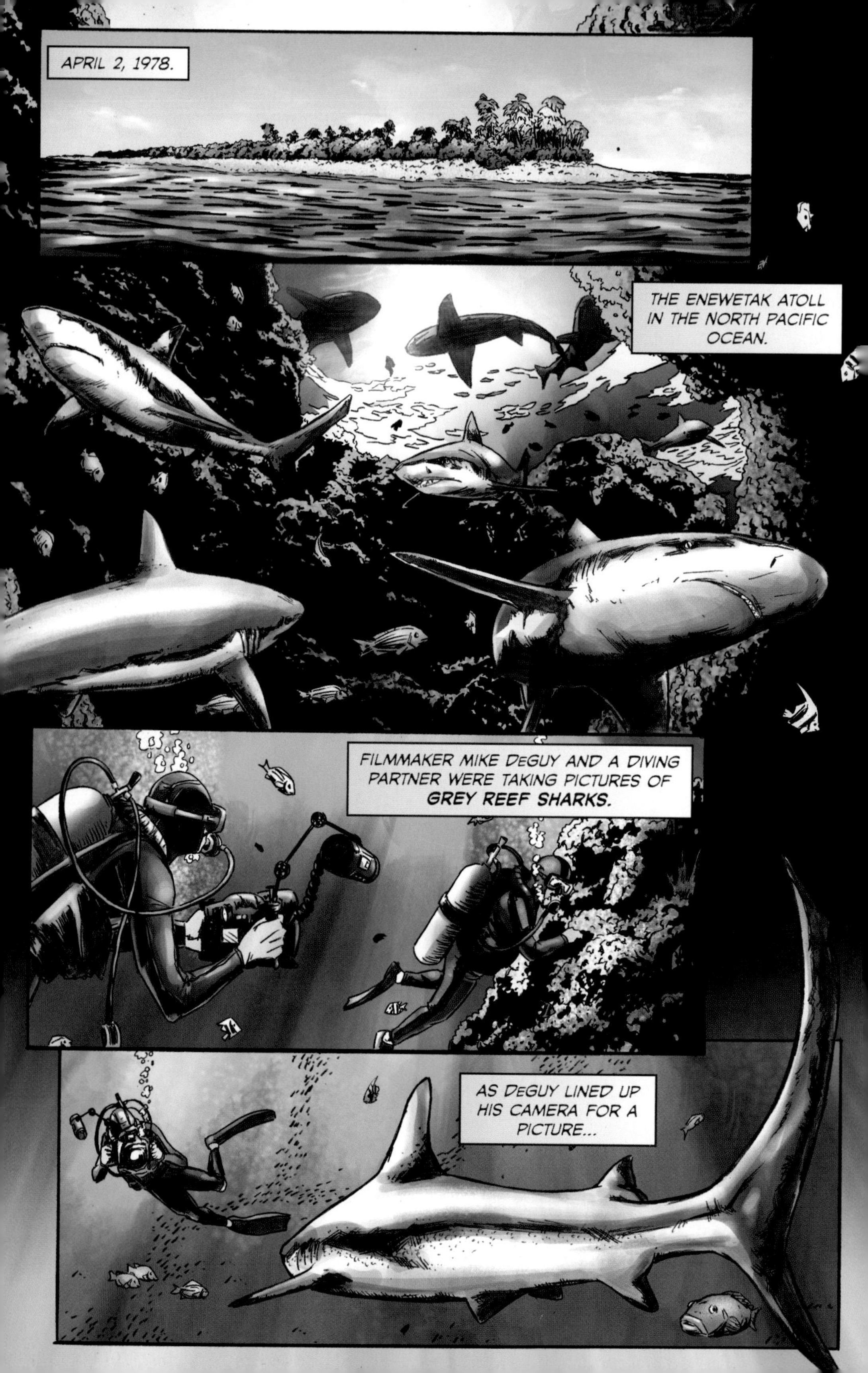
APRIL 2, 1978.
THE ENEWETAK ATOLL IN THE NORTH PACIFIC OCEAN.
FILMMAKER MIKE DeGUY AND A DIVING PARTNER WERE TAKING PICTURES OF **GREY REEF SHARKS.**
AS DeGUY LINED UP HIS CAMERA FOR A PICTURE...

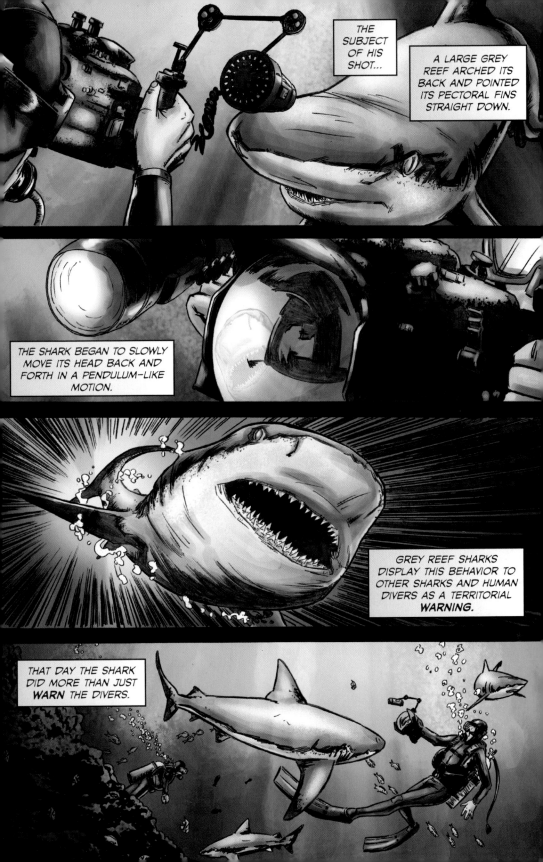

THE SUBJECT OF HIS SHOT...

A LARGE GREY REEF ARCHED ITS BACK AND POINTED ITS PECTORAL FINS STRAIGHT DOWN.

THE SHARK BEGAN TO SLOWLY MOVE ITS HEAD BACK AND FORTH IN A PENDULUM-LIKE MOTION.

GREY REEF SHARKS DISPLAY THIS BEHAVIOR TO OTHER SHARKS AND HUMAN DIVERS AS A TERRITORIAL **WARNING.**

THAT DAY THE SHARK DID MORE THAN JUST **WARN** THE DIVERS.

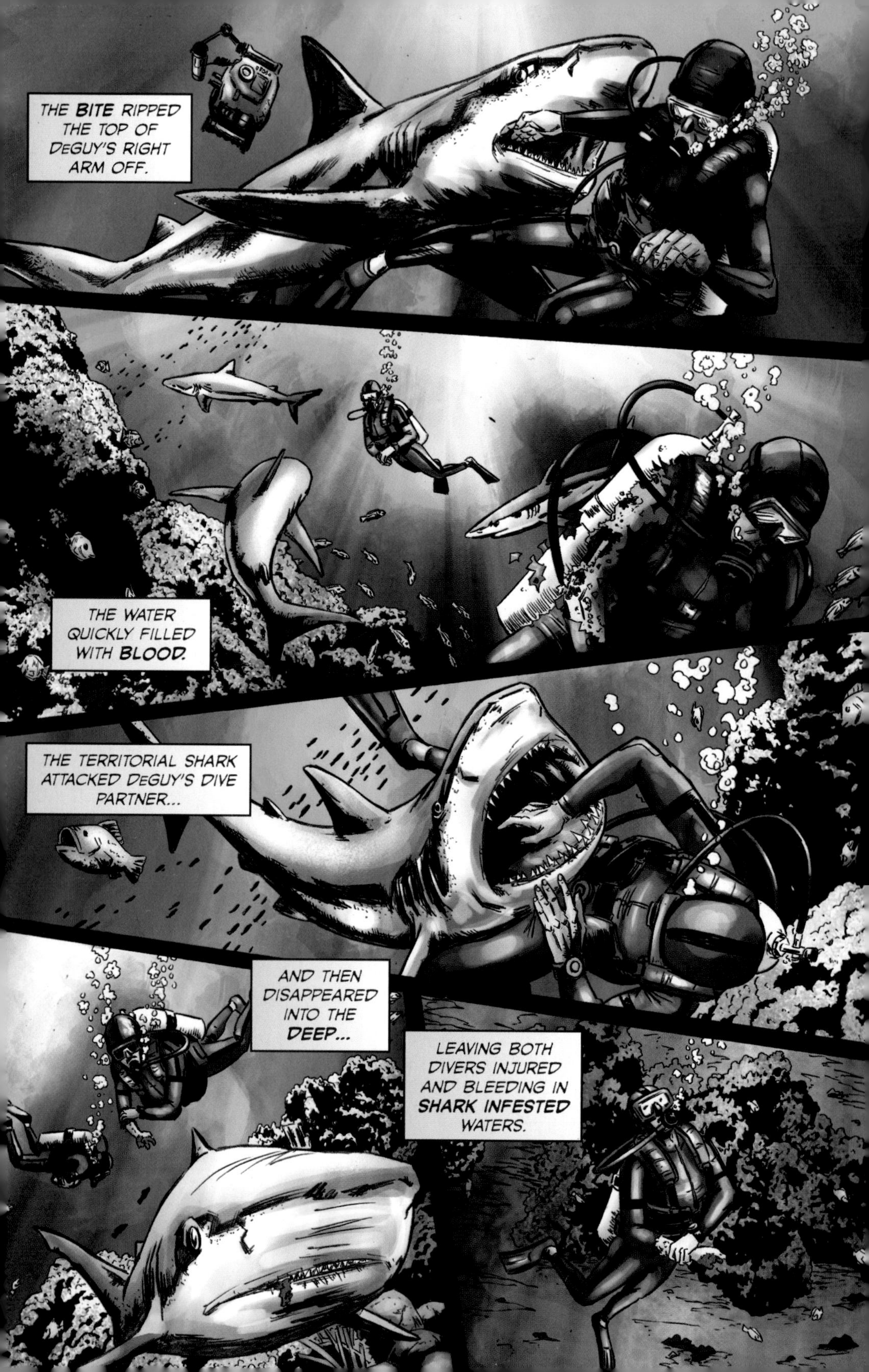
THE BITE RIPPED THE TOP OF DEGUY'S RIGHT ARM OFF.
THE WATER QUICKLY FILLED WITH BLOOD.
THE TERRITORIAL SHARK ATTACKED DEGUY'S DIVE PARTNER...
AND THEN DISAPPEARED INTO THE DEEP...
LEAVING BOTH DIVERS INJURED AND BLEEDING IN SHARK INFESTED WATERS.

DEGUY SURFACED **ONE HUNDRED YARDS** FROM HIS **BOAT**. HIS DIVE PARTNER WAS NOWHERE TO BE SEEN.

HE KNEW THAT **DOZENS** OF SHARKS WERE IN THE WATER BELOW HIM.

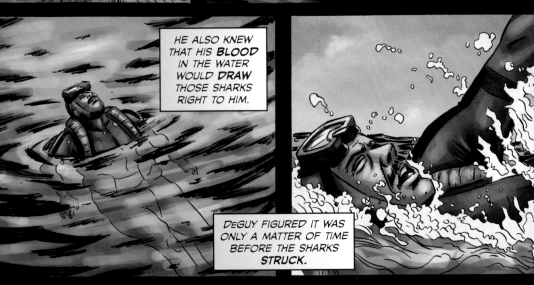

HE ALSO KNEW THAT HIS **BLOOD** IN THE WATER WOULD **DRAW** THOSE SHARKS RIGHT TO HIM.

DEGUY FIGURED IT WAS ONLY A MATTER OF TIME BEFORE THE SHARKS **STRUCK.**

BUT THE ATTACK NEVER CAME.

DEGUY REACHED THE BOAT TO FIND HIS DIVE PARTNER HAD ALREADY BEATEN HIM THERE.

BOTH MEN **ESCAPED** THE ORDEAL WITHOUT FURTHER INJURY.

TO THIS DAY HE STILL DOESN'T **KNOW** WHY THE SHARKS DIDN'T **ATTACK** HIM.

HIS EXPERIENCE GAVE HIM A NEW **RESPECT** FOR THE OCEANS' **OLDEST PREDATOR.**

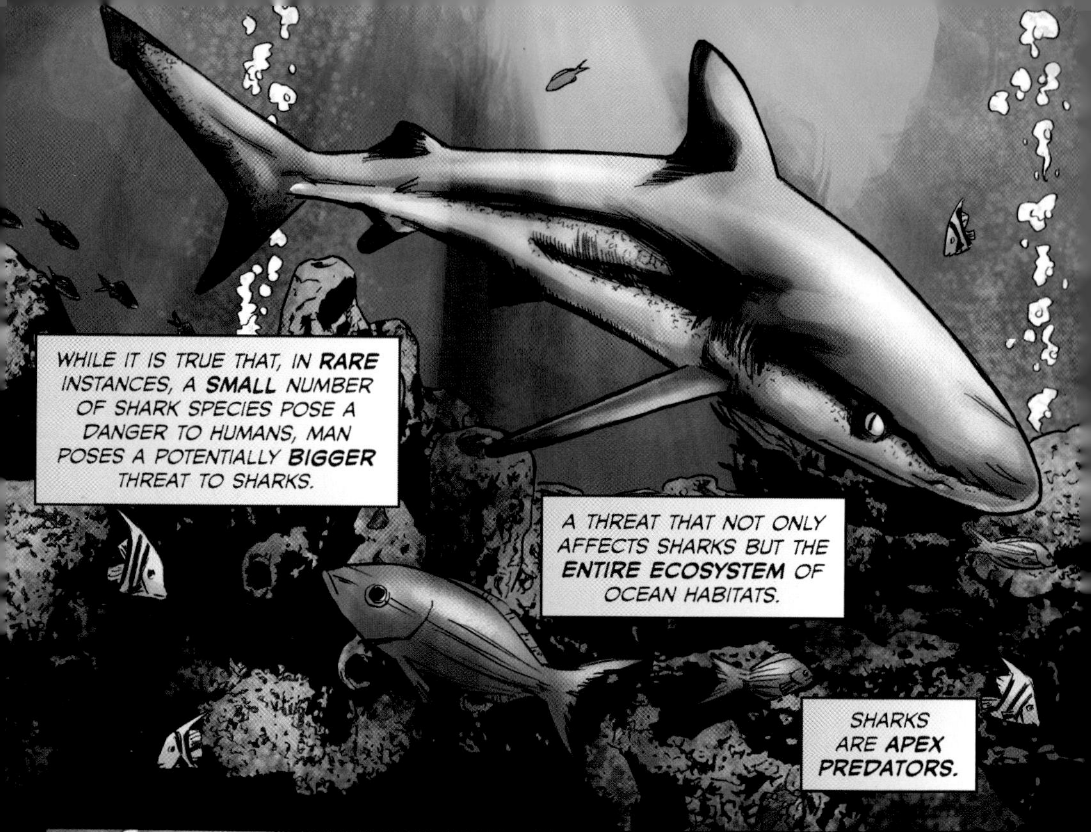
WHILE IT IS TRUE THAT, IN RARE INSTANCES, A SMALL NUMBER OF SHARK SPECIES POSE A DANGER TO HUMANS, MAN POSES A POTENTIALLY BIGGER THREAT TO SHARKS.
A THREAT THAT NOT ONLY AFFECTS SHARKS BUT THE ENTIRE ECOSYSTEM OF OCEAN HABITATS.
SHARKS ARE APEX PREDATORS.

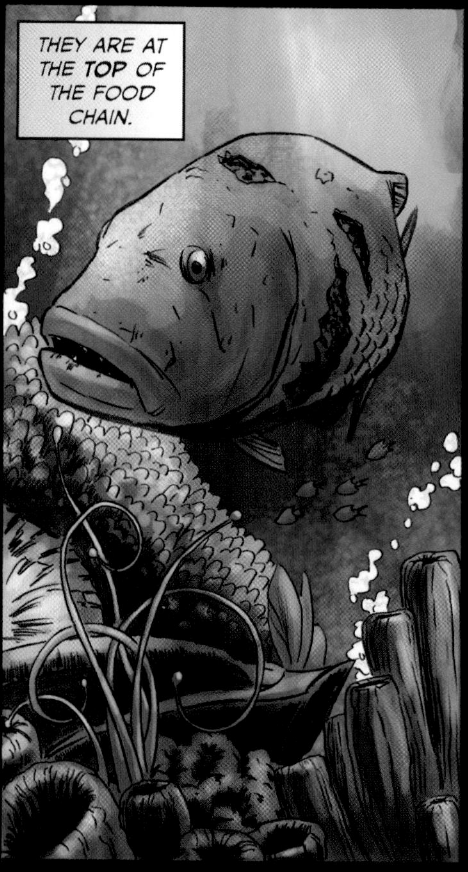
THEY ARE AT THE TOP OF THE FOOD CHAIN.

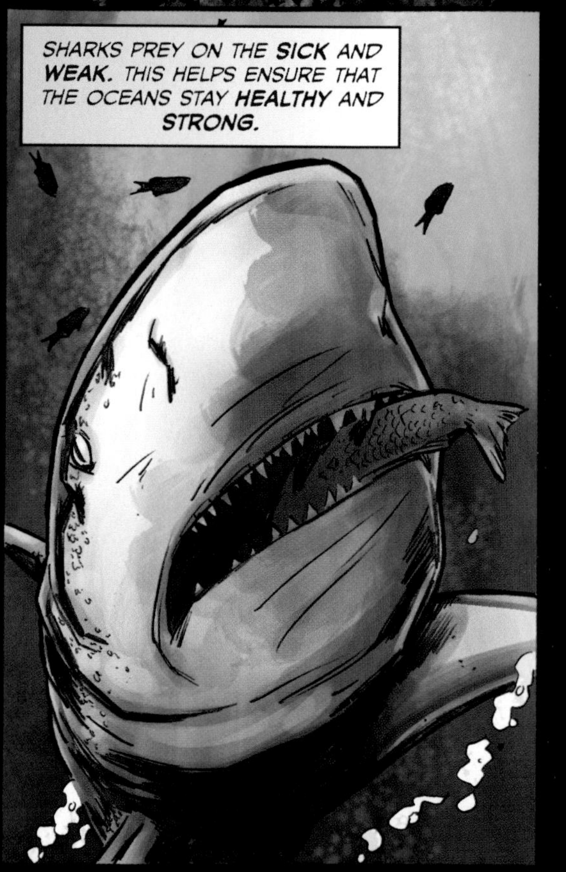
SHARKS PREY ON THE SICK AND WEAK. THIS HELPS ENSURE THAT THE OCEANS STAY HEALTHY AND STRONG.

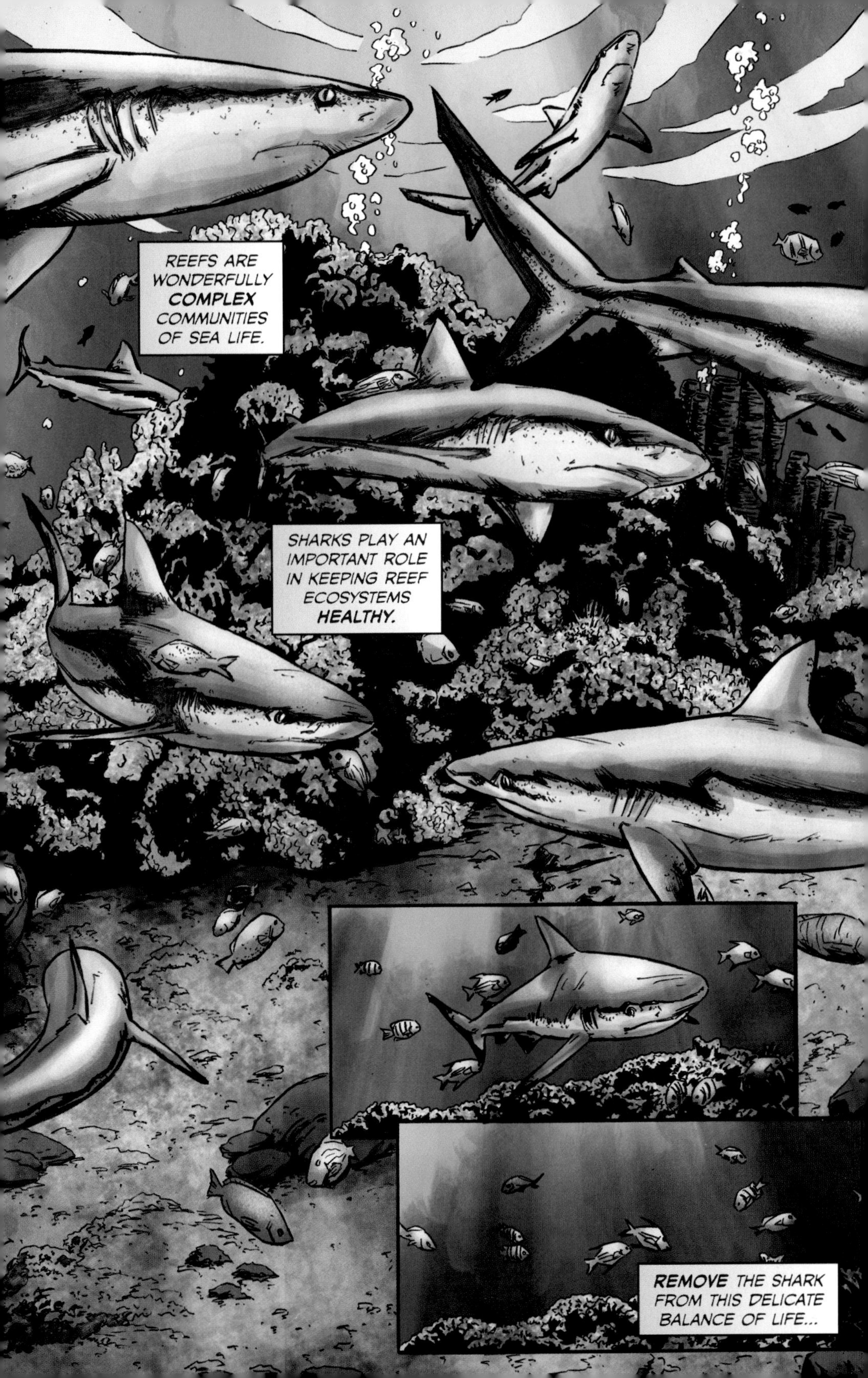
REEFS ARE WONDERFULLY COMPLEX COMMUNITIES OF SEA LIFE.
SHARKS PLAY AN IMPORTANT ROLE IN KEEPING REEF ECOSYSTEMS HEALTHY.
REMOVE THE SHARK FROM THIS DELICATE BALANCE OF LIFE...

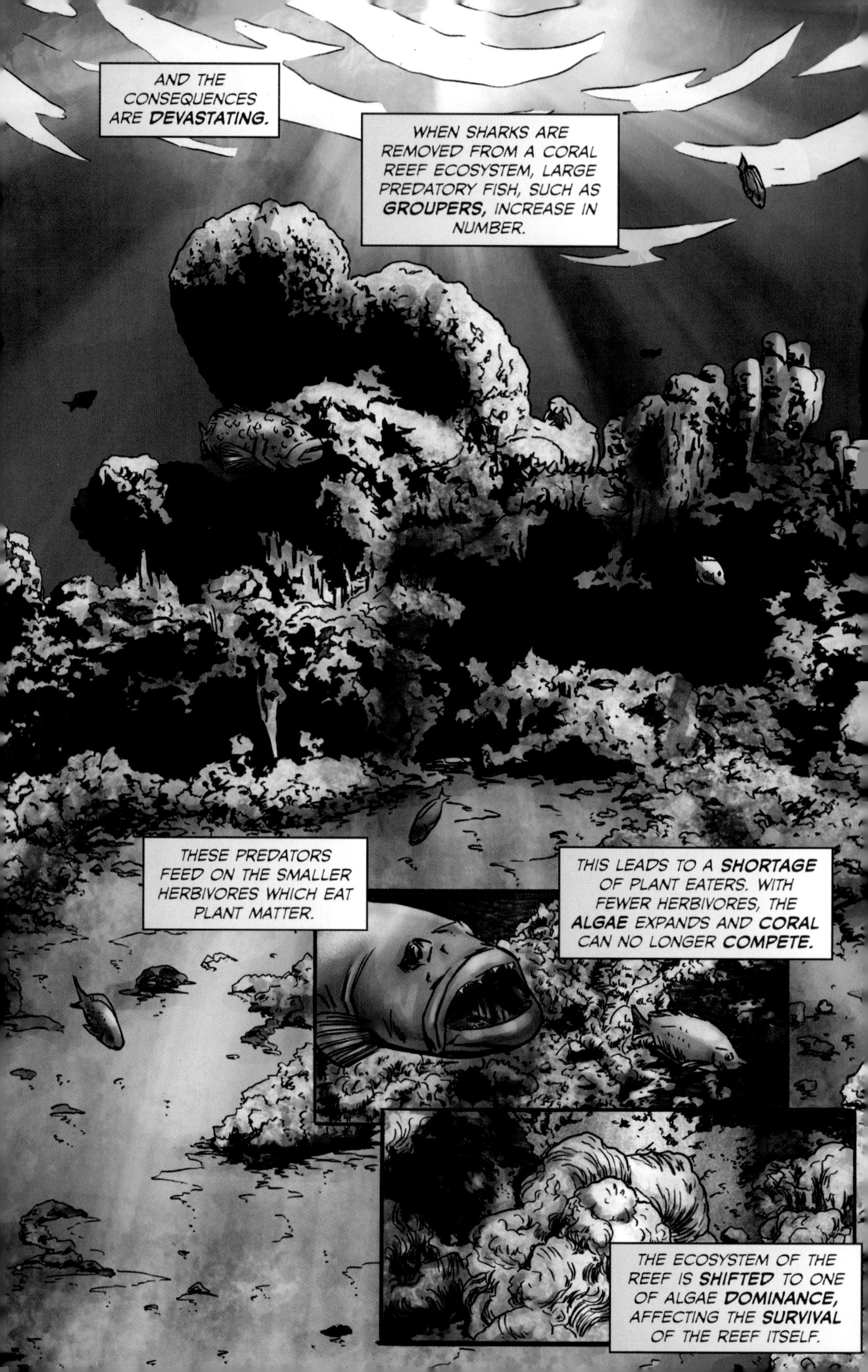
AND THE CONSEQUENCES ARE DEVASTATING.
WHEN SHARKS ARE REMOVED FROM A CORAL REEF ECOSYSTEM, LARGE PREDATORY FISH, SUCH AS GROUPERS, INCREASE IN NUMBER.
THESE PREDATORS FEED ON THE SMALLER HERBIVORES WHICH EAT PLANT MATTER.
THIS LEADS TO A SHORTAGE OF PLANT EATERS. WITH FEWER HERBIVORES, THE ALGAE EXPANDS AND CORAL CAN NO LONGER COMPETE.
THE ECOSYSTEM OF THE REEF IS SHIFTED TO ONE OF ALGAE DOMINANCE, AFFECTING THE SURVIVAL OF THE REEF ITSELF.

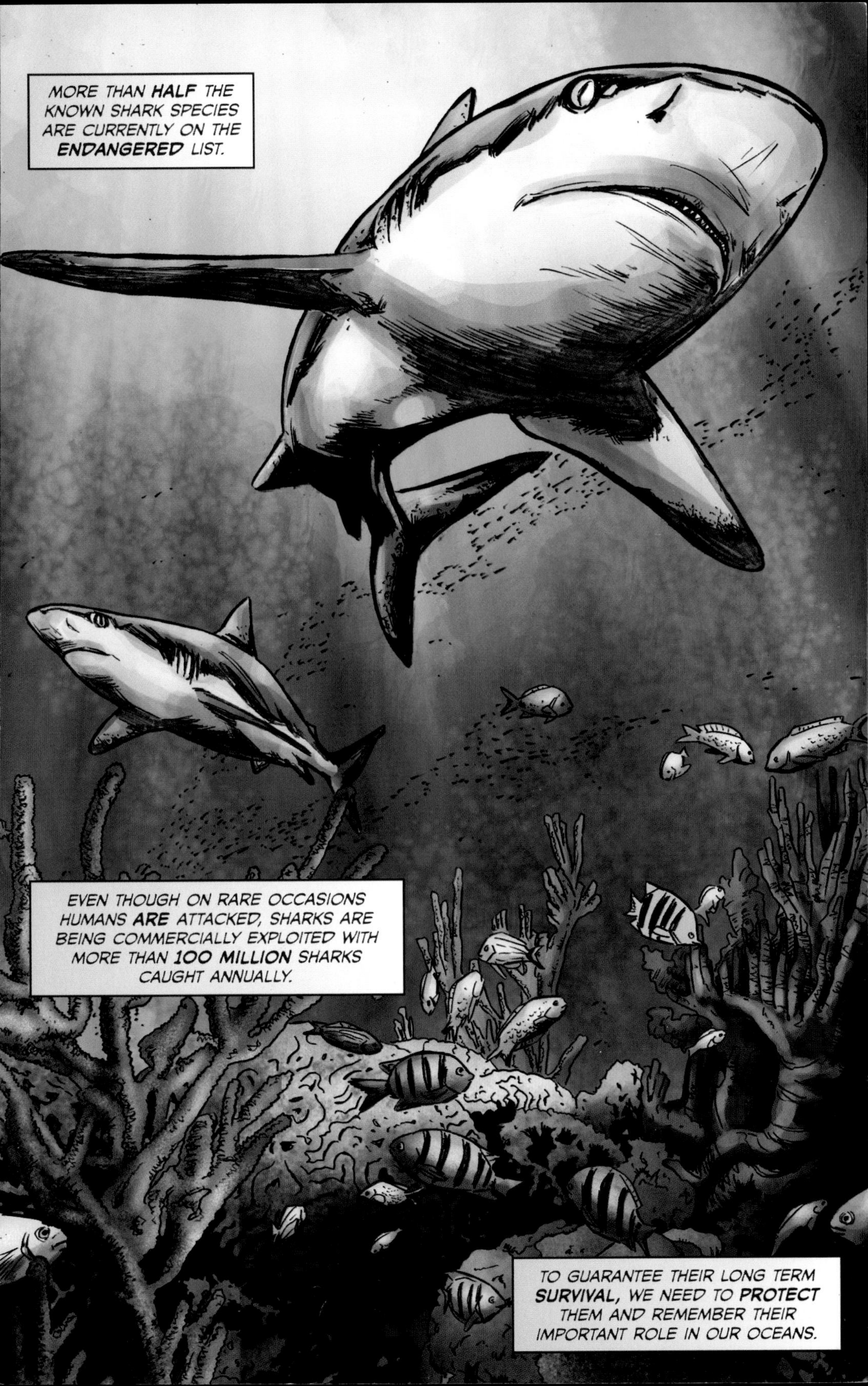
MORE THAN HALF THE KNOWN SHARK SPECIES ARE CURRENTLY ON THE ENDANGERED LIST.
EVEN THOUGH ON RARE OCCASIONS HUMANS ARE ATTACKED, SHARKS ARE BEING COMMERCIALLY EXPLOITED WITH MORE THAN 100 MILLION SHARKS CAUGHT ANNUALLY.
TO GUARANTEE THEIR LONG TERM SURVIVAL, WE NEED TO PROTECT THEM AND REMEMBER THEIR IMPORTANT ROLE IN OUR OCEANS.

#5 THE SHORTFIN MAKO SHARK

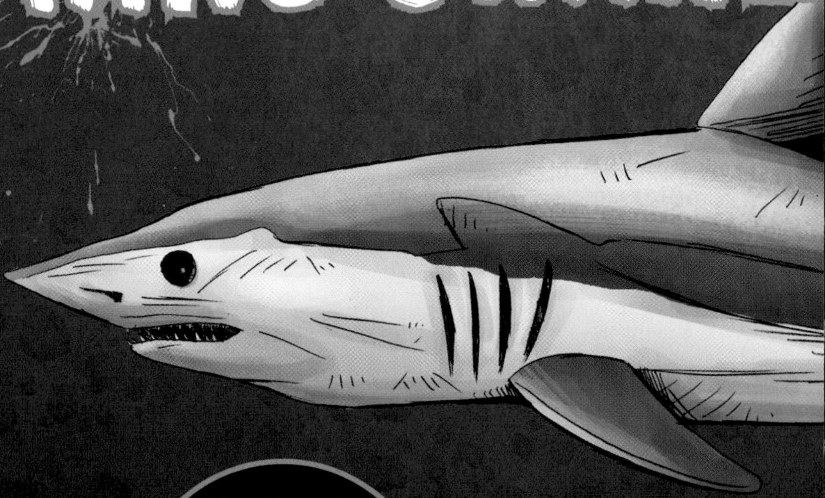

The Shortfin Mako's teeth are visible even when their mouth is closed. Like the Sand Tiger, this gives the Mako a sinister appearance.

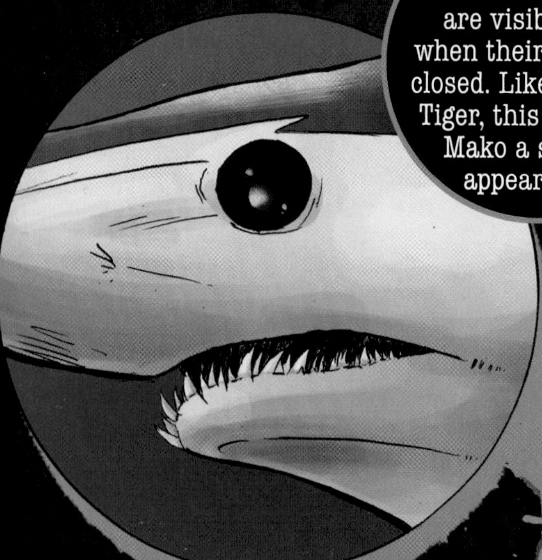

ATTACK FILE:

Recorded Attacks: 25

Unprovoked Fatalities: 1

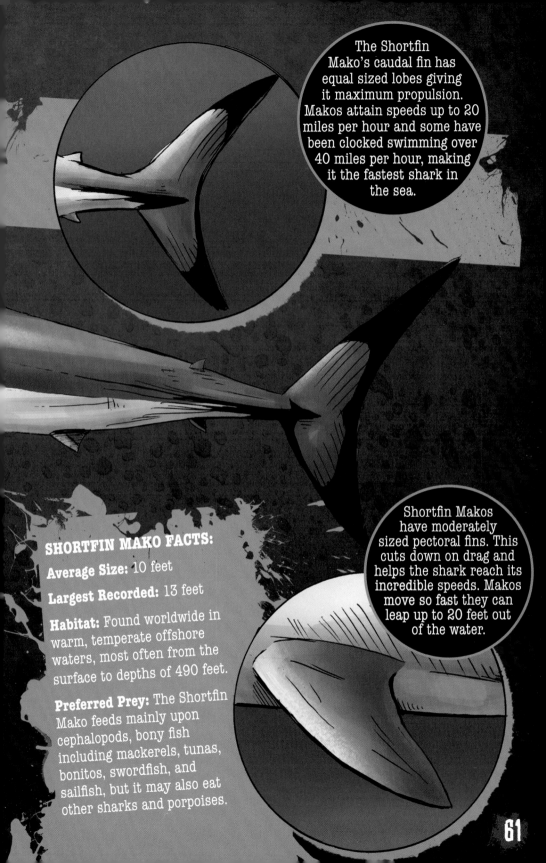

The Shortfin Mako's caudal fin has equal sized lobes giving it maximum propulsion. Makos attain speeds up to 20 miles per hour and some have been clocked swimming over 40 miles per hour, making it the fastest shark in the sea.

Shortfin Makos have moderately sized pectoral fins. This cuts down on drag and helps the shark reach its incredible speeds. Makos move so fast they can leap up to 20 feet out of the water.

SHORTFIN MAKO FACTS:

Average Size: 10 feet

Largest Recorded: 13 feet

Habitat: Found worldwide in warm, temperate offshore waters, most often from the surface to depths of 490 feet.

Preferred Prey: The Shortfin Mako feeds mainly upon cephalopods, bony fish including mackerels, tunas, bonitos, swordfish, and sailfish, but it may also eat other sharks and porpoises.

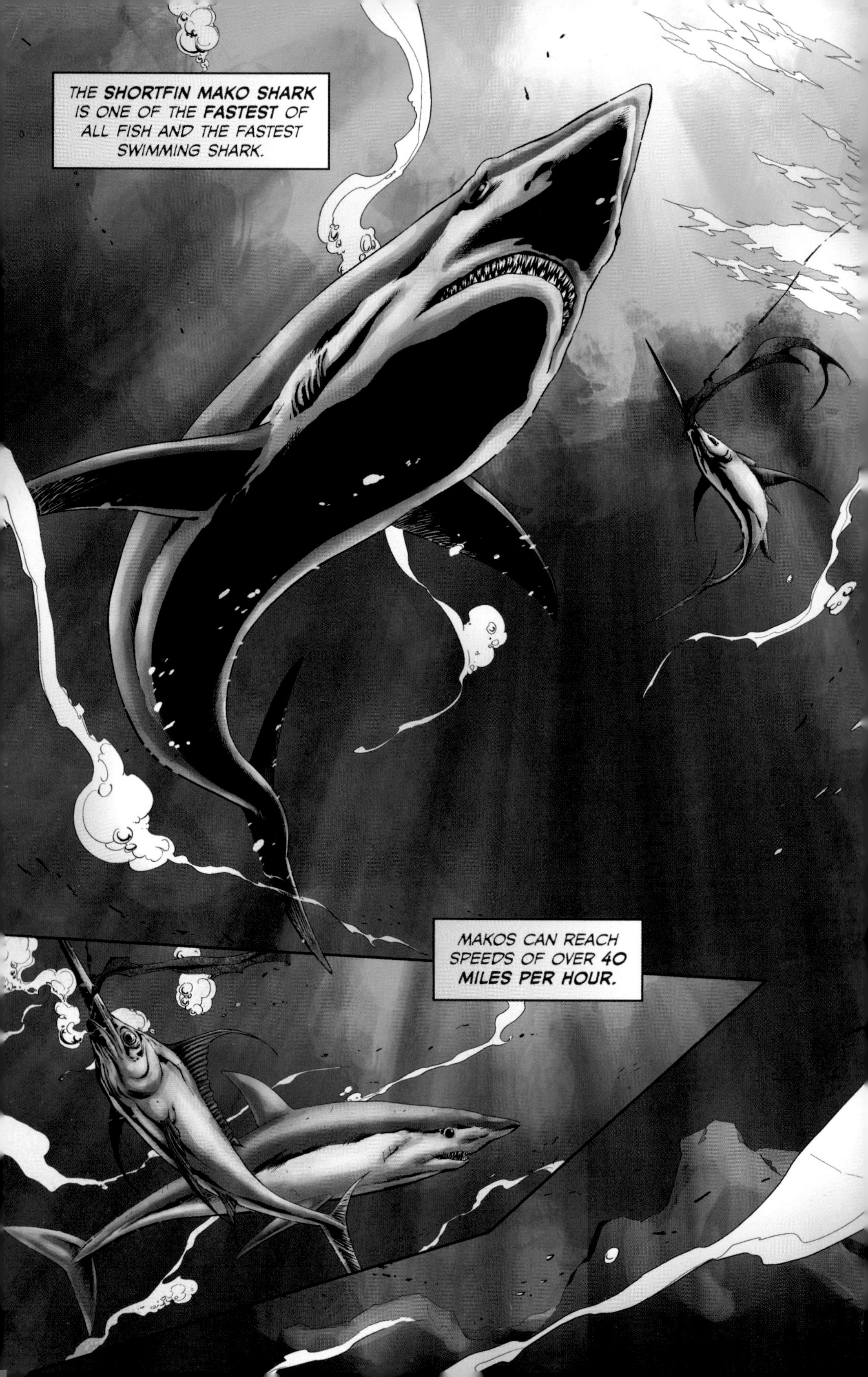
THE SHORTFIN MAKO SHARK IS ONE OF THE FASTEST OF ALL FISH AND THE FASTEST SWIMMING SHARK.
MAKOS CAN REACH SPEEDS OF OVER 40 MILES PER HOUR.

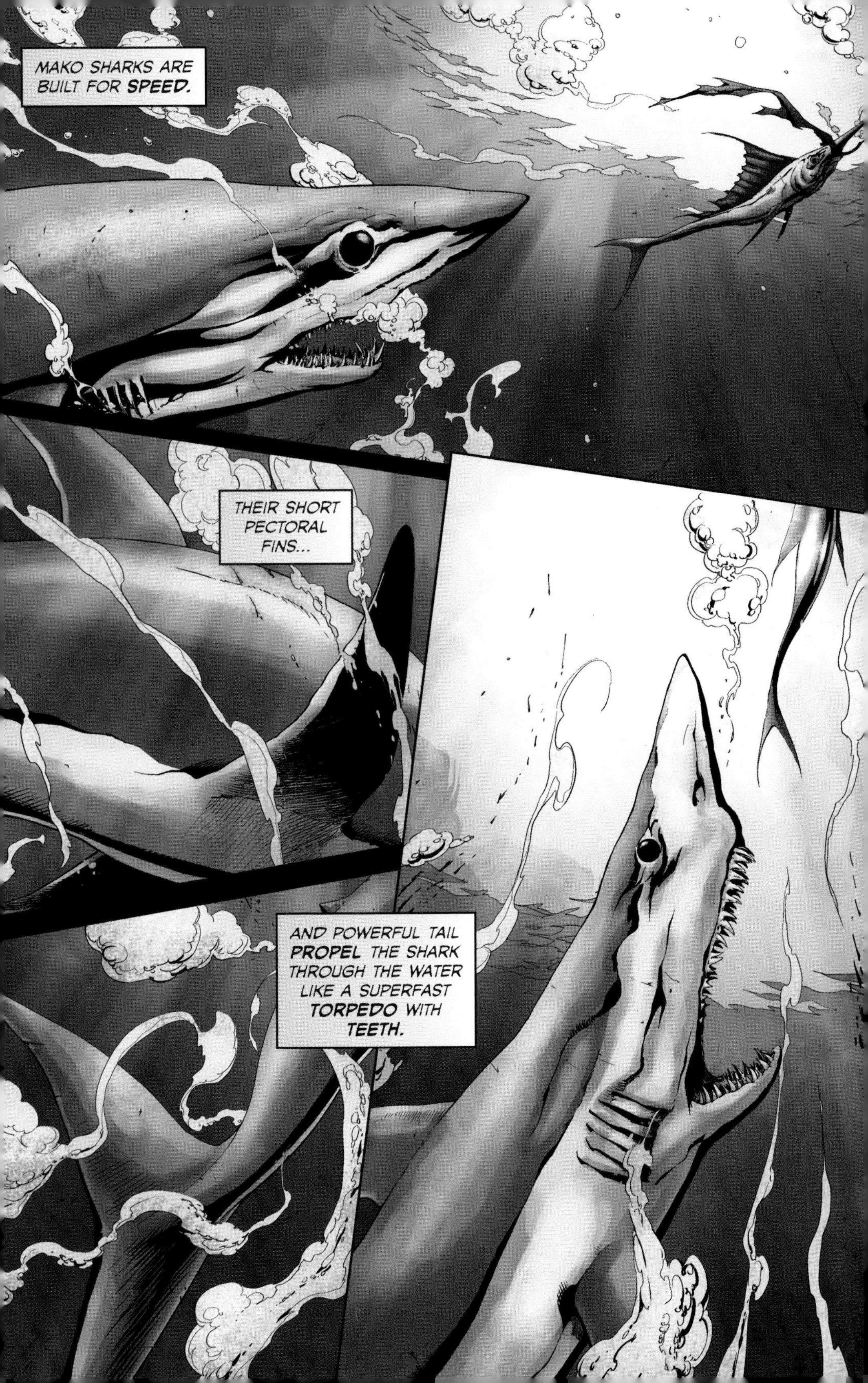
MAKO SHARKS ARE BUILT FOR SPEED.
THEIR SHORT PECTORAL FINS...
AND POWERFUL TAIL PROPEL THE SHARK THROUGH THE WATER LIKE A SUPERFAST TORPEDO WITH TEETH.

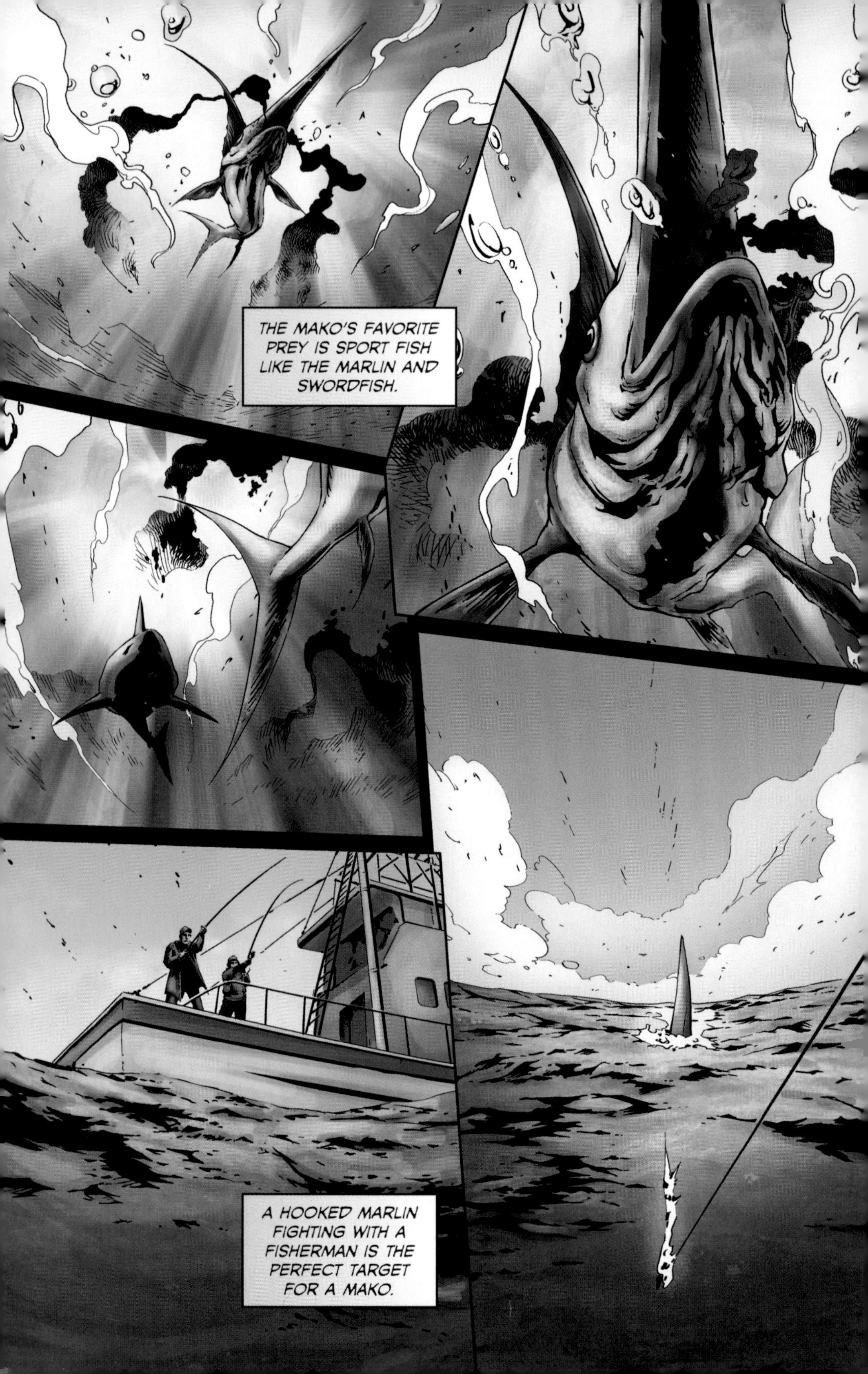
THE MAKO'S FAVORITE PREY IS SPORT FISH LIKE THE MARLIN AND SWORDFISH.
A HOOKED MARLIN FIGHTING WITH A FISHERMAN IS THE PERFECT TARGET FOR A MAKO.

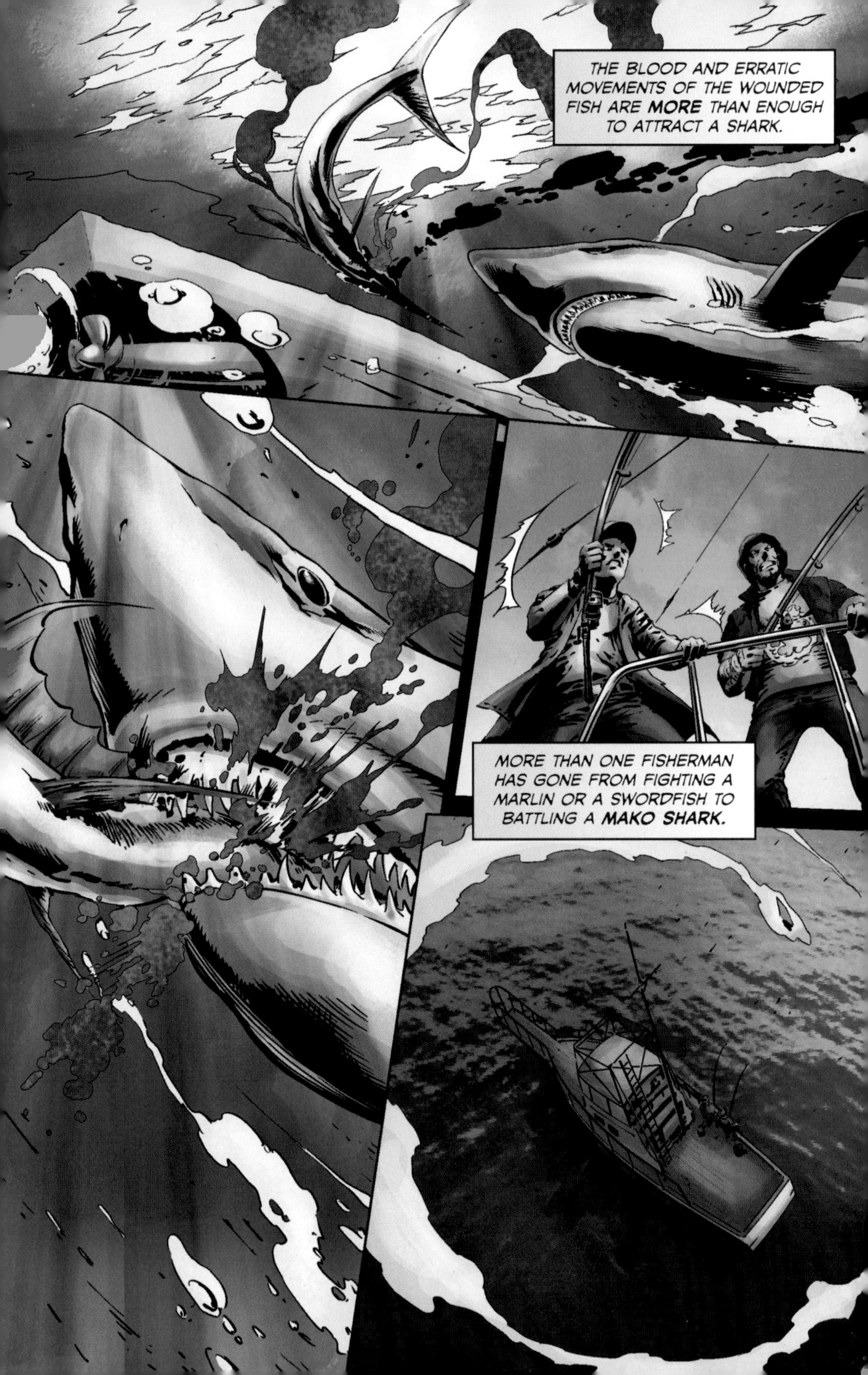
THE BLOOD AND ERRATIC MOVEMENTS OF THE WOUNDED FISH ARE **MORE** THAN ENOUGH TO ATTRACT A SHARK.
MORE THAN ONE FISHERMAN HAS GONE FROM FIGHTING A MARLIN OR A SWORDFISH TO BATTLING A **MAKO SHARK.**

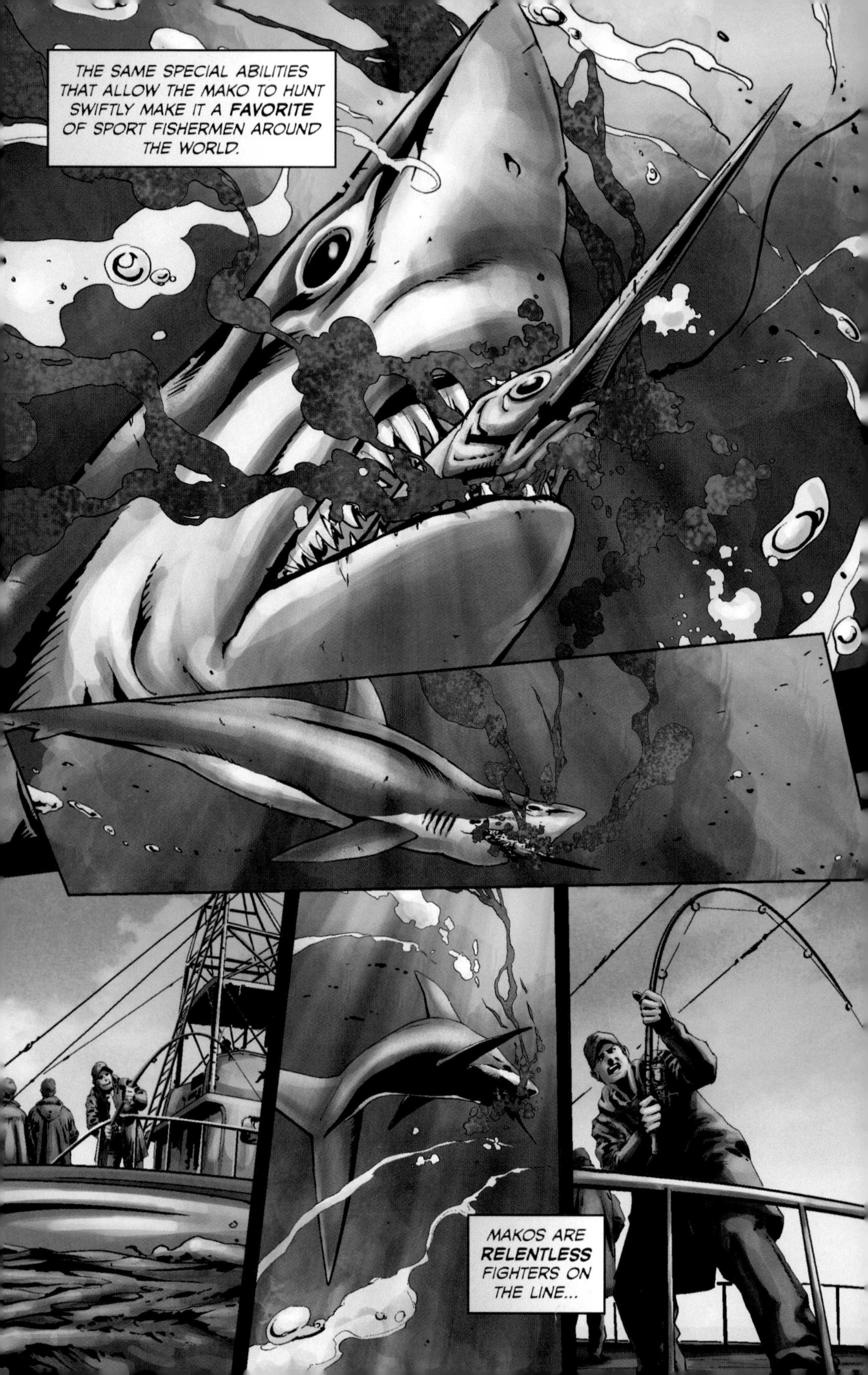
THE SAME SPECIAL ABILITIES THAT ALLOW THE MAKO TO HUNT SWIFTLY MAKE IT A **FAVORITE** OF SPORT FISHERMEN AROUND THE WORLD.
MAKOS ARE **RELENTLESS** FIGHTERS ON THE LINE...

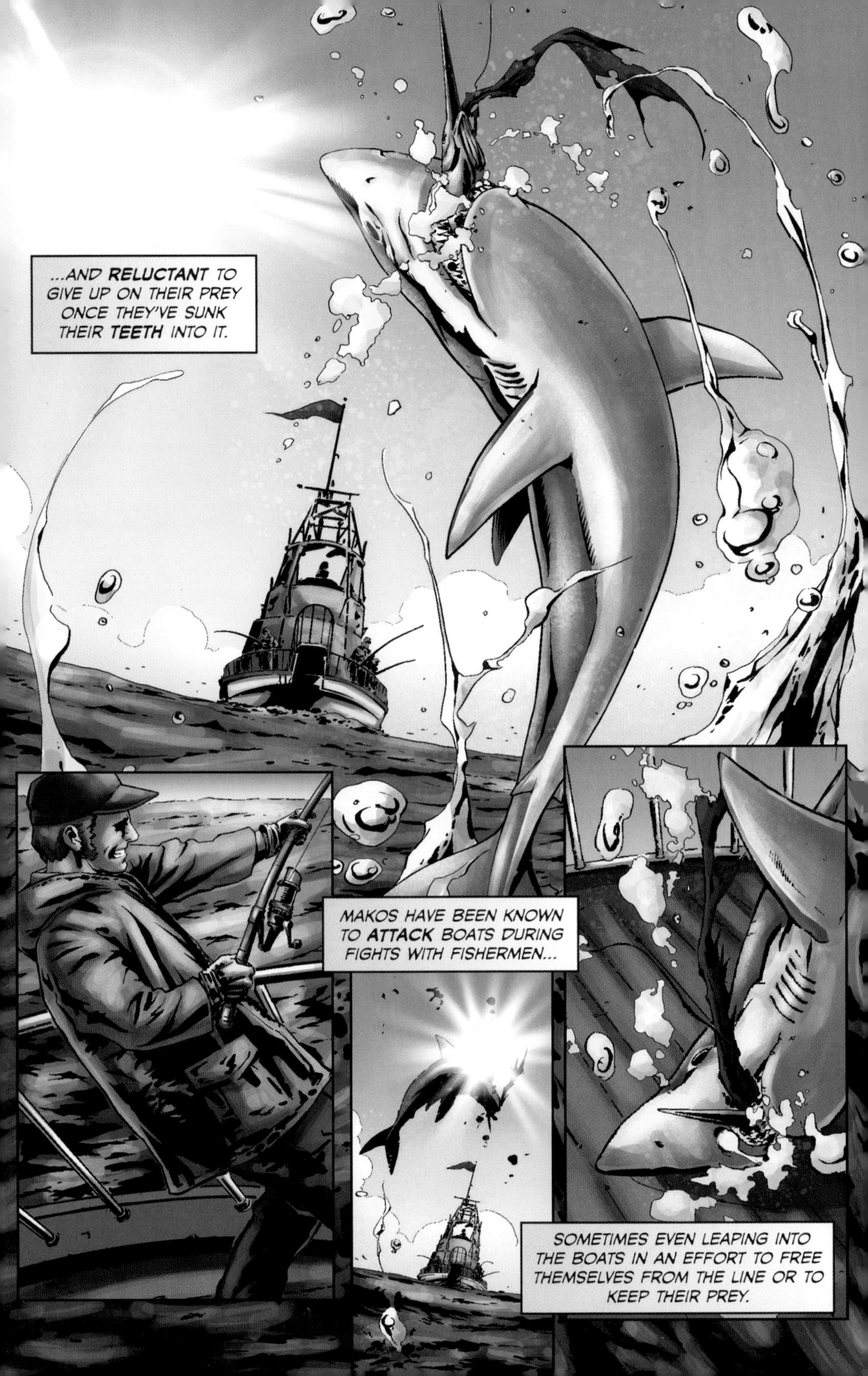
...AND **RELUCTANT** TO GIVE UP ON THEIR PREY ONCE THEY'VE SUNK THEIR **TEETH** INTO IT.
MAKOS HAVE BEEN KNOWN TO **ATTACK** BOATS DURING FIGHTS WITH FISHERMEN...
SOMETIMES EVEN LEAPING INTO THE BOATS IN AN EFFORT TO FREE THEMSELVES FROM THE LINE OR TO KEEP THEIR PREY.

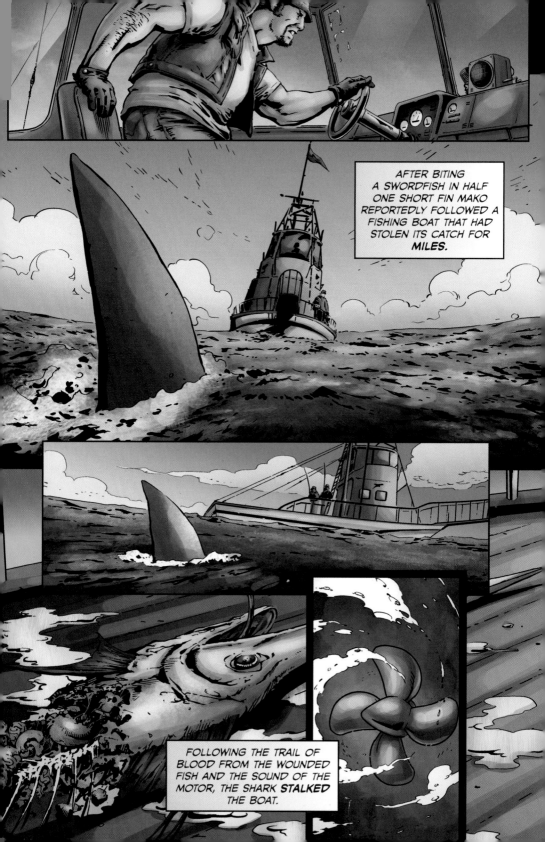

AFTER BITING A SWORDFISH IN HALF ONE SHORT FIN MAKO REPORTEDLY FOLLOWED A FISHING BOAT THAT HAD STOLEN ITS CATCH FOR **MILES.**

FOLLOWING THE TRAIL OF BLOOD FROM THE WOUNDED FISH AND THE SOUND OF THE MOTOR, THE SHARK **STALKED** THE BOAT.

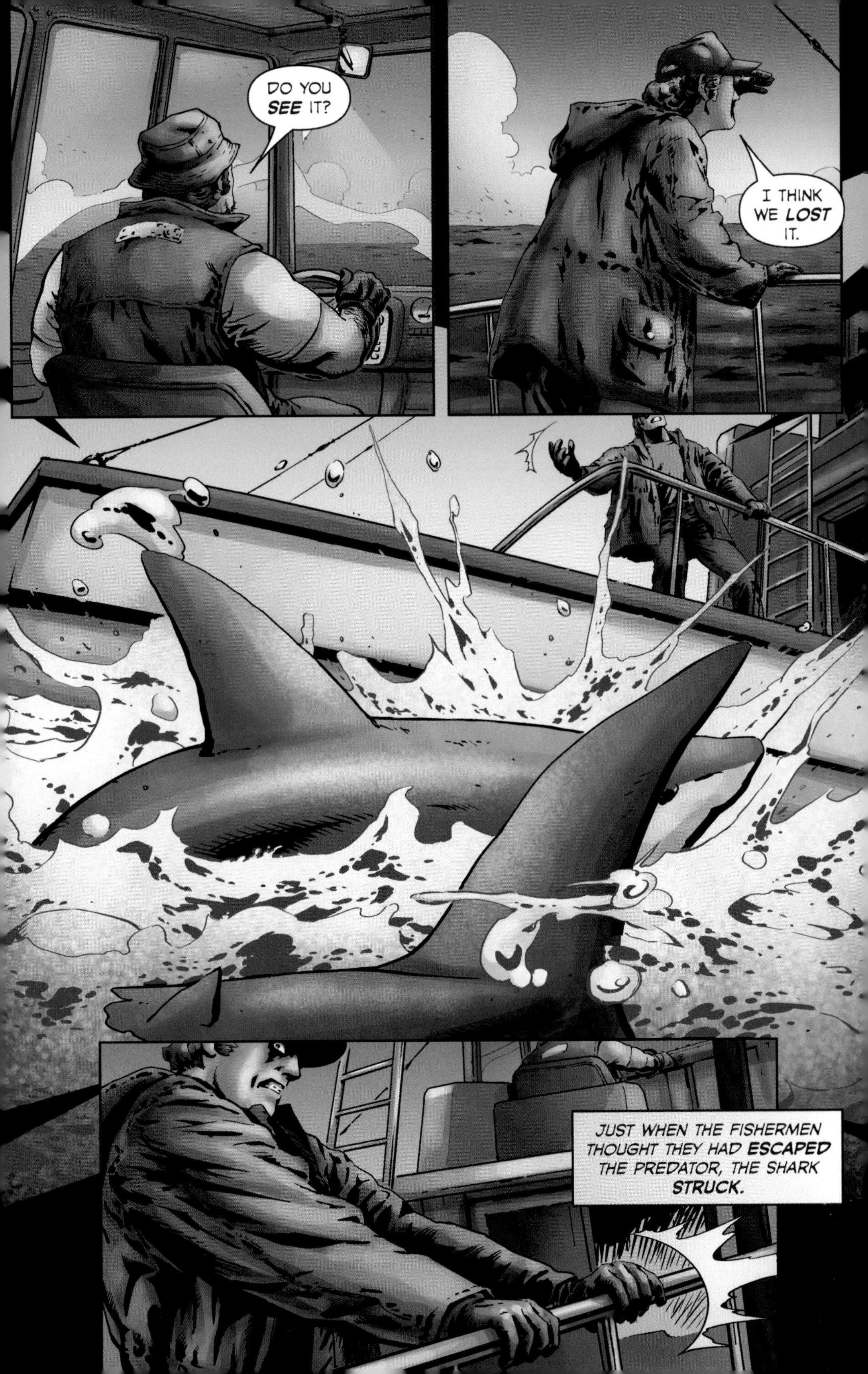
DO YOU SEE IT?
I THINK WE LOST IT.
JUST WHEN THE FISHERMEN THOUGHT THEY HAD ESCAPED THE PREDATOR, THE SHARK STRUCK.

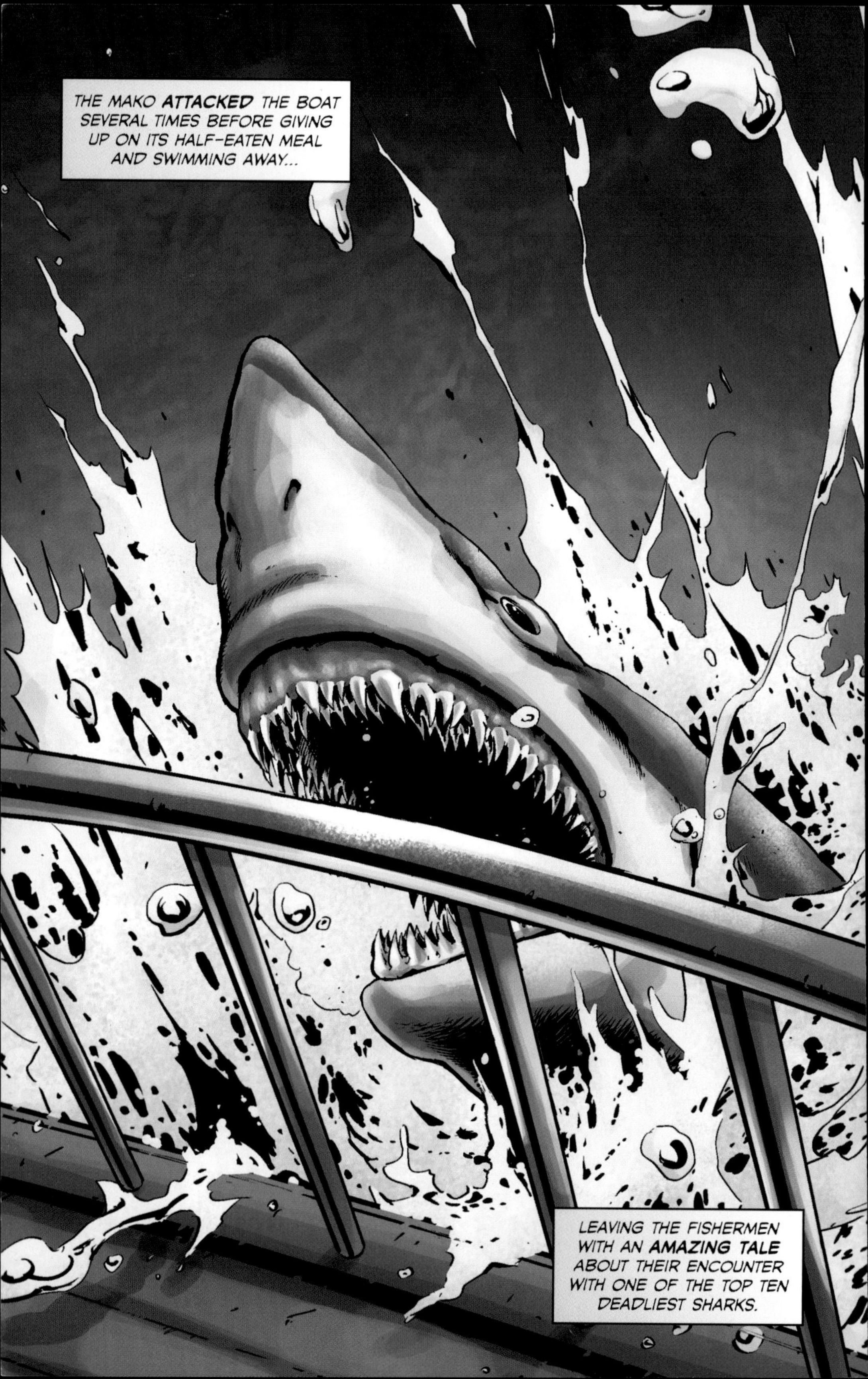
THE MAKO ATTACKED THE BOAT SEVERAL TIMES BEFORE GIVING UP ON ITS HALF-EATEN MEAL AND SWIMMING AWAY...
LEAVING THE FISHERMEN WITH AN AMAZING TALE ABOUT THEIR ENCOUNTER WITH ONE OF THE TOP TEN DEADLIEST SHARKS.

Shark Fact File:
Shortfin Mako Sharks can leap up to 20 feet out of the water into the air.

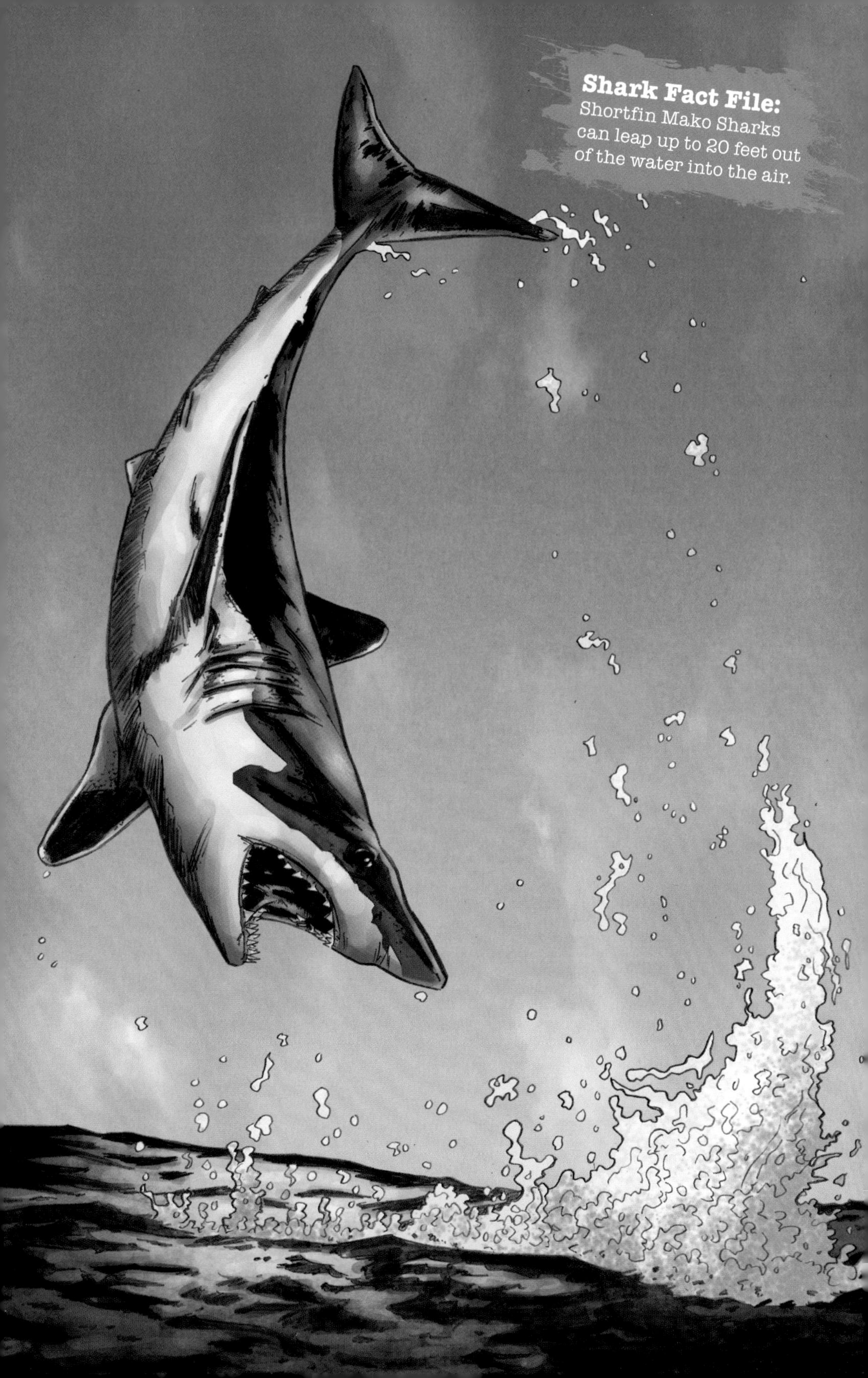

#4 THE OCEANIC WHITETIP SHARK

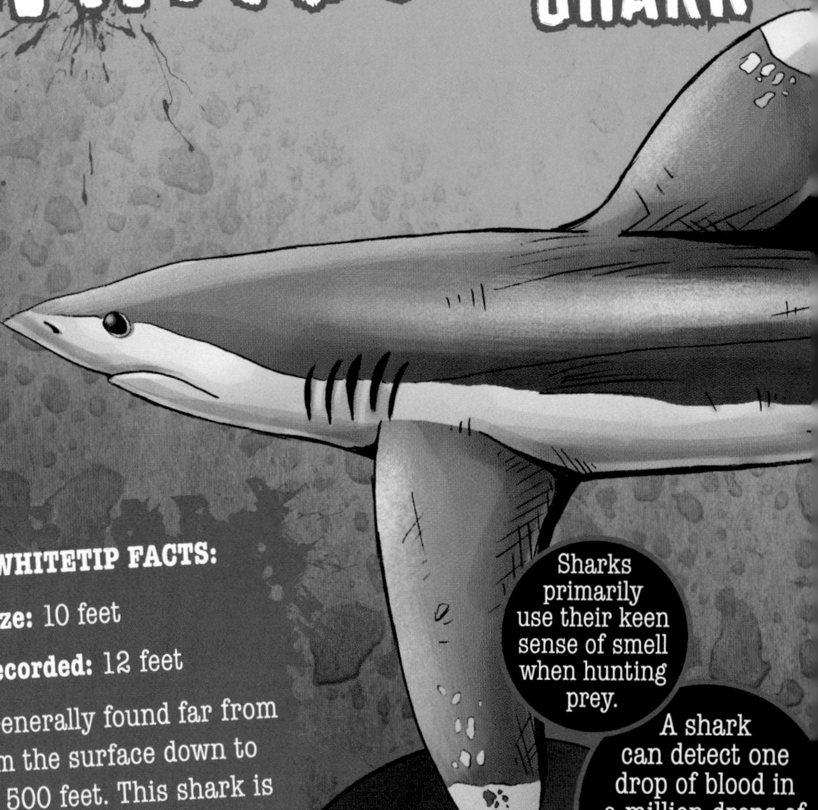

OCEANIC WHITETIP FACTS:

Average Size: 10 feet

Largest Recorded: 12 feet

Habitat: Generally found far from shore, from the surface down to a depth of 500 feet. This shark is common in warm oceanic water and occasionally found in coastal areas of the tropics or warm temperate waters.

Preferred Prey:
Fast moving fishes such as tuna, barracuda and white marlin. However it also consumes squid, turtles, seabirds and even garbage that has been disposed of at sea.

Sharks primarily use their keen sense of smell when hunting prey.

A shark can detect one drop of blood in a million drops of water and can sme blood a 1/4 mile away.

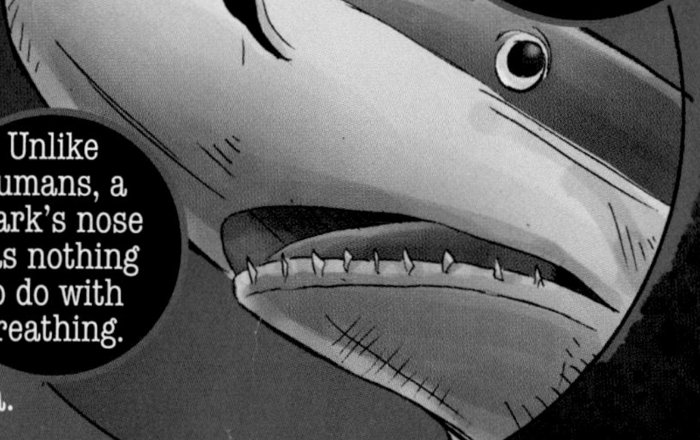

Unlike humans, a shark's nose has nothing to do with breathing.

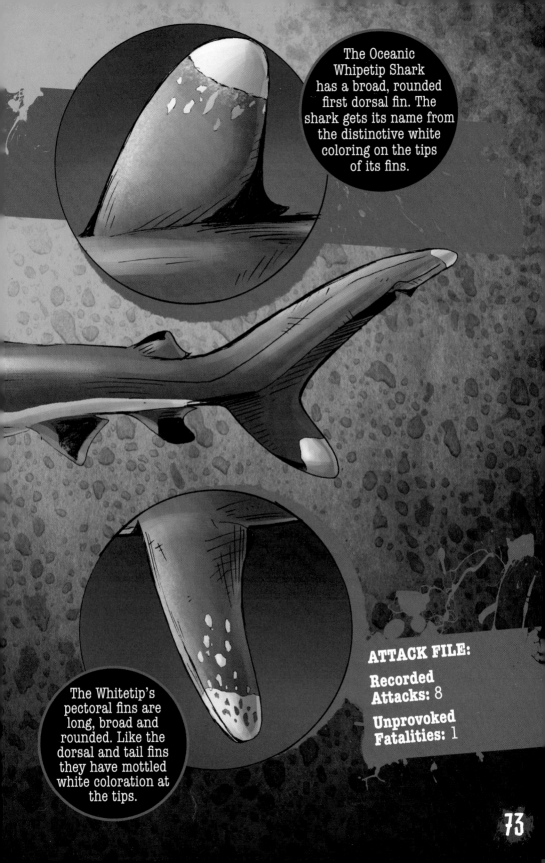

The Oceanic Whipetip Shark has a broad, rounded first dorsal fin. The shark gets its name from the distinctive white coloring on the tips of its fins.

The Whitetip's pectoral fins are long, broad and rounded. Like the dorsal and tail fins they have mottled white coloration at the tips.

ATTACK FILE:

Recorded Attacks: 8

Unprovoked Fatalities: 1

73

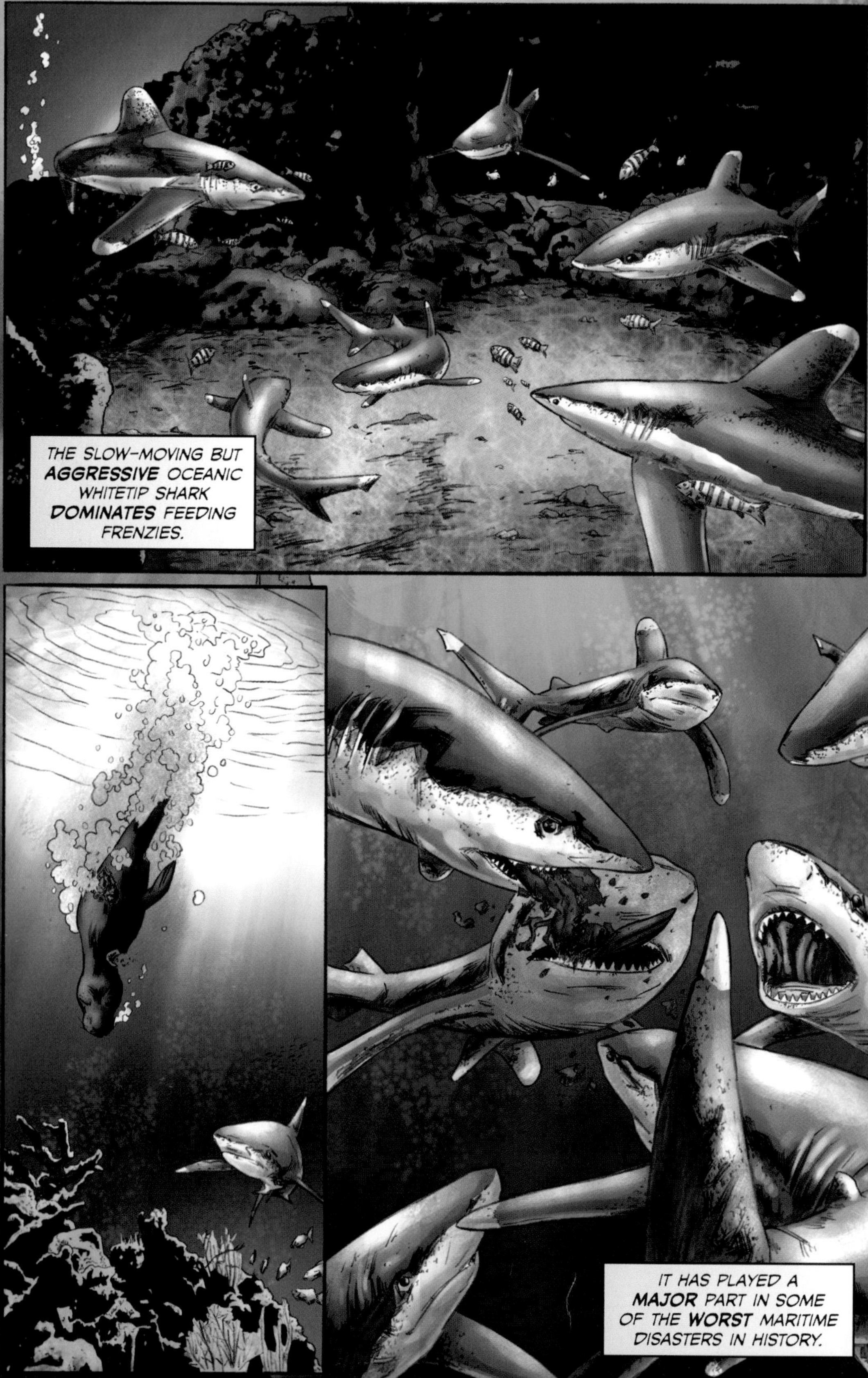
THE SLOW-MOVING BUT AGGRESSIVE OCEANIC WHITETIP SHARK DOMINATES FEEDING FRENZIES.
IT HAS PLAYED A MAJOR PART IN SOME OF THE WORST MARITIME DISASTERS IN HISTORY.

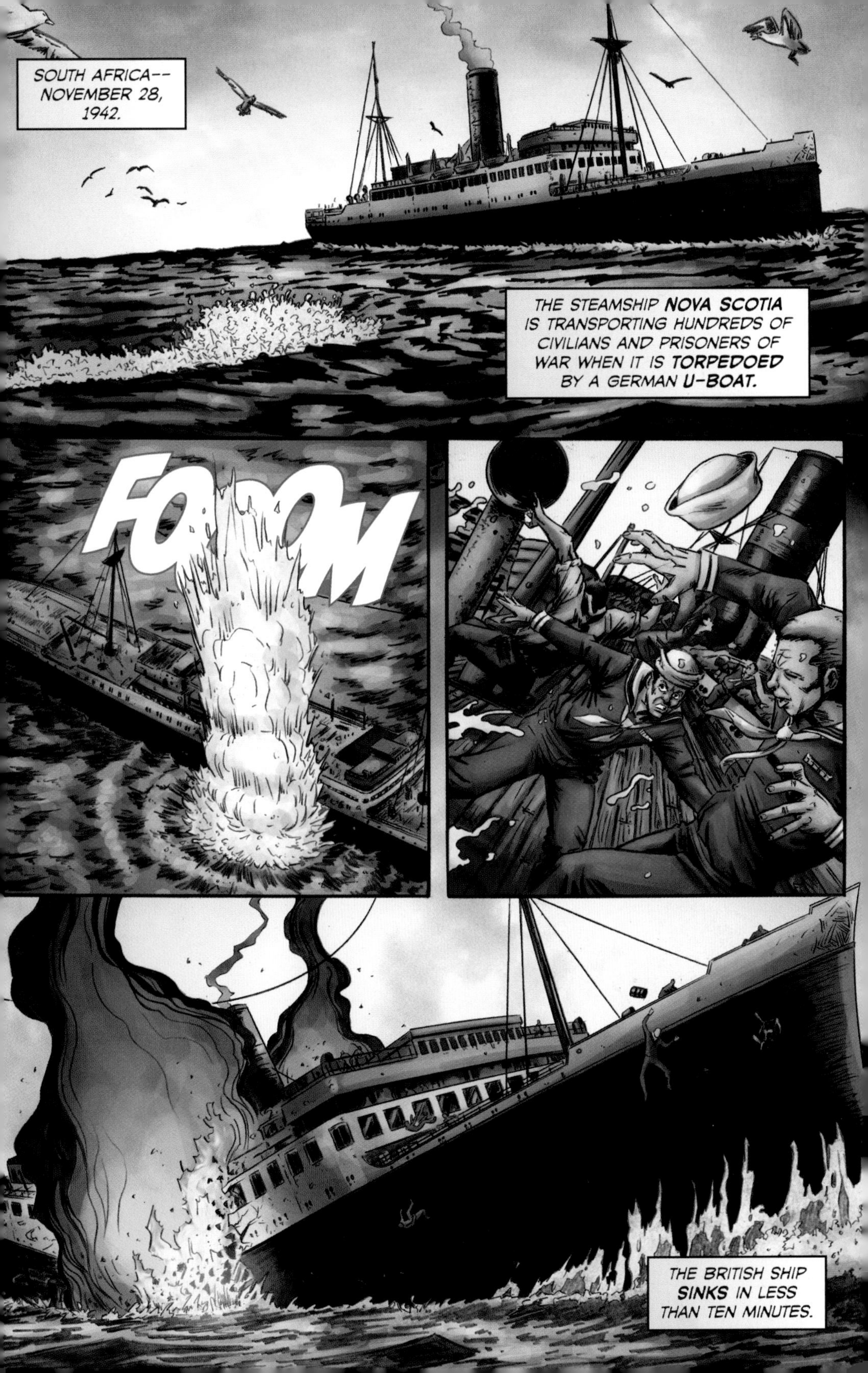
SOUTH AFRICA-- NOVEMBER 28, 1942.
THE STEAMSHIP NOVA SCOTIA IS TRANSPORTING HUNDREDS OF CIVILIANS AND PRISONERS OF WAR WHEN IT IS TORPEDOED BY A GERMAN U-BOAT.
FOOOM
THE BRITISH SHIP SINKS IN LESS THAN TEN MINUTES.

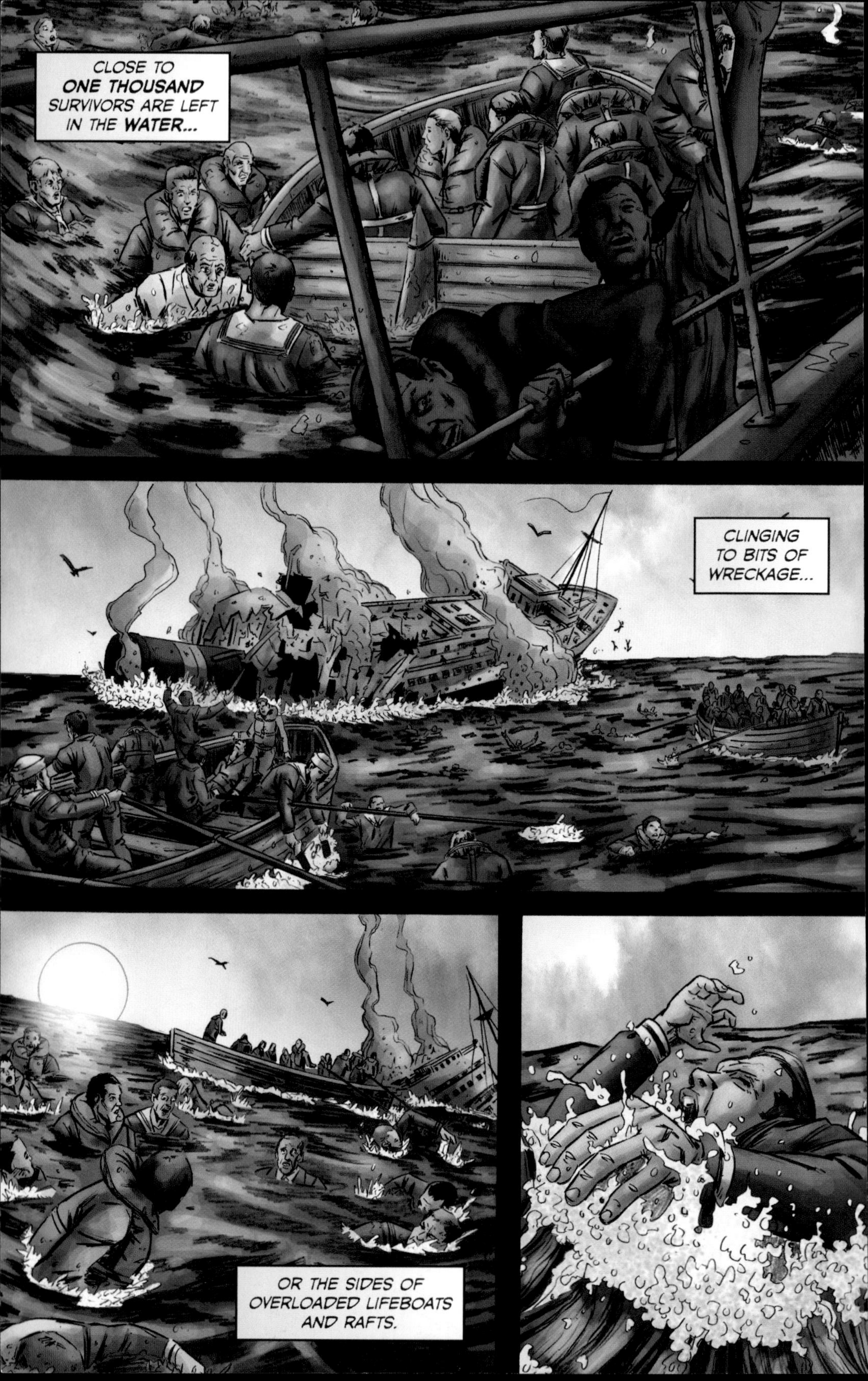
CLOSE TO ONE THOUSAND SURVIVORS ARE LEFT IN THE WATER...
CLINGING TO BITS OF WRECKAGE...
OR THE SIDES OF OVERLOADED LIFEBOATS AND RAFTS.

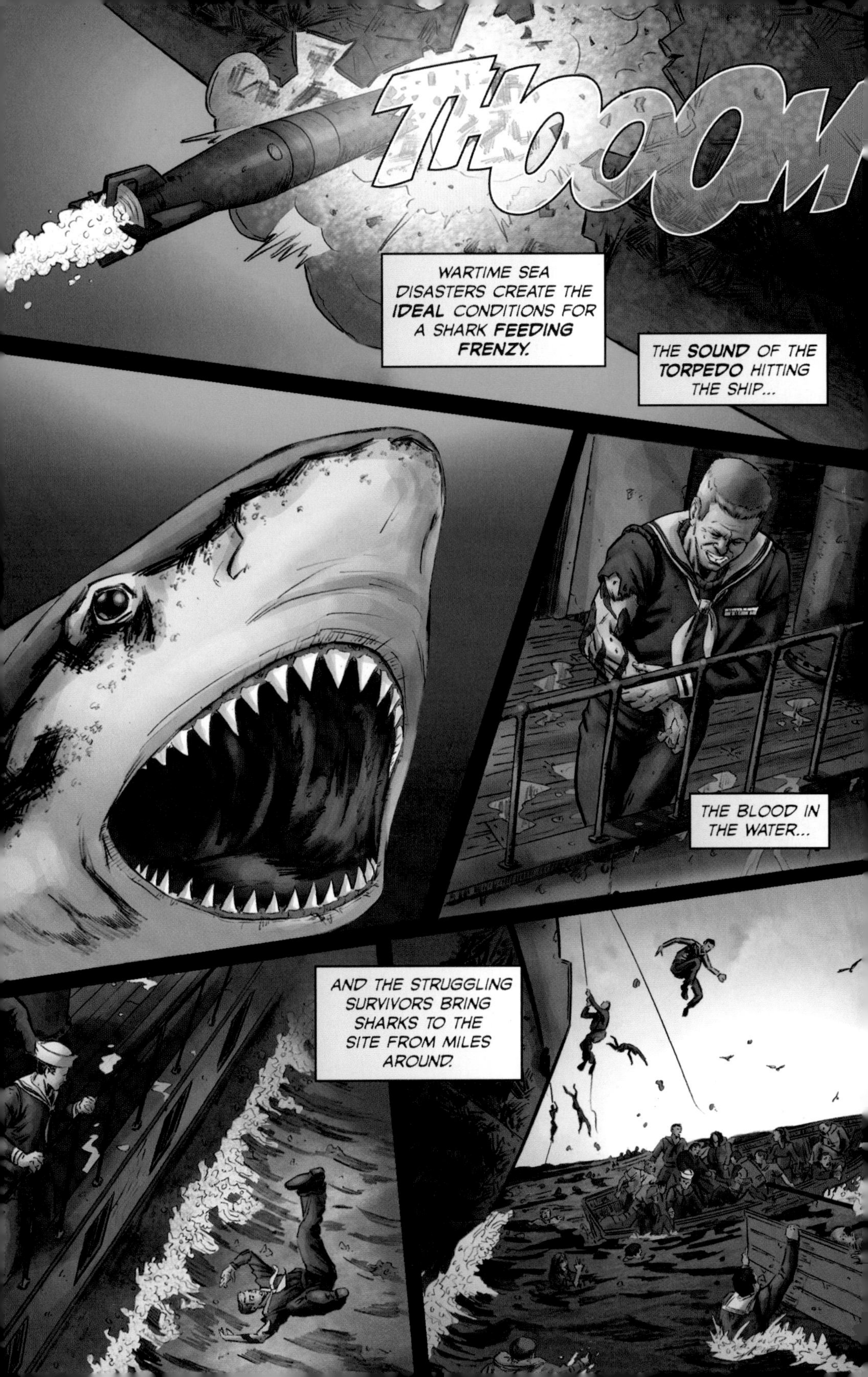
THOOOM
WARTIME SEA DISASTERS CREATE THE IDEAL CONDITIONS FOR A SHARK FEEDING FRENZY.
THE SOUND OF THE TORPEDO HITTING THE SHIP...
THE BLOOD IN THE WATER...
AND THE STRUGGLING SURVIVORS BRING SHARKS TO THE SITE FROM MILES AROUND.

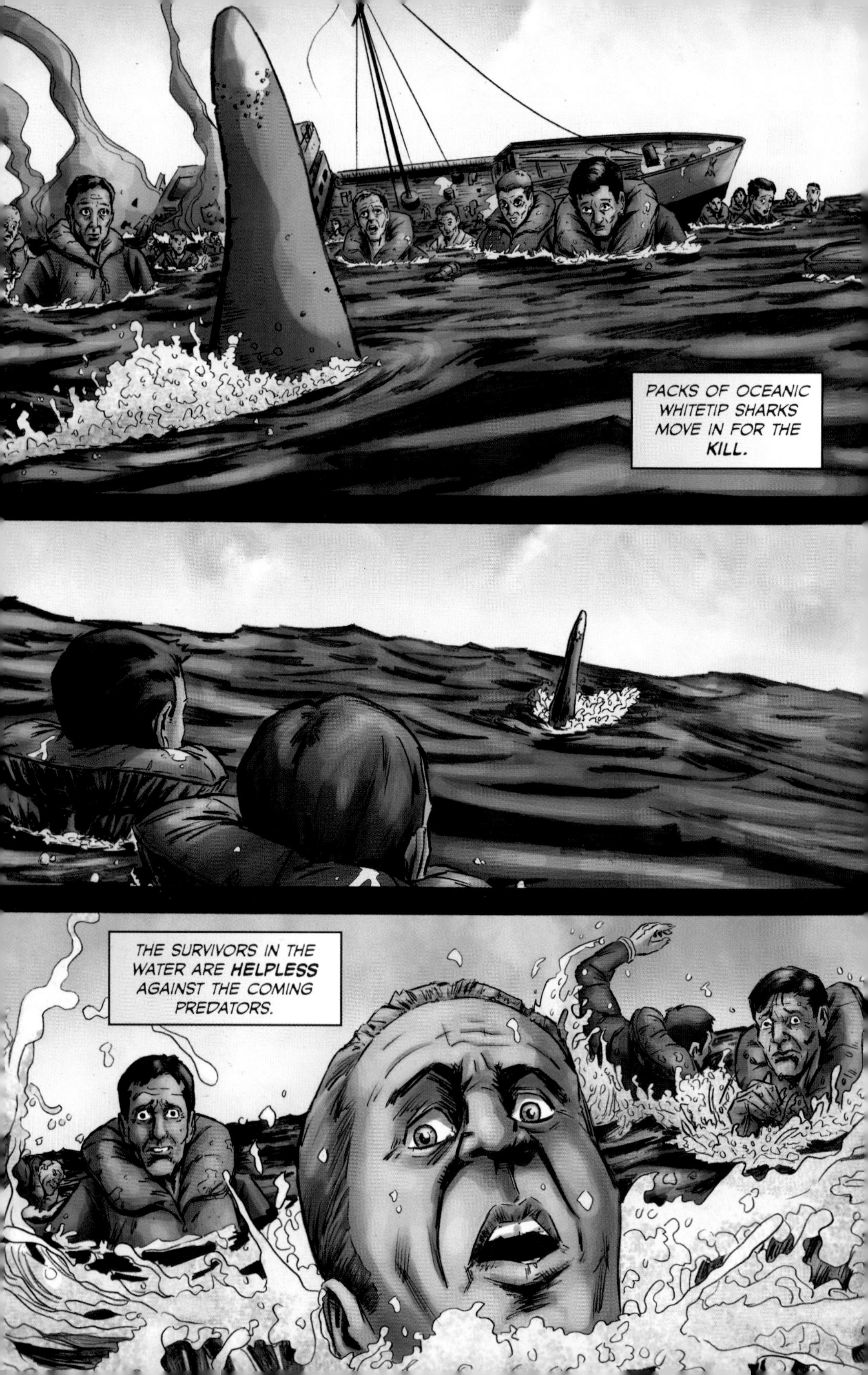
PACKS OF OCEANIC WHITETIP SHARKS MOVE IN FOR THE KILL.
THE SURVIVORS IN THE WATER ARE HELPLESS AGAINST THE COMING PREDATORS.

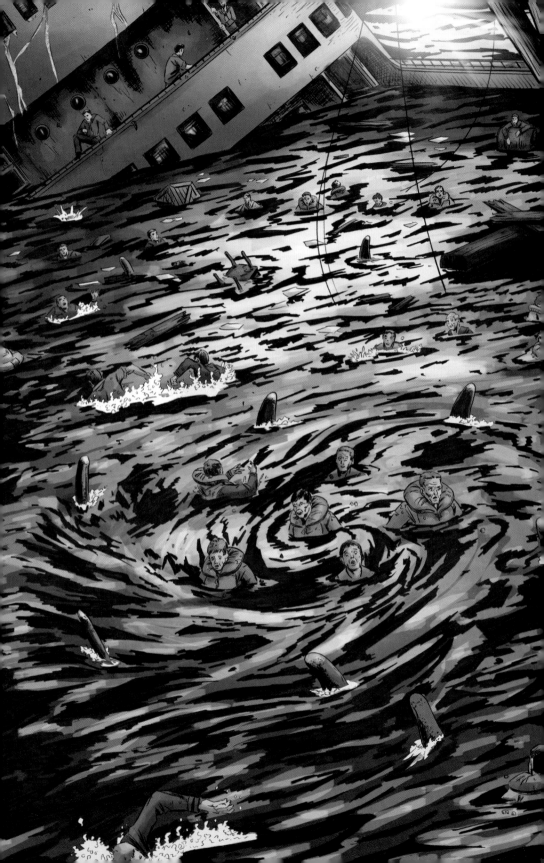

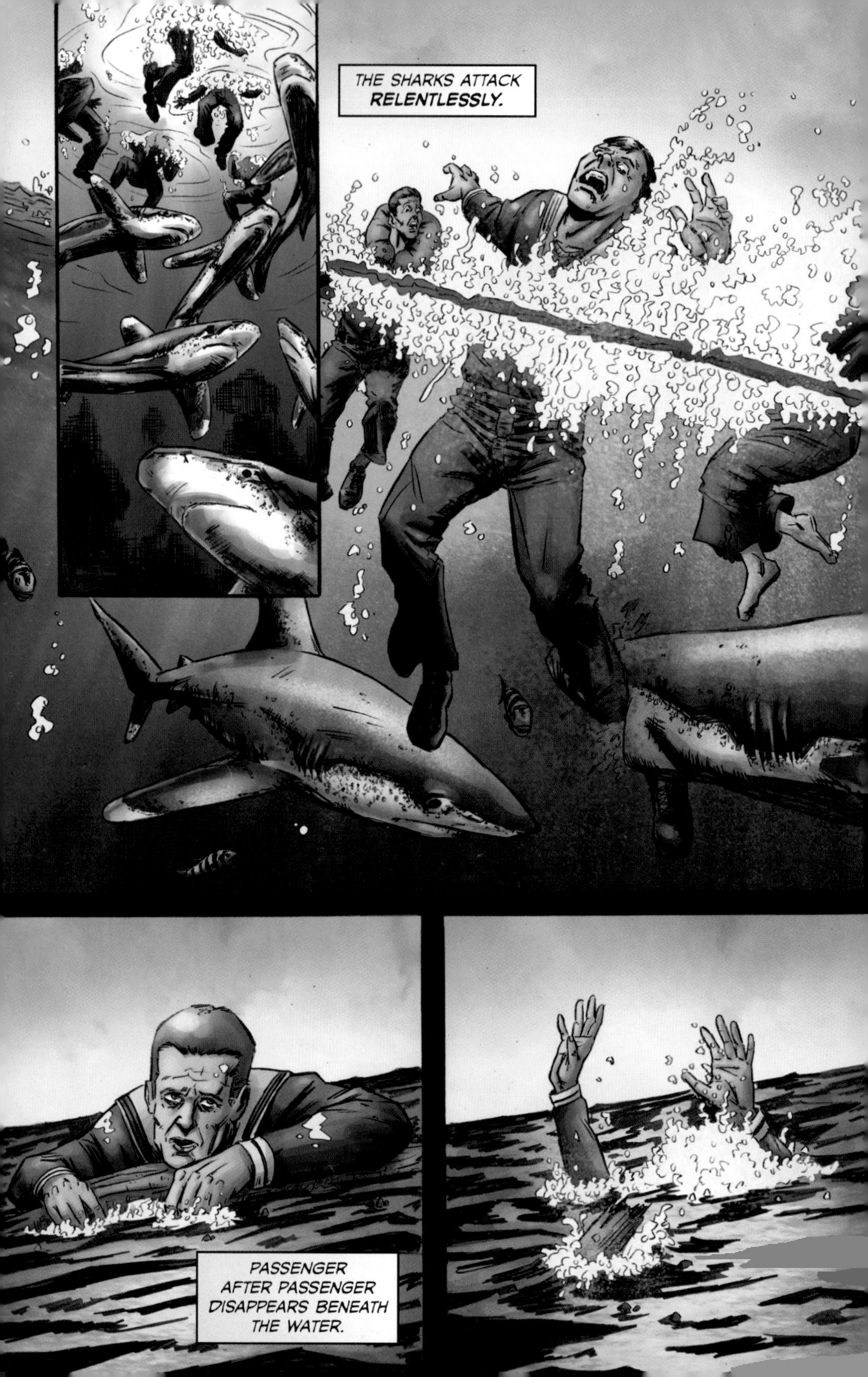
THE SHARKS ATTACK RELENTLESSLY.
PASSENGER AFTER PASSENGER DISAPPEARS BENEATH THE WATER.

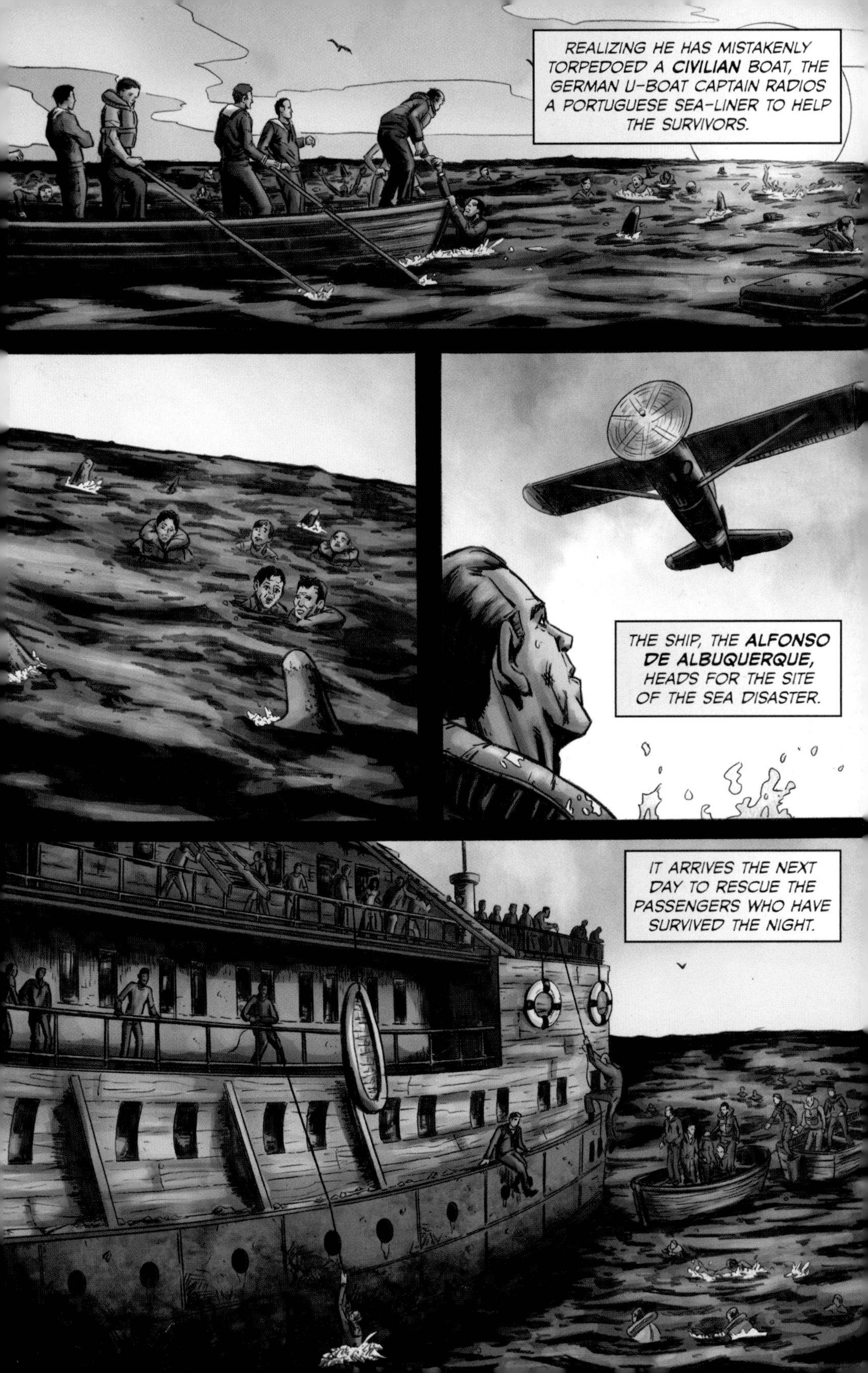
REALIZING HE HAS MISTAKENLY TORPEDOED A CIVILIAN BOAT, THE GERMAN U-BOAT CAPTAIN RADIOS A PORTUGUESE SEA-LINER TO HELP THE SURVIVORS.
THE SHIP, THE ALFONSO DE ALBUQUERQUE, HEADS FOR THE SITE OF THE SEA DISASTER.
IT ARRIVES THE NEXT DAY TO RESCUE THE PASSENGERS WHO HAVE SURVIVED THE NIGHT.

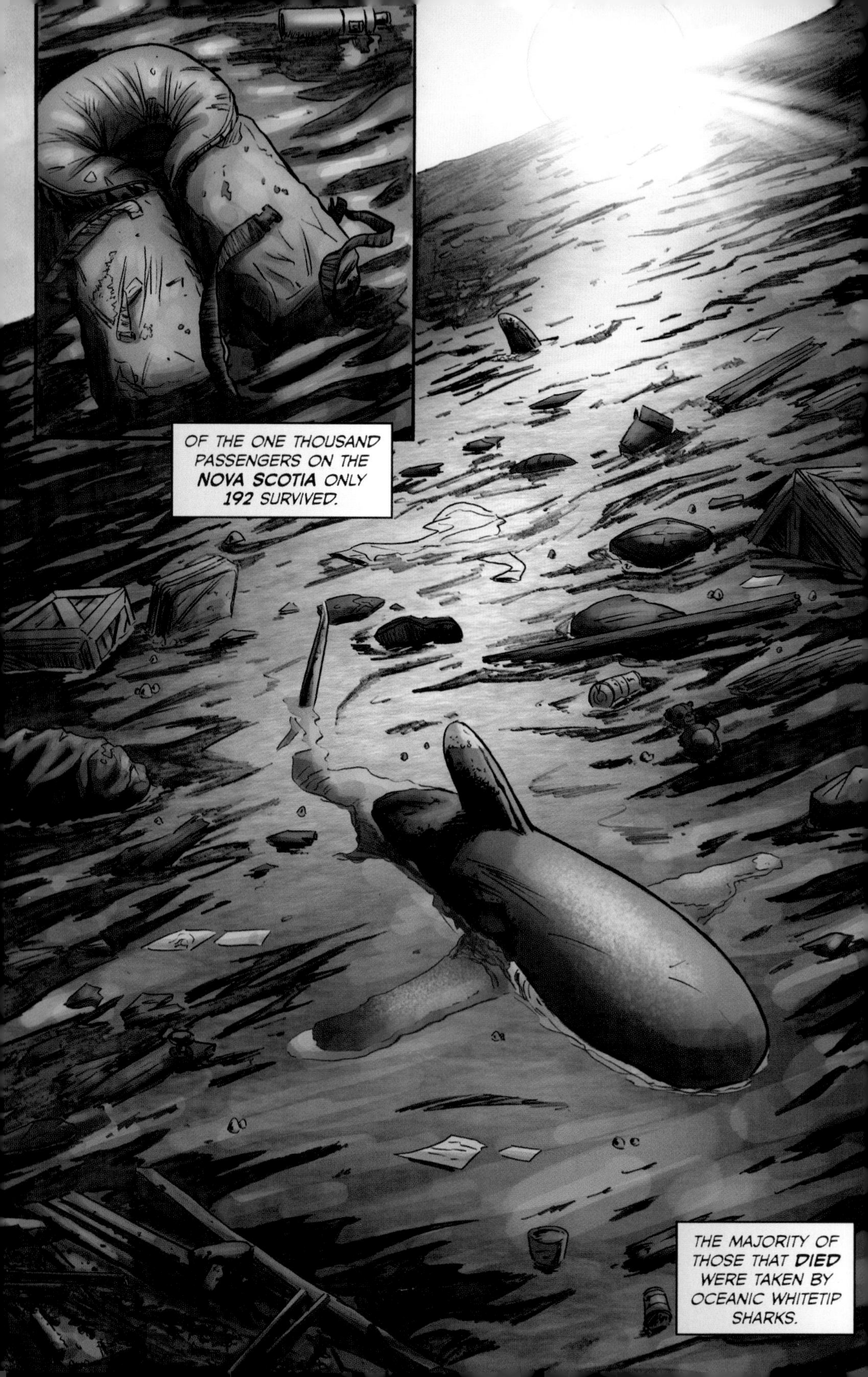
OF THE ONE THOUSAND PASSENGERS ON THE NOVA SCOTIA ONLY 192 SURVIVED.
THE MAJORITY OF THOSE THAT DIED WERE TAKEN BY OCEANIC WHITETIP SHARKS.

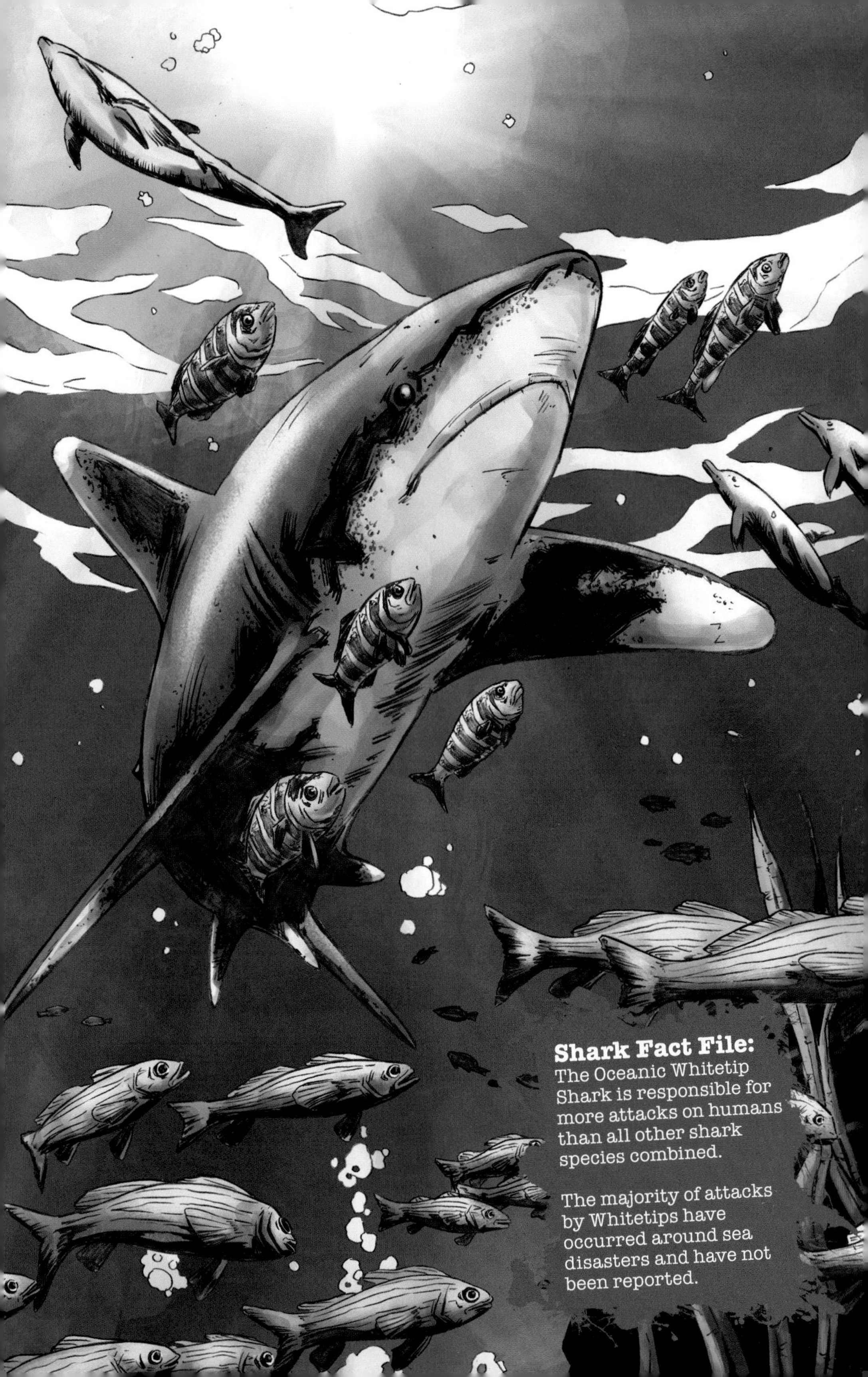
Shark Fact File:
The Oceanic Whitetip Shark is responsible for more attacks on humans than all other shark species combined.
The majority of attacks by Whitetips have occurred around sea disasters and have not been reported.

#3 THE TIGER SHARK

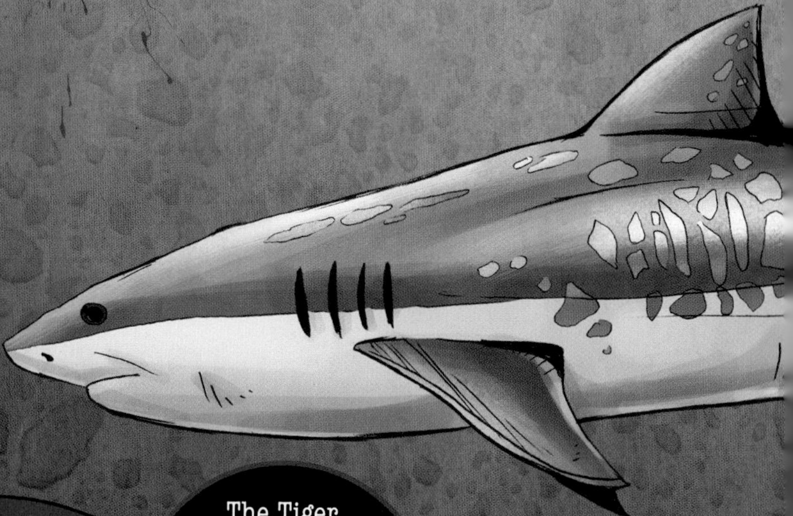

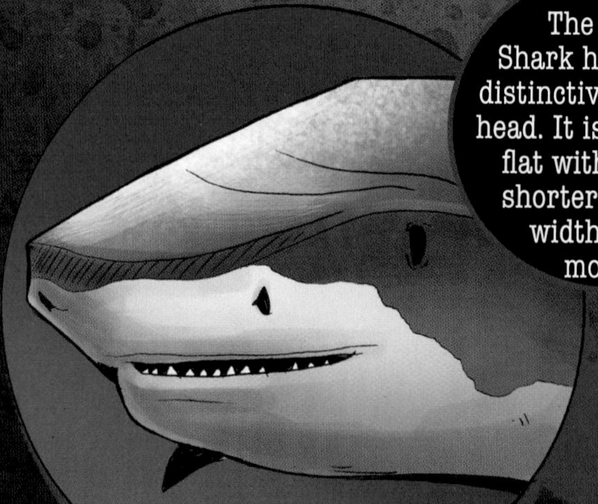

The Tiger Shark has a very distinctively shaped head. It is broad and flat with a snout shorter than the width of the mouth.

ATTACK FILE:

Recorded Attacks: 147

Unprovoked Fatalities: 27

The Tiger Shark gets its name because juvenile members of this species have black or brown stripes arranged over their gray backs and sides.

The Tiger Shark's teeth are shaped like those found on a circular saw, with a flat and curved hook at the end. These powerful teeth can cut through a turtle shell with a single bite.

TIGER SHARK FACTS:

Average Size: 15 feet

Largest Recorded: 18 feet

Habitat: Murky waters in coastal areas, river estuaries and harbors. Shallow areas around large island chains and oceanic islands including lagoons.

Preferred Prey: Sea turtles, rays, other sharks, bony fishes, sea birds, dolphins, squid, various crustaceans, carrion and even garbage.

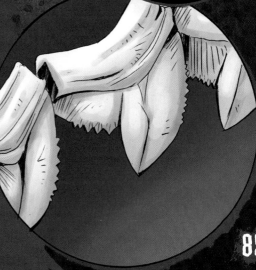

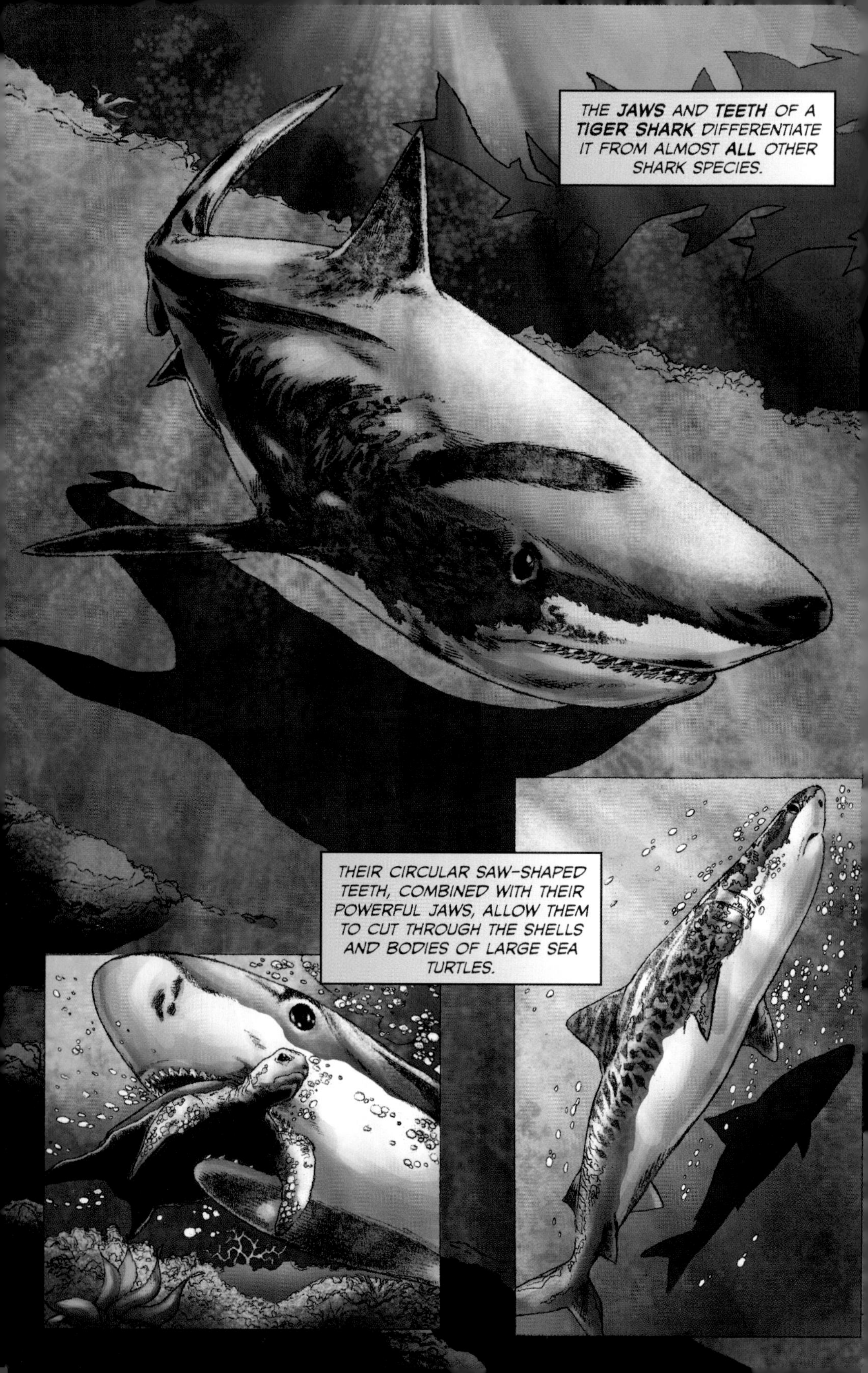
THE **JAWS** AND **TEETH** OF A **TIGER SHARK** DIFFERENTIATE IT FROM ALMOST **ALL** OTHER SHARK SPECIES.
THEIR CIRCULAR SAW-SHAPED TEETH, COMBINED WITH THEIR POWERFUL JAWS, ALLOW THEM TO CUT THROUGH THE SHELLS AND BODIES OF LARGE SEA TURTLES.

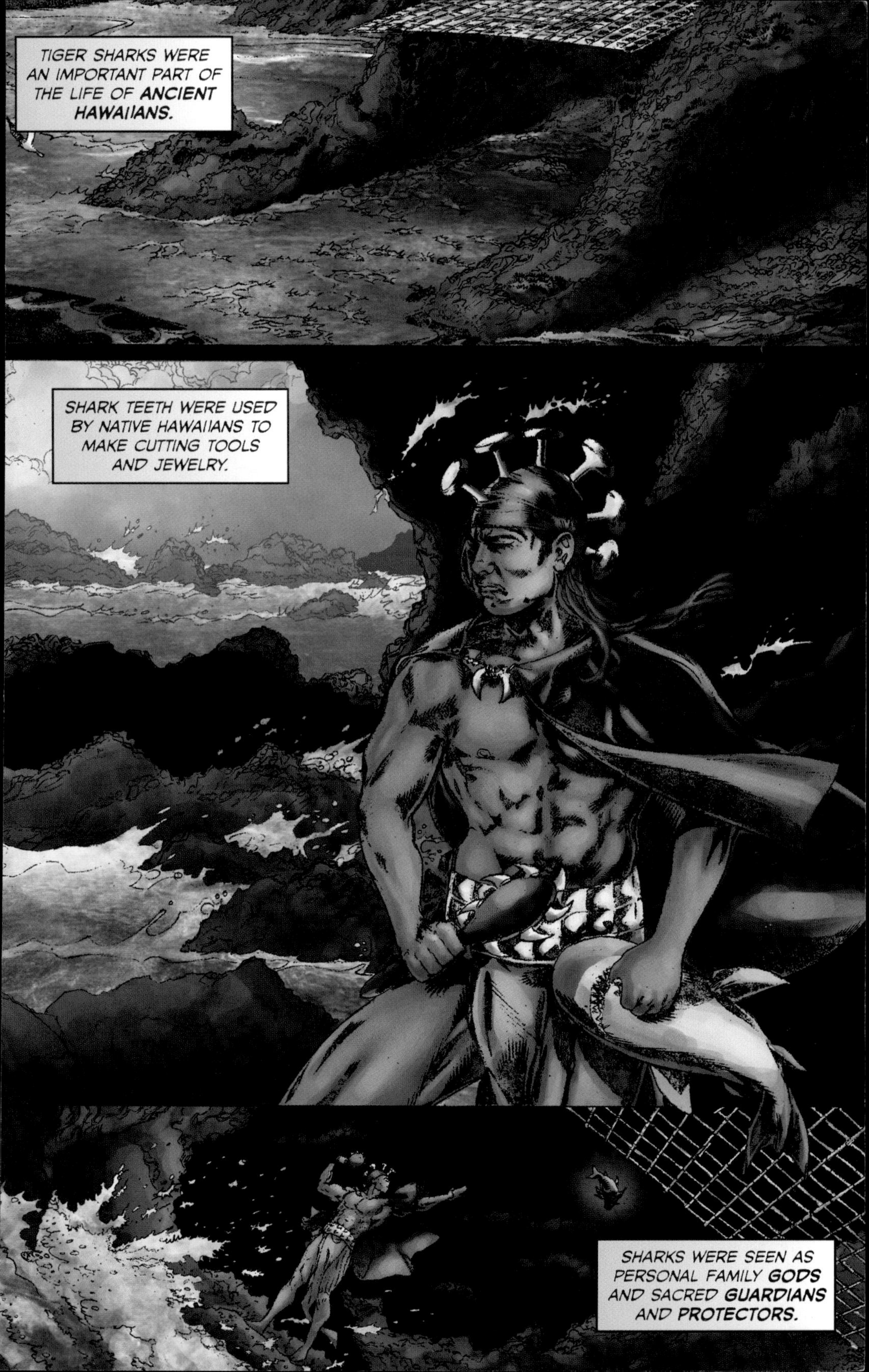
TIGER SHARKS WERE AN IMPORTANT PART OF THE LIFE OF ANCIENT HAWAIIANS.
SHARK TEETH WERE USED BY NATIVE HAWAIIANS TO MAKE CUTTING TOOLS AND JEWELRY.
SHARKS WERE SEEN AS PERSONAL FAMILY GODS AND SACRED GUARDIANS AND PROTECTORS.

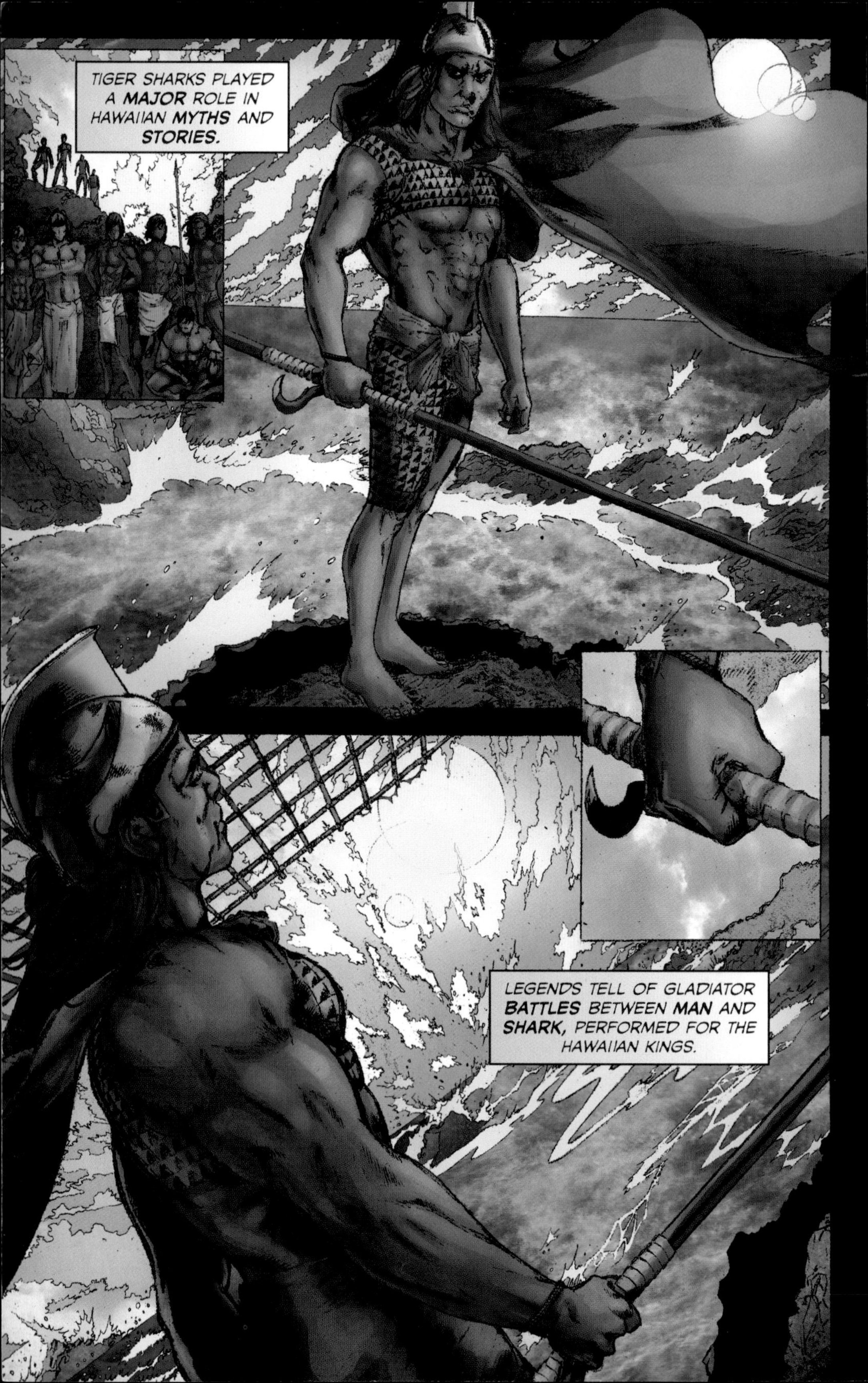
TIGER SHARKS PLAYED A MAJOR ROLE IN HAWAIIAN MYTHS AND STORIES.
LEGENDS TELL OF GLADIATOR BATTLES BETWEEN MAN AND SHARK, PERFORMED FOR THE HAWAIIAN KINGS.

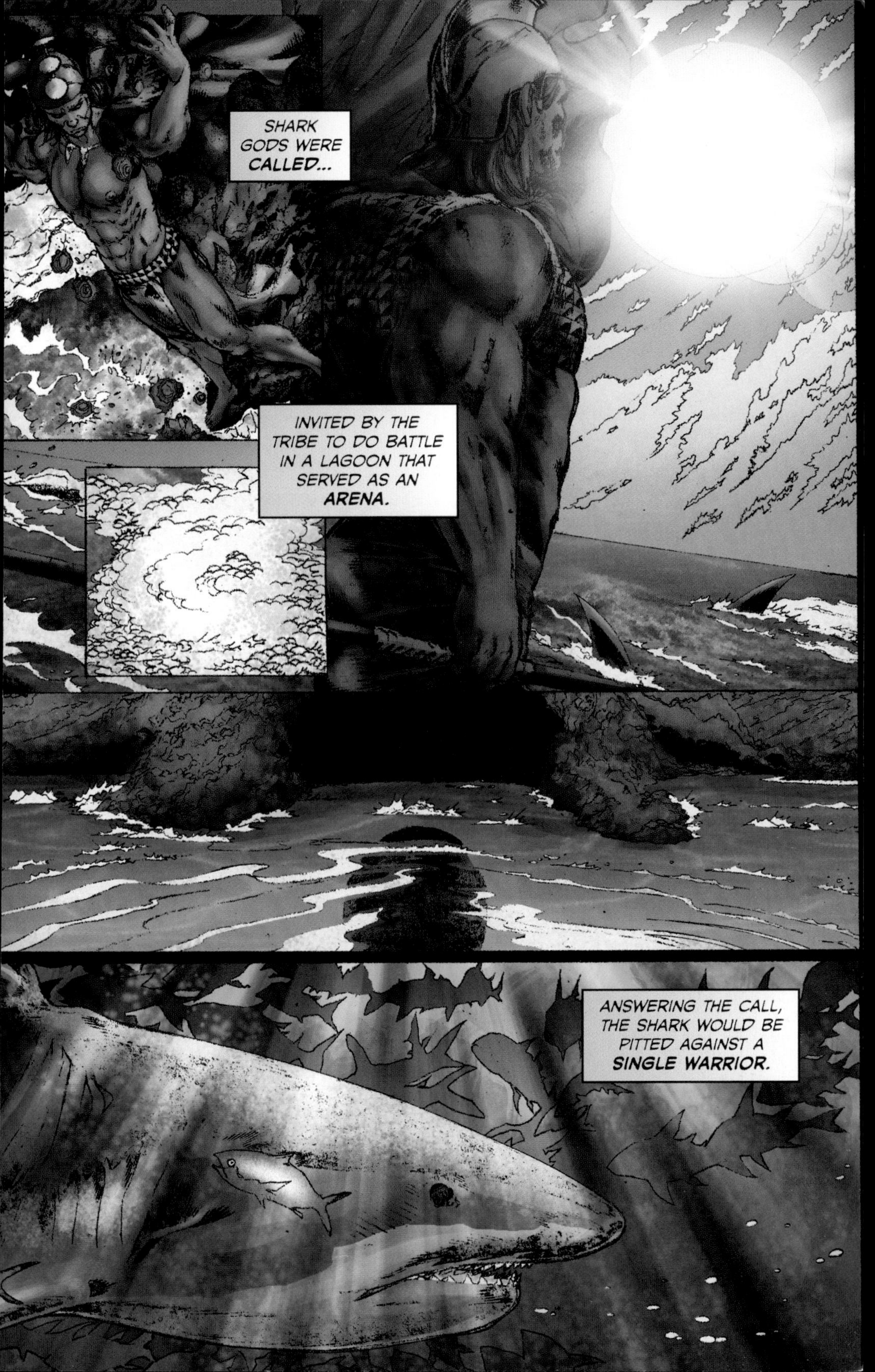
SHARK GODS WERE CALLED...
INVITED BY THE TRIBE TO DO BATTLE IN A LAGOON THAT SERVED AS AN ARENA.
ANSWERING THE CALL, THE SHARK WOULD BE PITTED AGAINST A SINGLE WARRIOR.

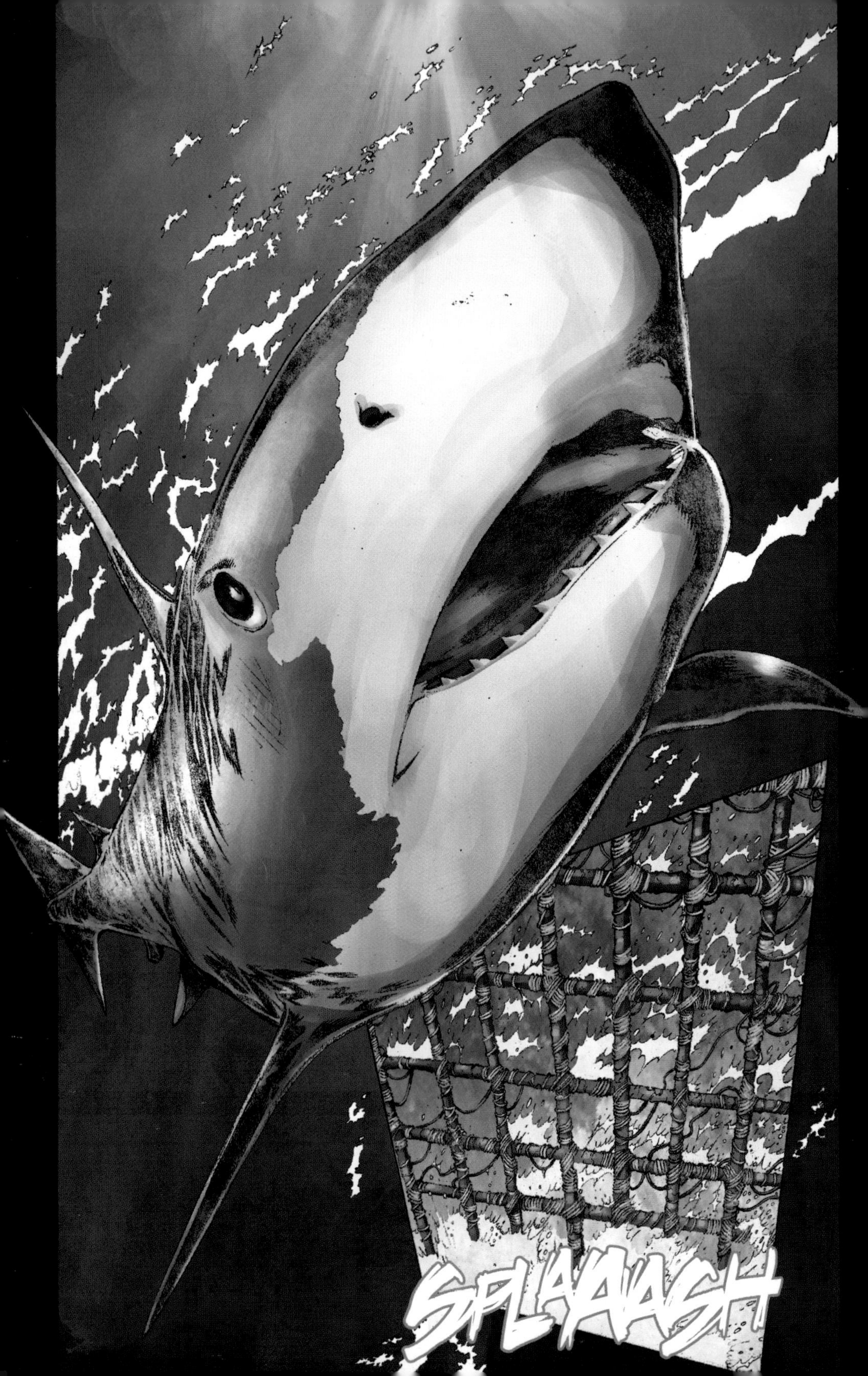
SPLAAASH

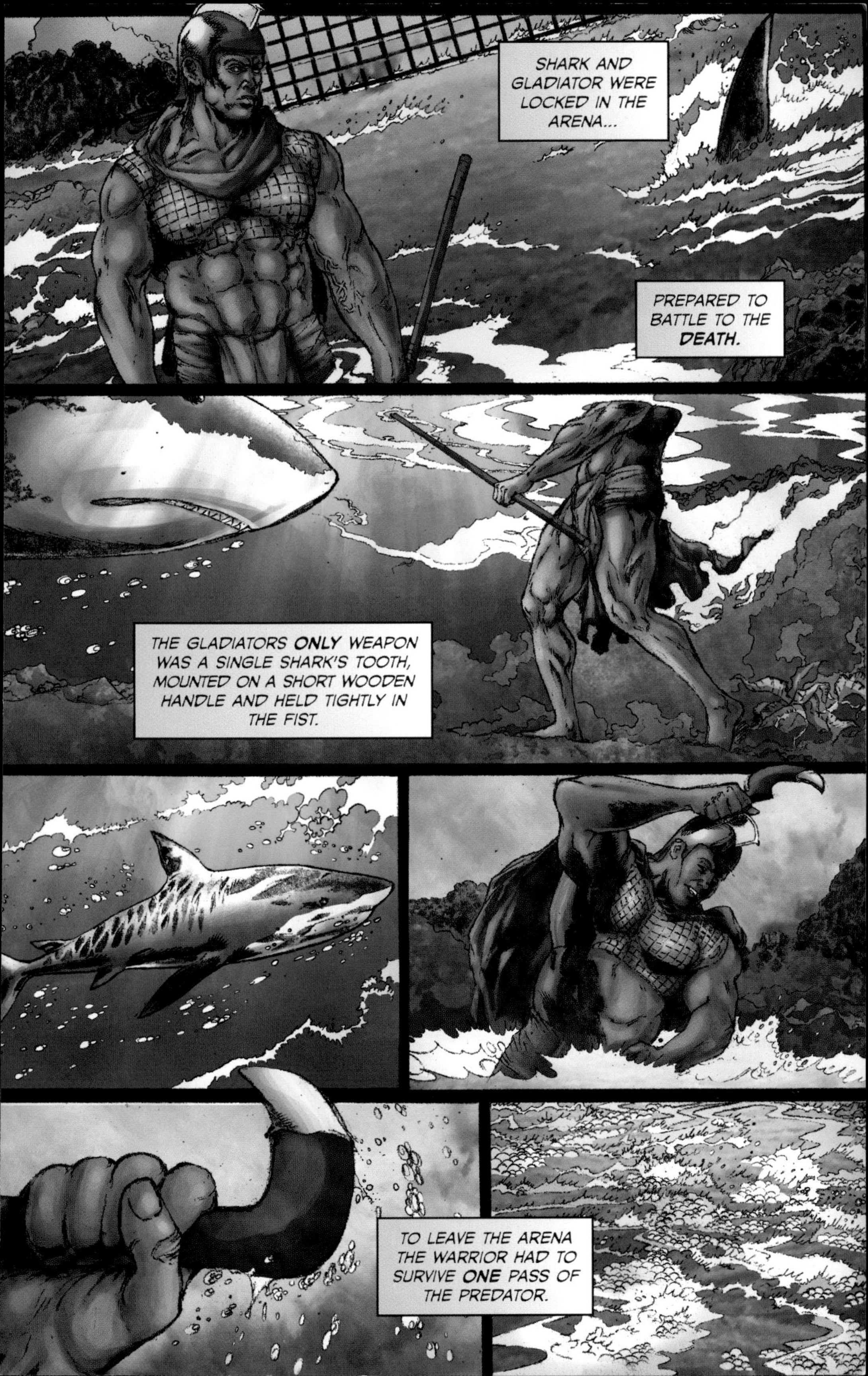
SHARK AND GLADIATOR WERE LOCKED IN THE ARENA...
PREPARED TO BATTLE TO THE **DEATH.**
THE GLADIATORS **ONLY** WEAPON WAS A SINGLE SHARK'S TOOTH, MOUNTED ON A SHORT WOODEN HANDLE AND HELD TIGHTLY IN THE FIST.
TO LEAVE THE ARENA THE WARRIOR HAD TO SURVIVE **ONE** PASS OF THE PREDATOR.

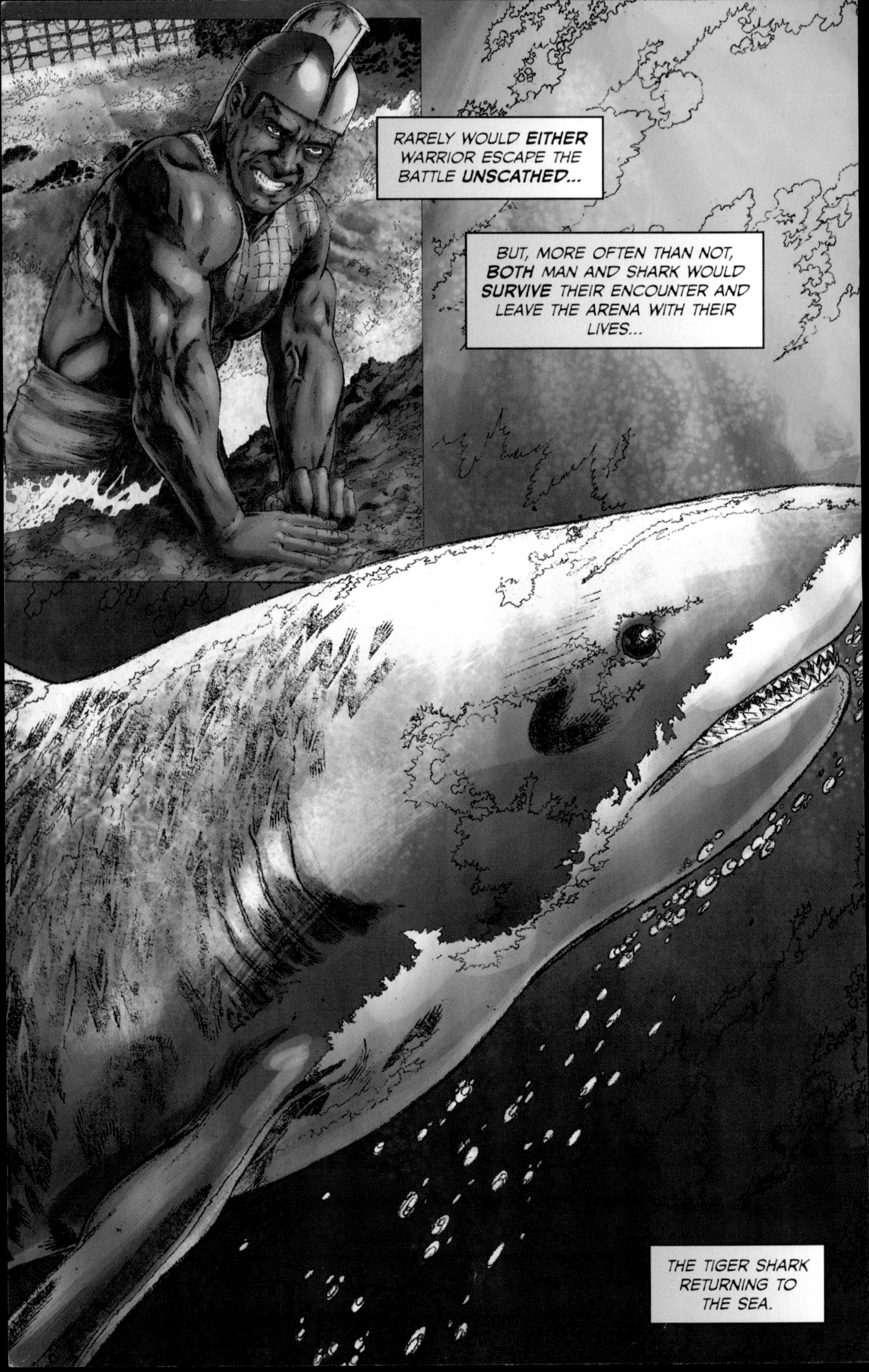
RARELY WOULD **EITHER** WARRIOR ESCAPE THE BATTLE **UNSCATHED...**
BUT, MORE OFTEN THAN NOT, **BOTH** MAN AND SHARK WOULD **SURVIVE** THEIR ENCOUNTER AND LEAVE THE ARENA WITH THEIR LIVES...
THE TIGER SHARK RETURNING TO THE SEA.

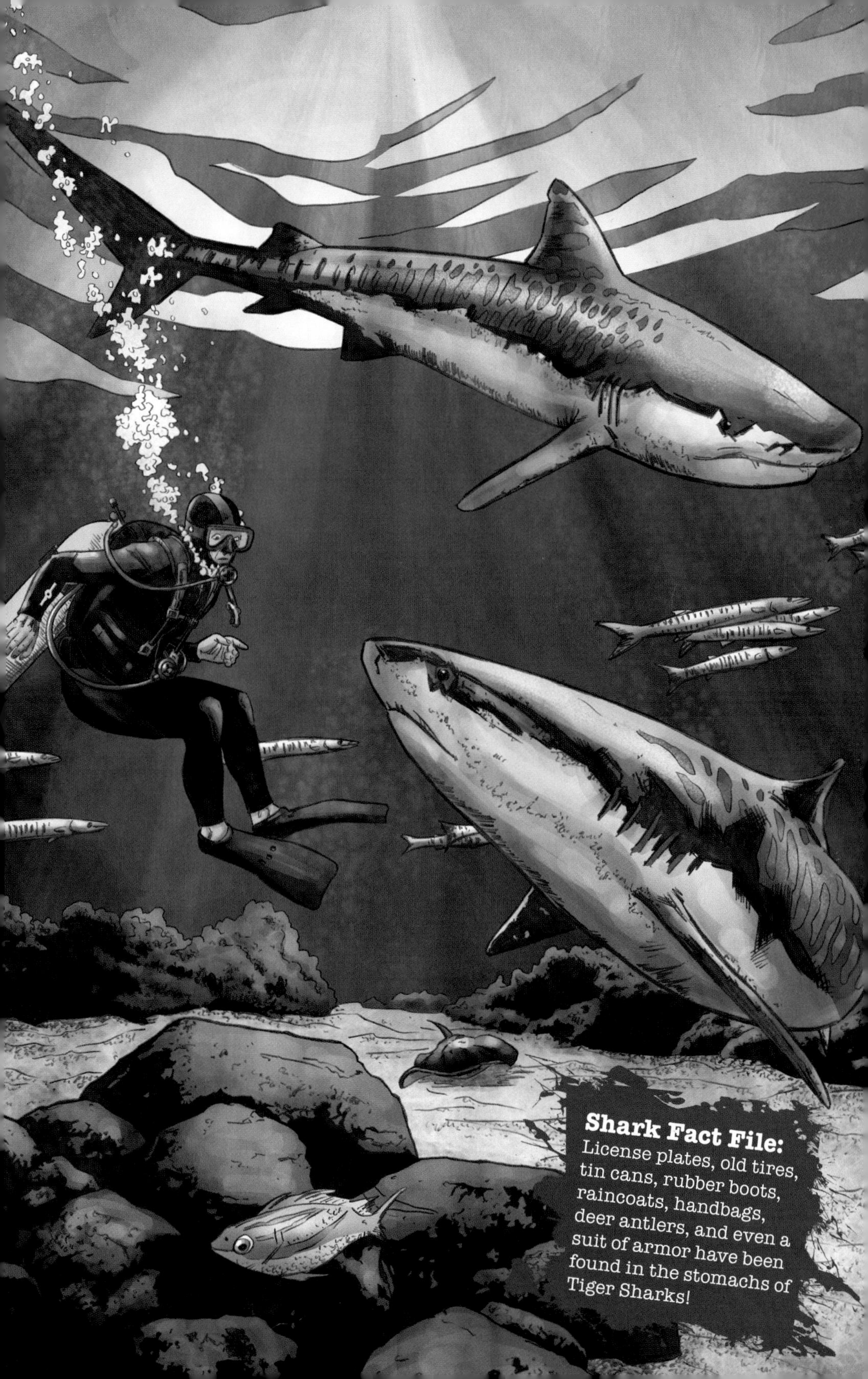

Shark Fact File:
License plates, old tires, tin cans, rubber boots, raincoats, handbags, deer antlers, and even a suit of armor have been found in the stomachs of Tiger Sharks!

#2 THE GREAT WHITE

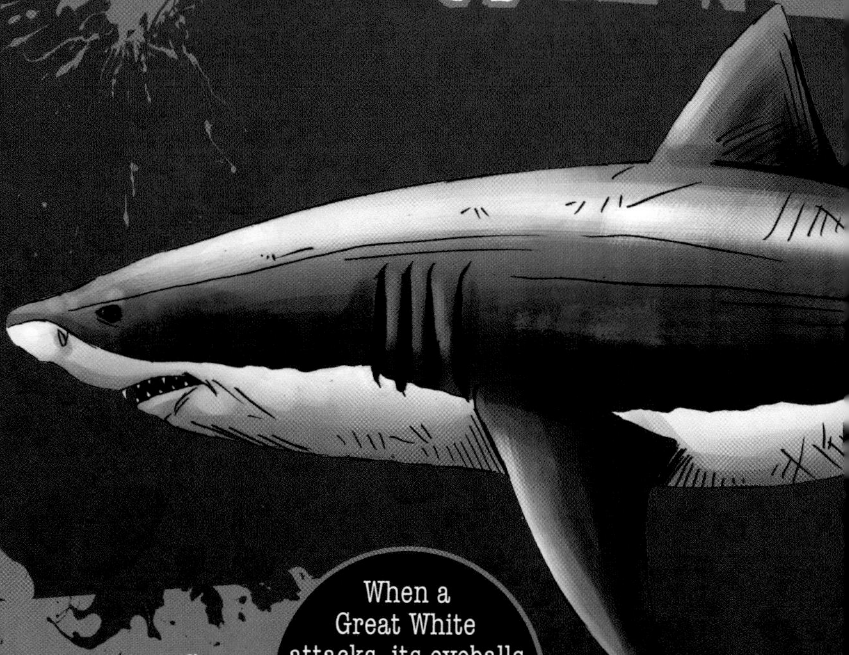

When a Great White attacks, its eyeballs roll back into its head to protect them from injury.

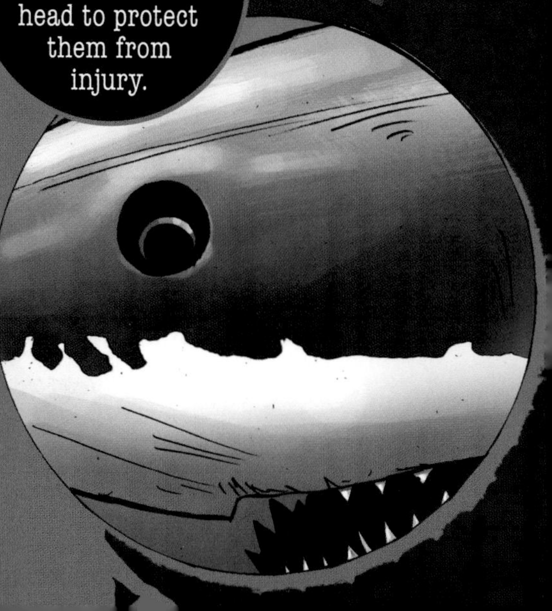

GREAT WHITE FACTS:

Average Size: 18 feet

Largest Recorded: 21 feet

Habitat: Coastal and offshore waters which have water temperature between 54 and 75 °F.

Preferred Prey:
Tuna, rays, other sharks, dolphins, porpoises, whales, seals, sea lions, sea turtles, sea otters, and seabirds.

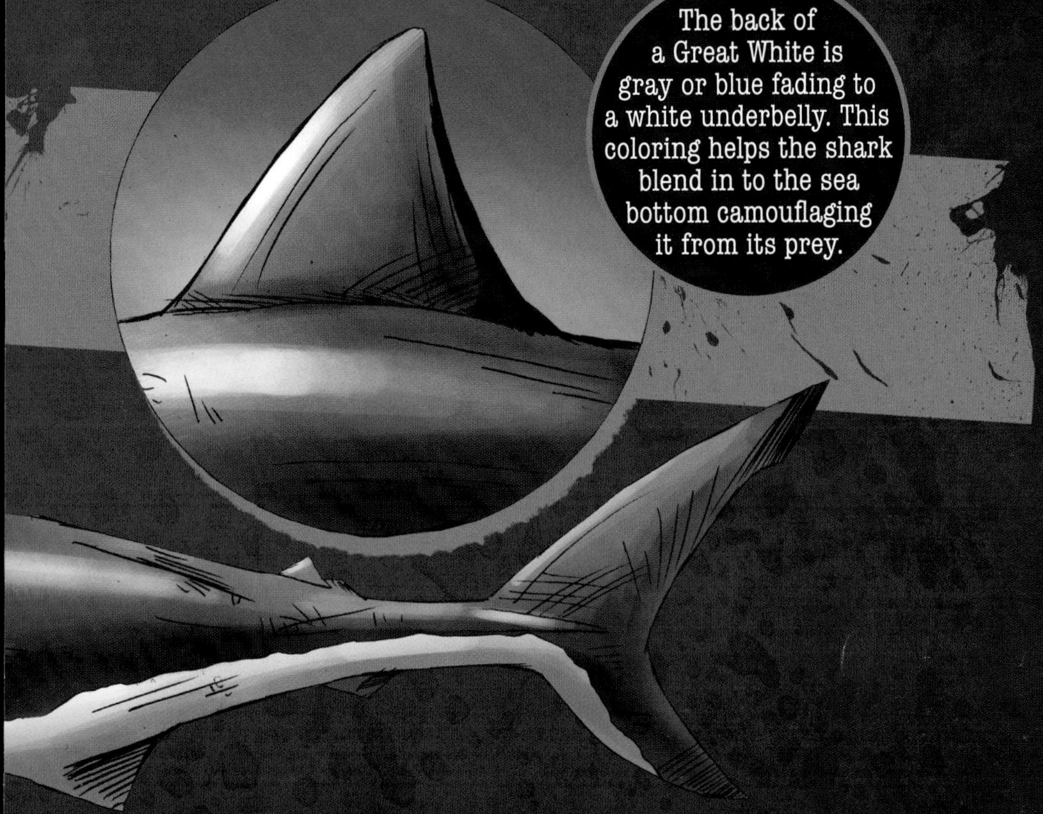

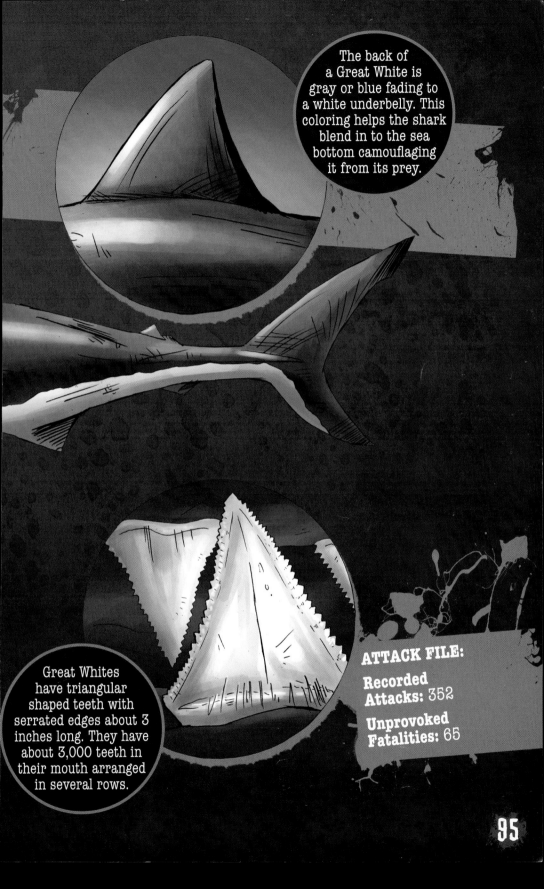

The back of a Great White is gray or blue fading to a white underbelly. This coloring helps the shark blend in to the sea bottom camouflaging it from its prey.

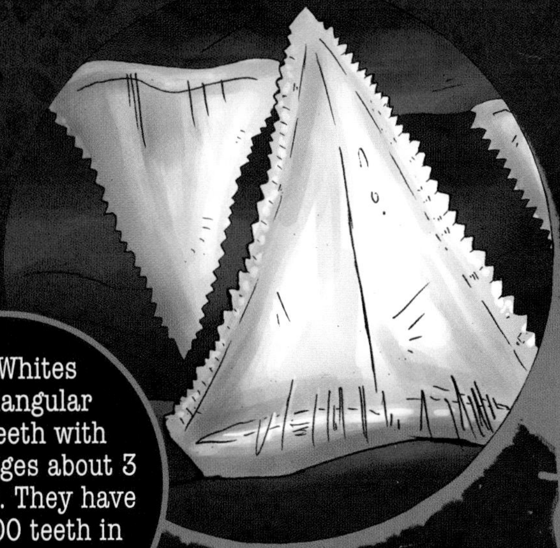

Great Whites have triangular shaped teeth with serrated edges about 3 inches long. They have about 3,000 teeth in their mouth arranged in several rows.

ATTACK FILE:

Recorded Attacks: 352

Unprovoked Fatalities: 65

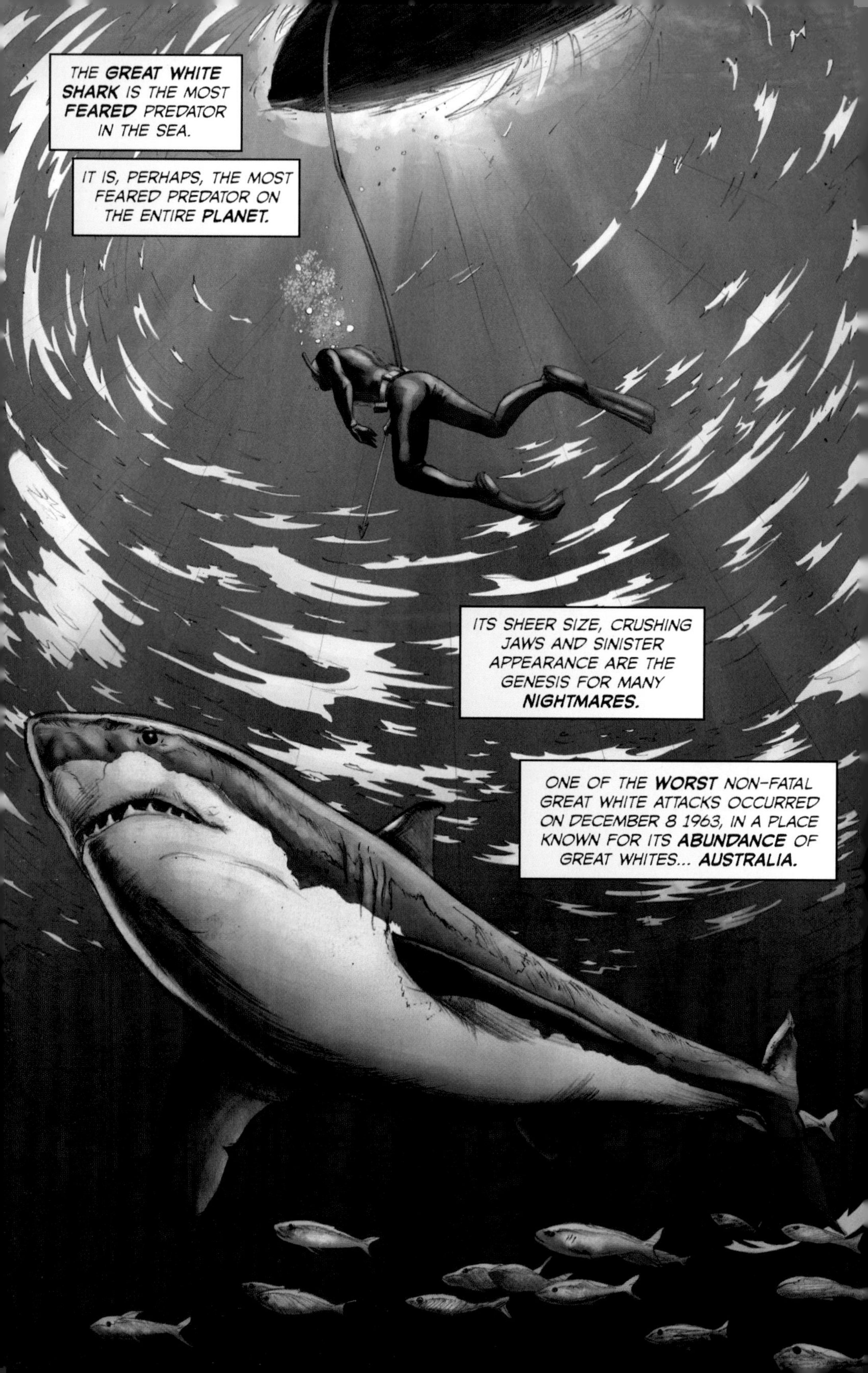
THE **GREAT WHITE SHARK** IS THE MOST **FEARED** PREDATOR IN THE SEA.
IT IS, PERHAPS, THE MOST FEARED PREDATOR ON THE ENTIRE **PLANET.**
ITS SHEER SIZE, CRUSHING JAWS AND SINISTER APPEARANCE ARE THE GENESIS FOR MANY **NIGHTMARES.**
ONE OF THE **WORST** NON-FATAL GREAT WHITE ATTACKS OCCURRED ON DECEMBER 8 1963, IN A PLACE KNOWN FOR ITS **ABUNDANCE** OF GREAT WHITES... **AUSTRALIA.**

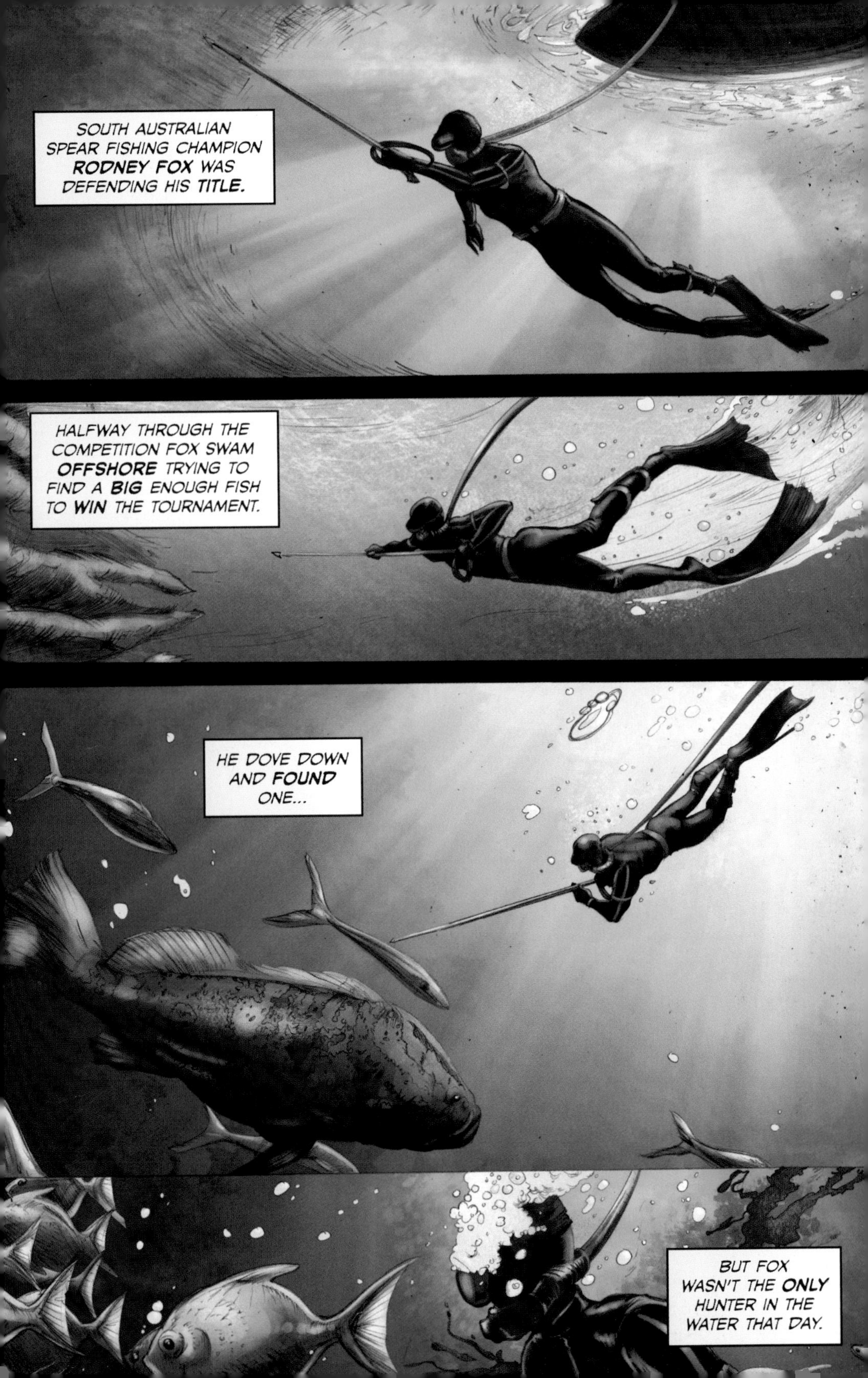

SOUTH AUSTRALIAN SPEAR FISHING CHAMPION RODNEY FOX WAS DEFENDING HIS TITLE.
HALFWAY THROUGH THE COMPETITION FOX SWAM OFFSHORE TRYING TO FIND A BIG ENOUGH FISH TO WIN THE TOURNAMENT.
HE DOVE DOWN AND FOUND ONE...
BUT FOX WASN'T THE ONLY HUNTER IN THE WATER THAT DAY.

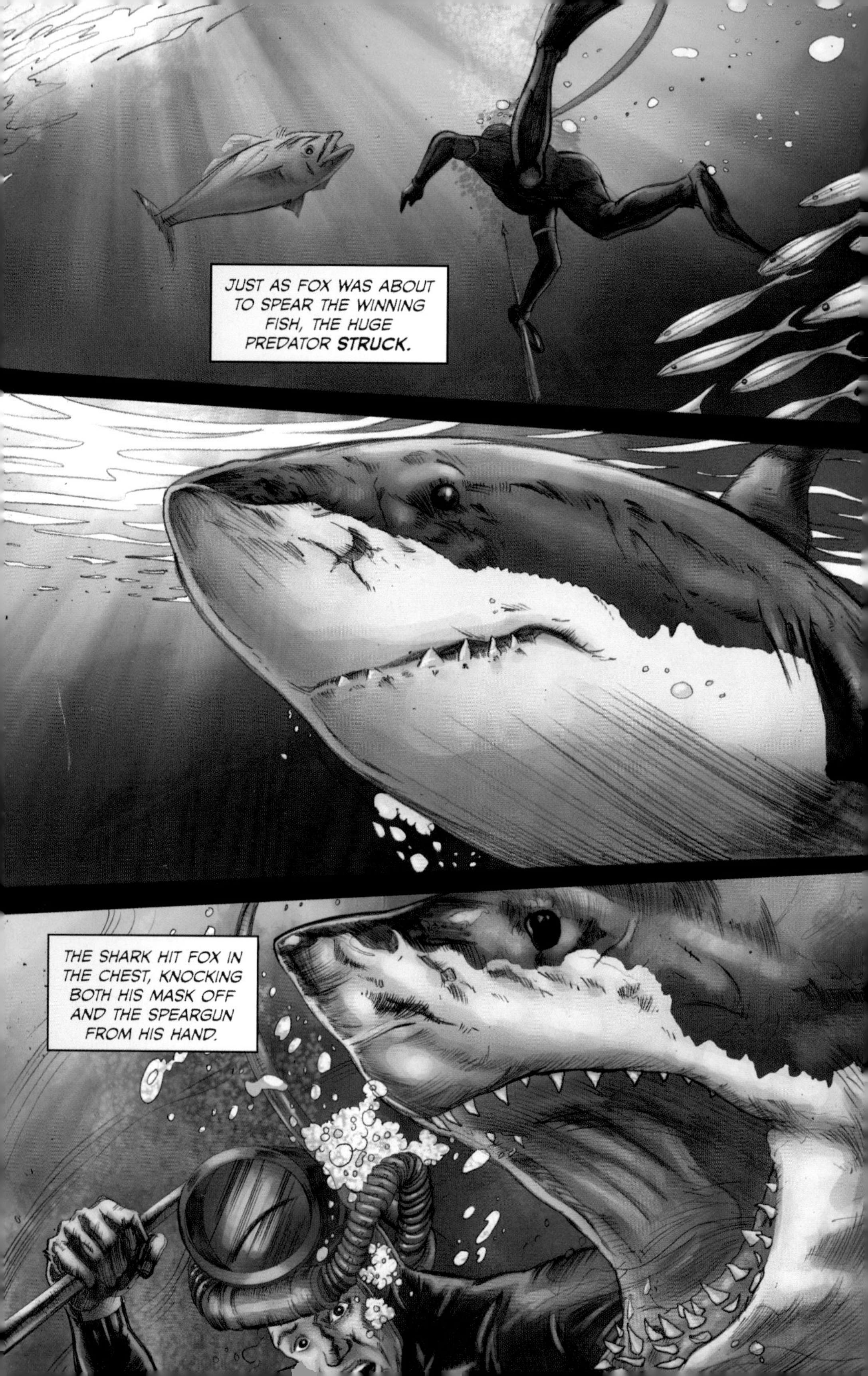
JUST AS FOX WAS ABOUT TO SPEAR THE WINNING FISH, THE HUGE PREDATOR **STRUCK.**
THE SHARK HIT FOX IN THE CHEST, KNOCKING BOTH HIS MASK OFF AND THE SPEARGUN FROM HIS HAND.

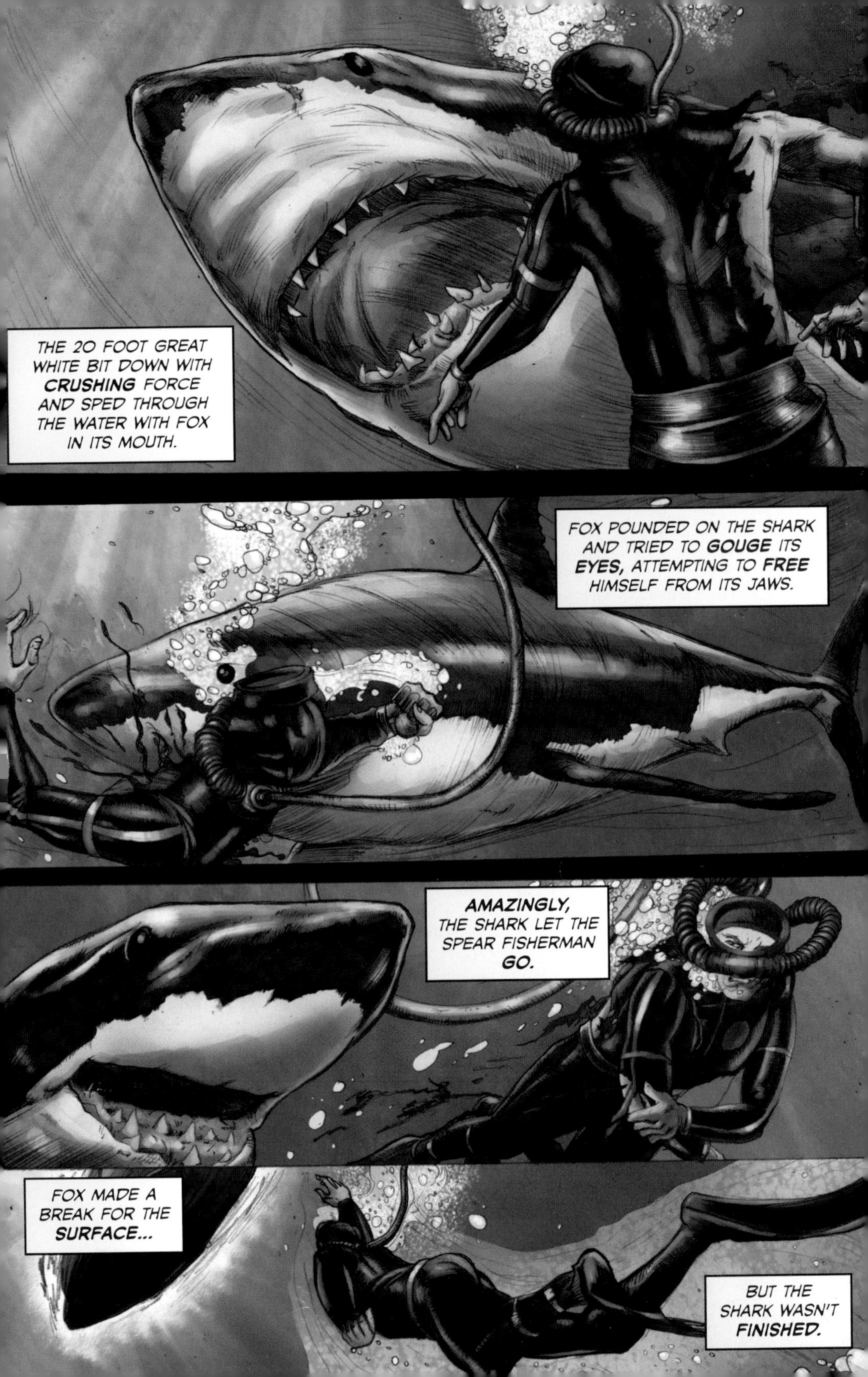
THE 20 FOOT GREAT WHITE BIT DOWN WITH **CRUSHING** FORCE AND SPED THROUGH THE WATER WITH FOX IN ITS MOUTH.
FOX POUNDED ON THE SHARK AND TRIED TO **GOUGE** ITS **EYES,** ATTEMPTING TO **FREE** HIMSELF FROM ITS JAWS.
AMAZINGLY, THE SHARK LET THE SPEAR FISHERMAN **GO.**
FOX MADE A BREAK FOR THE **SURFACE...**
BUT THE SHARK WASN'T **FINISHED.**

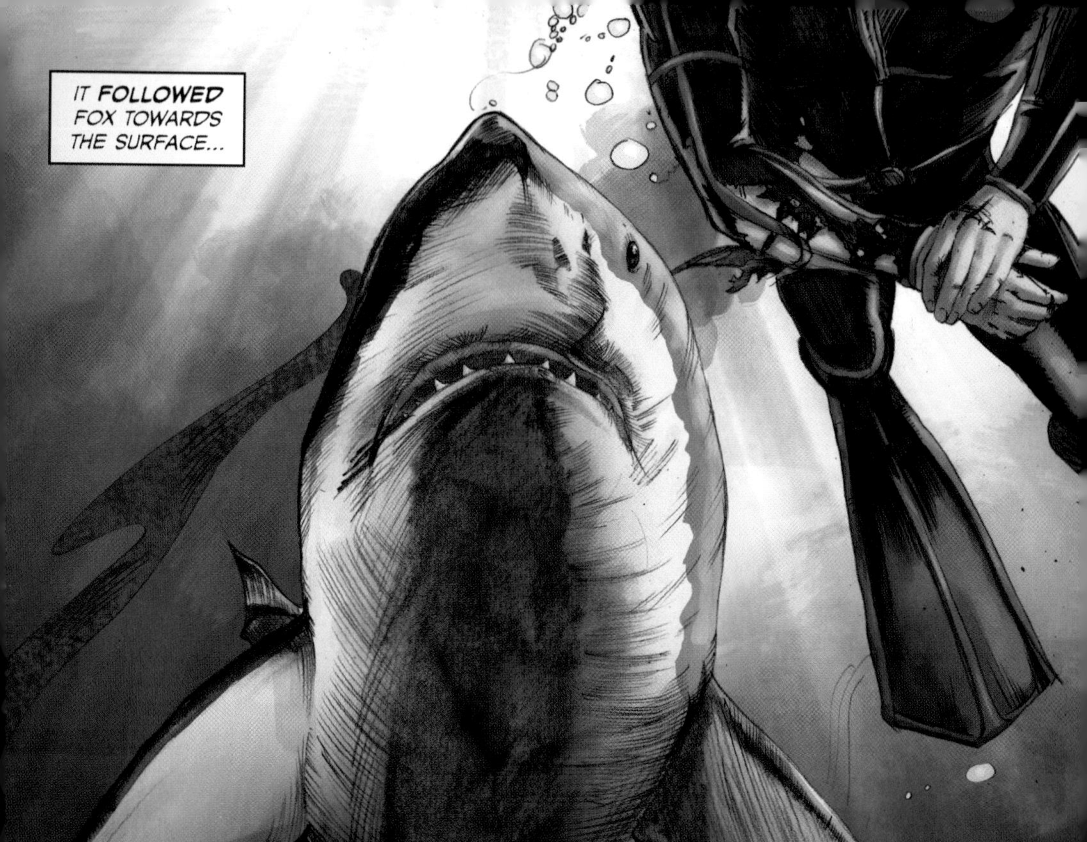
IT FOLLOWED FOX TOWARDS THE SURFACE...

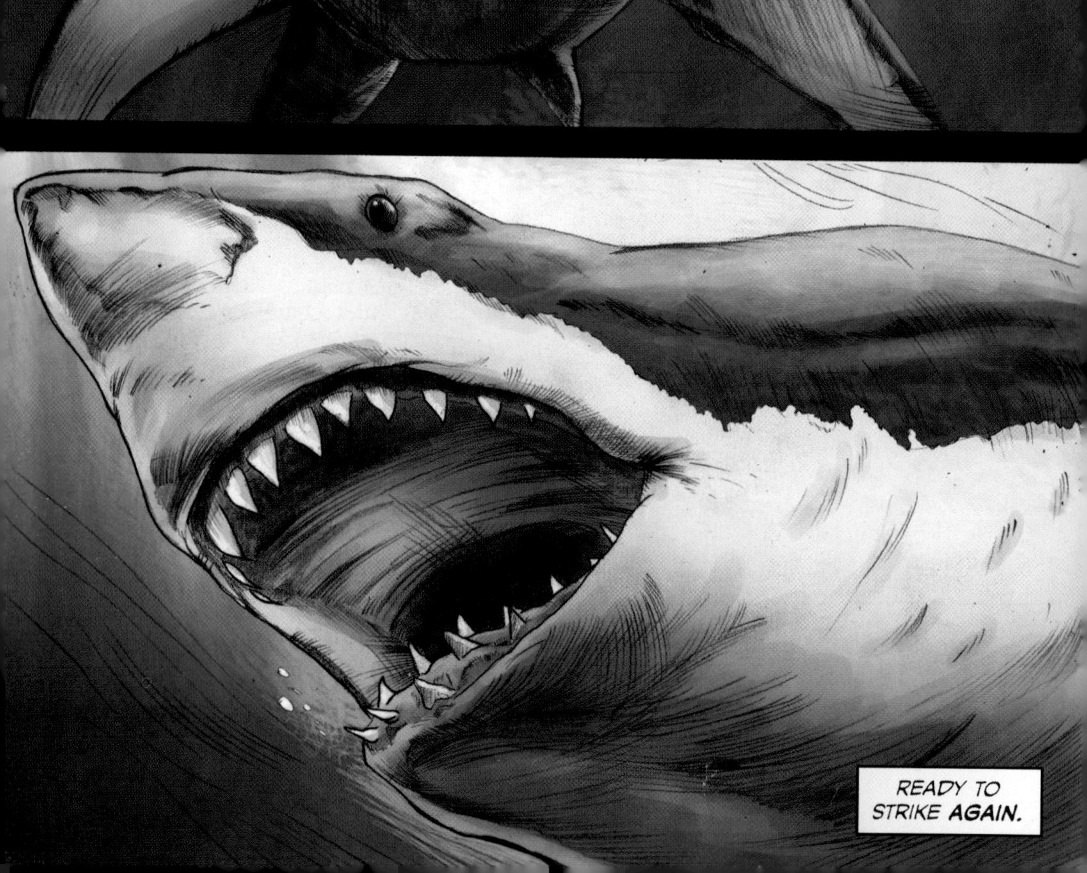
READY TO STRIKE AGAIN.

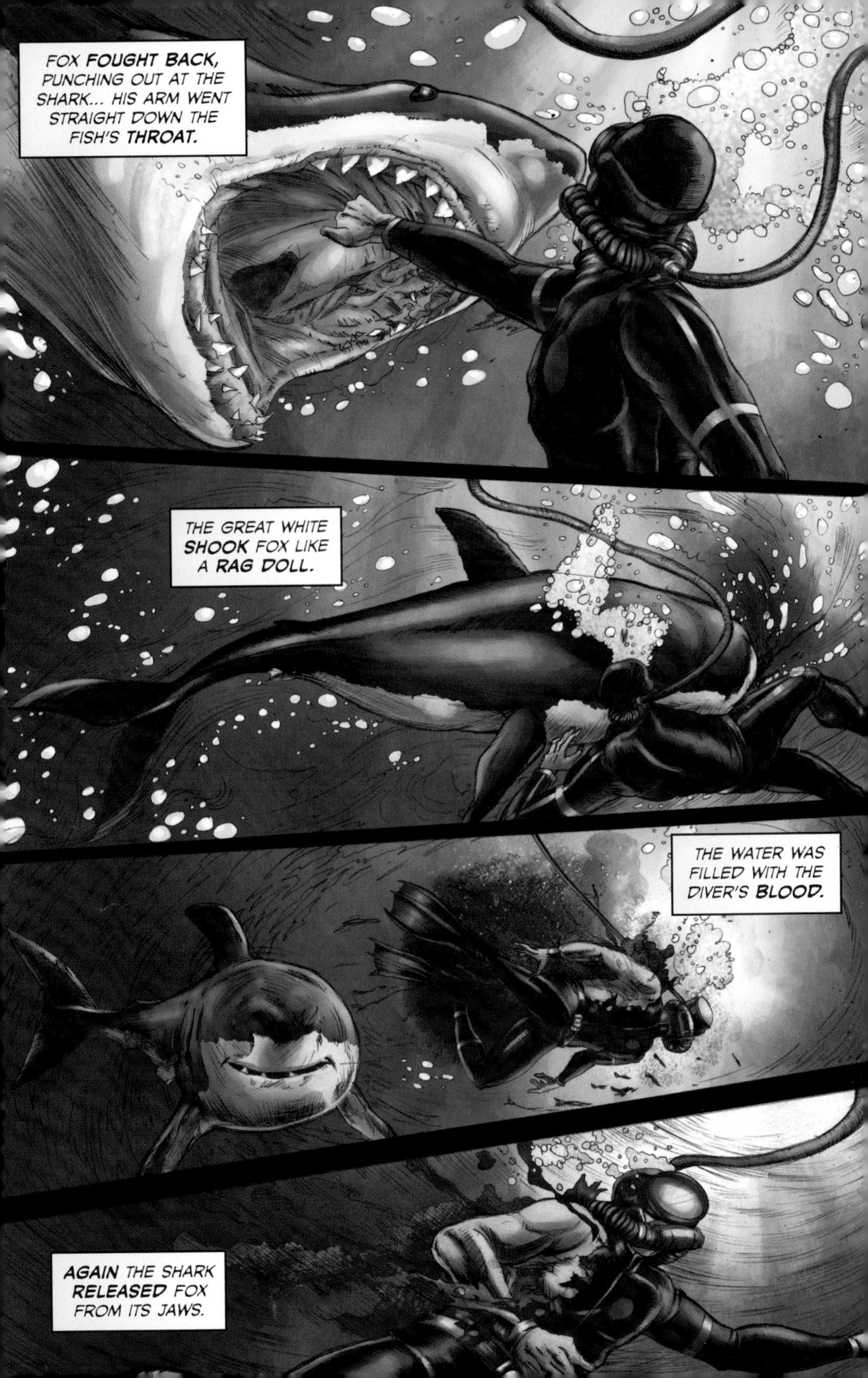
FOX FOUGHT BACK, PUNCHING OUT AT THE SHARK... HIS ARM WENT STRAIGHT DOWN THE FISH'S THROAT.
THE GREAT WHITE SHOOK FOX LIKE A RAG DOLL.
THE WATER WAS FILLED WITH THE DIVER'S BLOOD.
AGAIN THE SHARK RELEASED FOX FROM ITS JAWS.

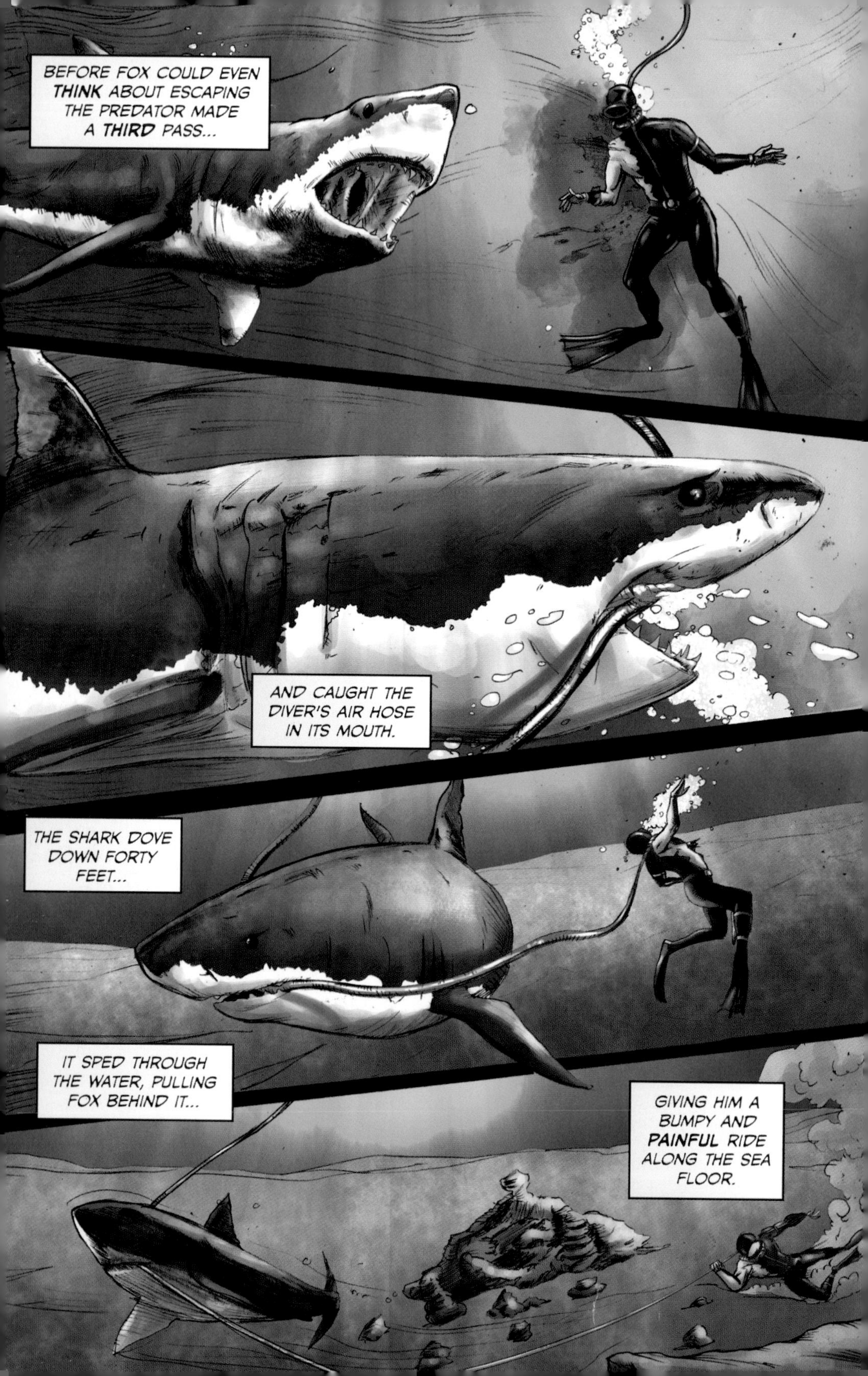
BEFORE FOX COULD EVEN THINK ABOUT ESCAPING THE PREDATOR MADE A THIRD PASS...
AND CAUGHT THE DIVER'S AIR HOSE IN ITS MOUTH.
THE SHARK DOVE DOWN FORTY FEET...
IT SPED THROUGH THE WATER, PULLING FOX BEHIND IT...
GIVING HIM A BUMPY AND PAINFUL RIDE ALONG THE SEA FLOOR.

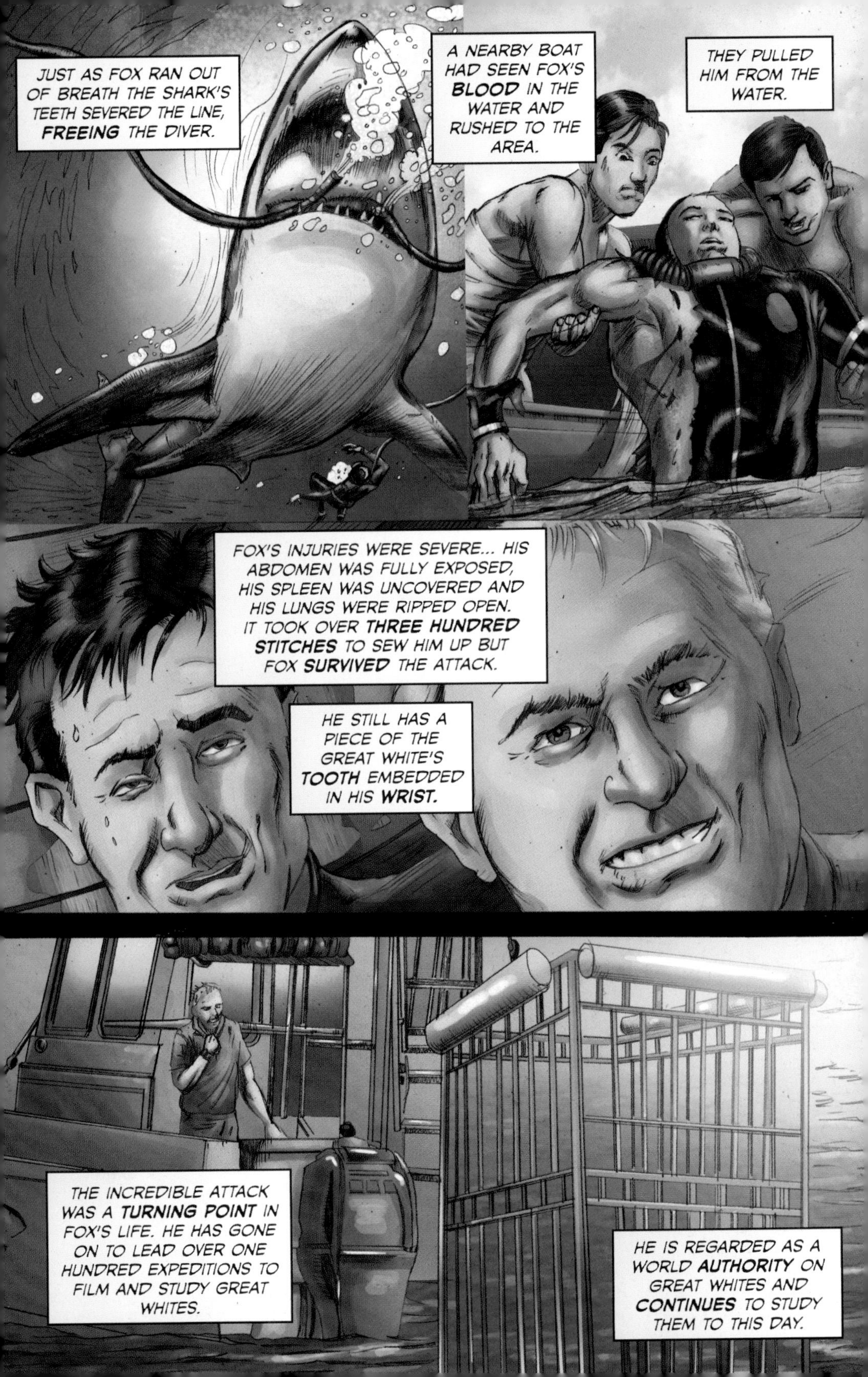
JUST AS FOX RAN OUT OF BREATH THE SHARK'S TEETH SEVERED THE LINE, **FREEING** THE DIVER.
A NEARBY BOAT HAD SEEN FOX'S **BLOOD** IN THE WATER AND RUSHED TO THE AREA.
THEY PULLED HIM FROM THE WATER.
FOX'S INJURIES WERE SEVERE... HIS ABDOMEN WAS FULLY EXPOSED, HIS SPLEEN WAS UNCOVERED AND HIS LUNGS WERE RIPPED OPEN. IT TOOK OVER **THREE HUNDRED STITCHES** TO SEW HIM UP BUT FOX **SURVIVED** THE ATTACK.
HE STILL HAS A PIECE OF THE GREAT WHITE'S **TOOTH** EMBEDDED IN HIS **WRIST.**
THE INCREDIBLE ATTACK WAS A **TURNING POINT** IN FOX'S LIFE. HE HAS GONE ON TO LEAD OVER ONE HUNDRED EXPEDITIONS TO FILM AND STUDY GREAT WHITES.
HE IS REGARDED AS A WORLD **AUTHORITY** ON GREAT WHITES AND **CONTINUES** TO STUDY THEM TO THIS DAY.

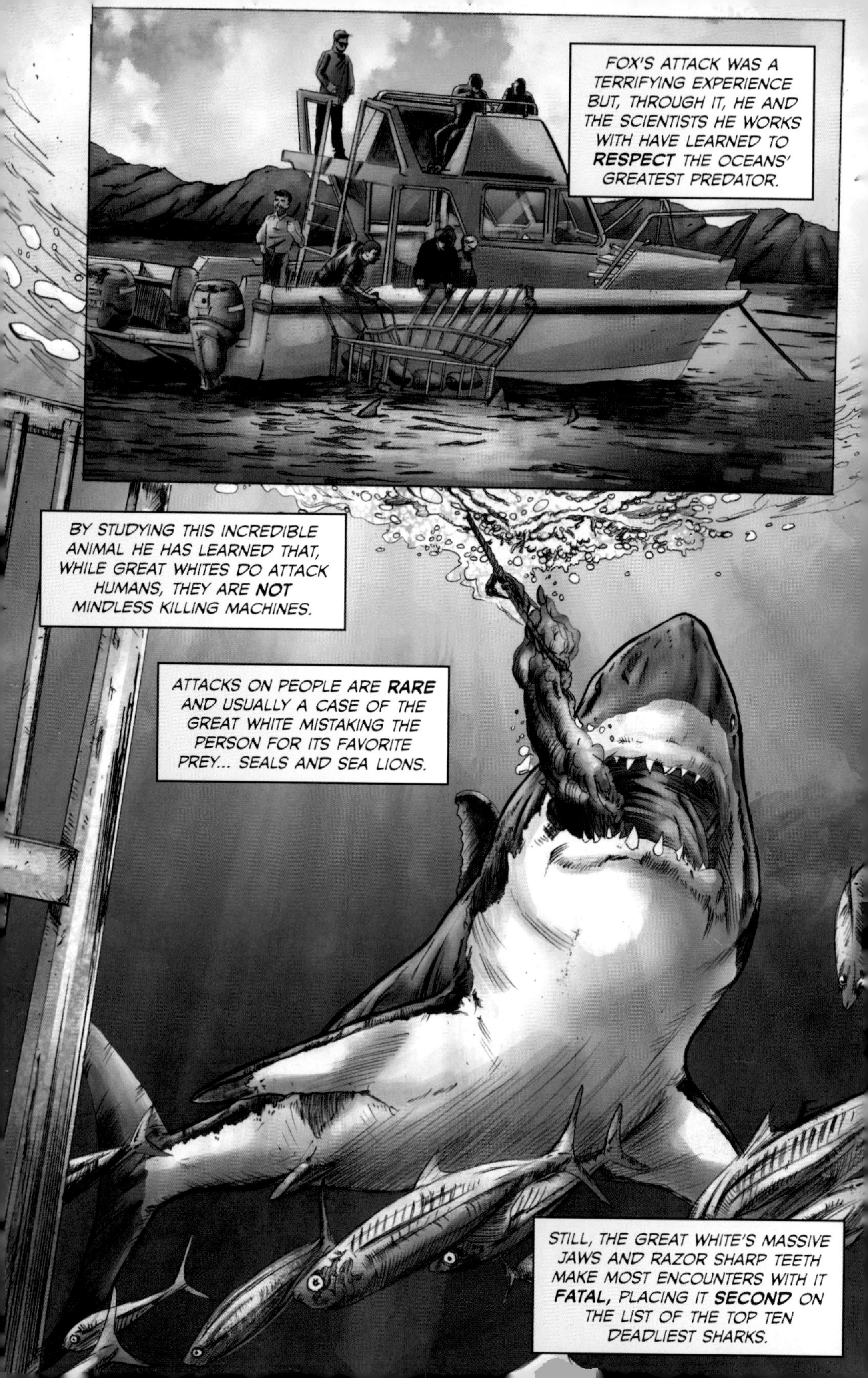
FOX'S ATTACK WAS A TERRIFYING EXPERIENCE BUT, THROUGH IT, HE AND THE SCIENTISTS HE WORKS WITH HAVE LEARNED TO **RESPECT** THE OCEANS' GREATEST PREDATOR.
BY STUDYING THIS INCREDIBLE ANIMAL HE HAS LEARNED THAT, WHILE GREAT WHITES DO ATTACK HUMANS, THEY ARE **NOT** MINDLESS KILLING MACHINES.
ATTACKS ON PEOPLE ARE **RARE** AND USUALLY A CASE OF THE GREAT WHITE MISTAKING THE PERSON FOR ITS FAVORITE PREY... SEALS AND SEA LIONS.
STILL, THE GREAT WHITE'S MASSIVE JAWS AND RAZOR SHARP TEETH MAKE MOST ENCOUNTERS WITH IT **FATAL,** PLACING IT **SECOND** ON THE LIST OF THE TOP TEN DEADLIEST SHARKS.

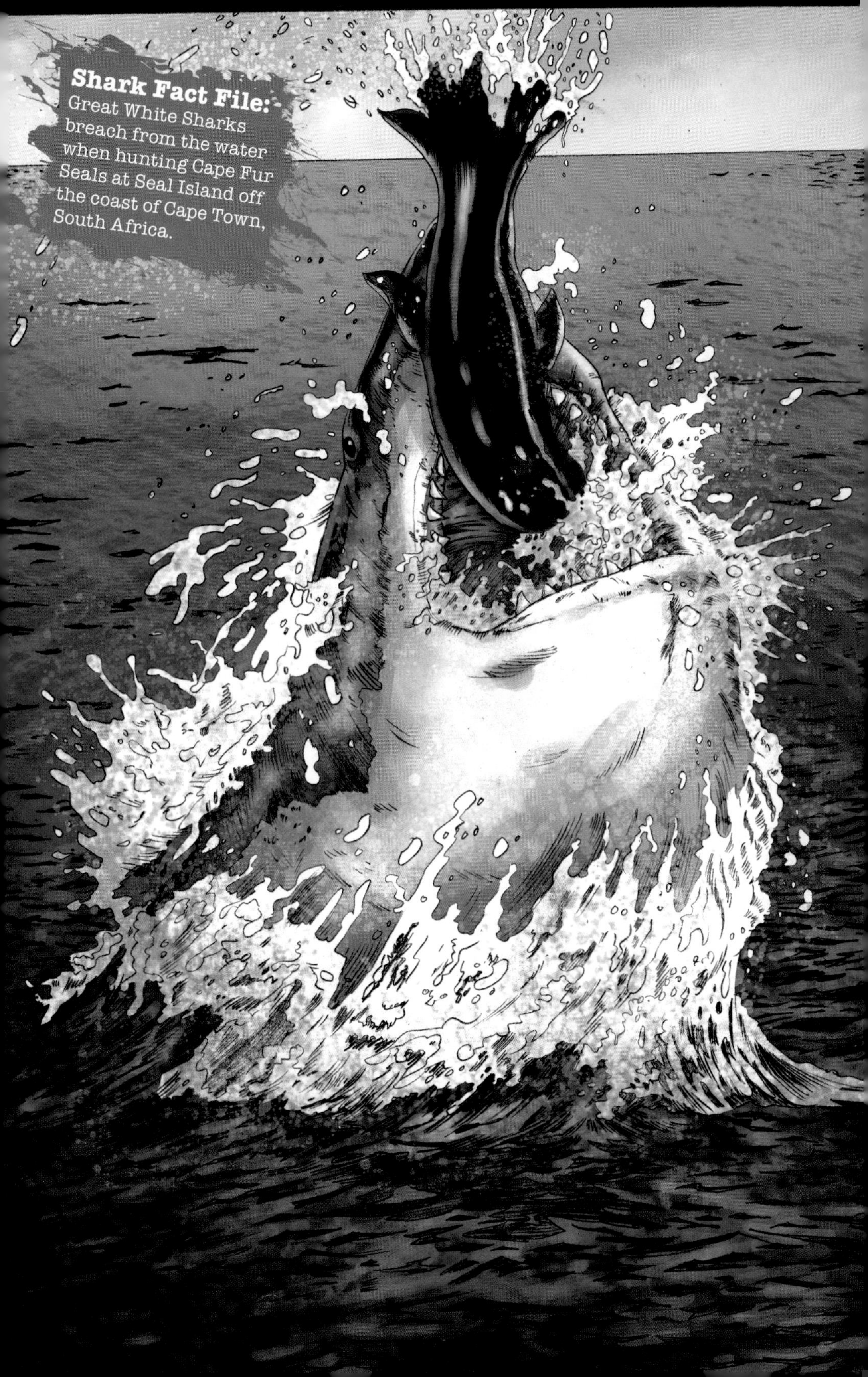
Shark Fact File:
Great White Sharks breach from the water when hunting Cape Fur Seals at Seal Island off the coast of Cape Town, South Africa.

#1 THE BULL SHARK

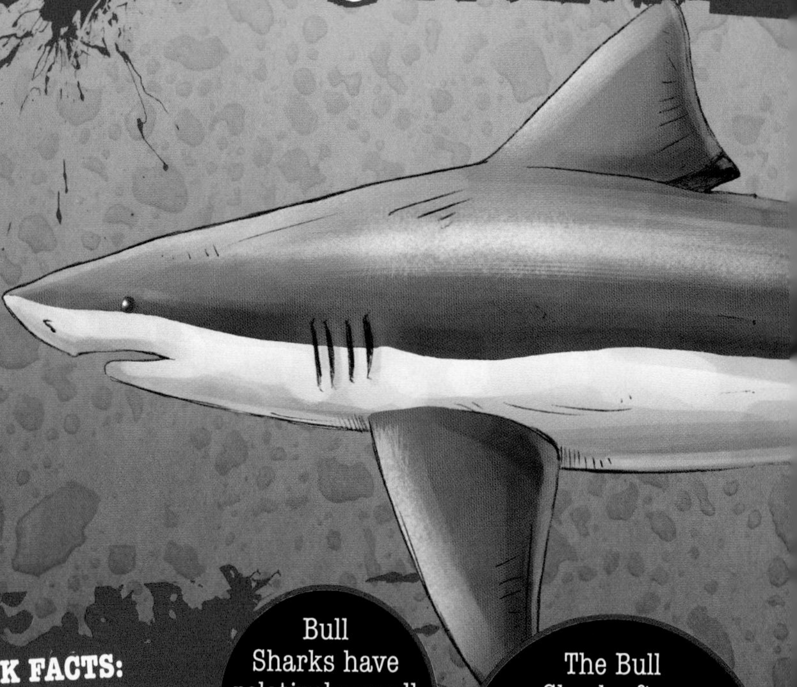

Bull Sharks have relatively small eyes compared to other shark species.

The Bull Shark often hunts in murky and turbid waters and their vision may not be as an important hunting tool as it is for other sharks.

BULL SHARK FACTS:

Average Size: 7.8 Feet

Largest Recorded: 11.5 feet

Habitat: Shallow coastal waters of warm oceans, in rivers and lakes, salt and freshwater streams if they are deep enough. They are the only shark capable of surviving in fresh water.

Preferred Prey: Bony fish, other sharks, dolphins, rays, turtles, seabirds, molluscs, echinoderms, and crustaceans.

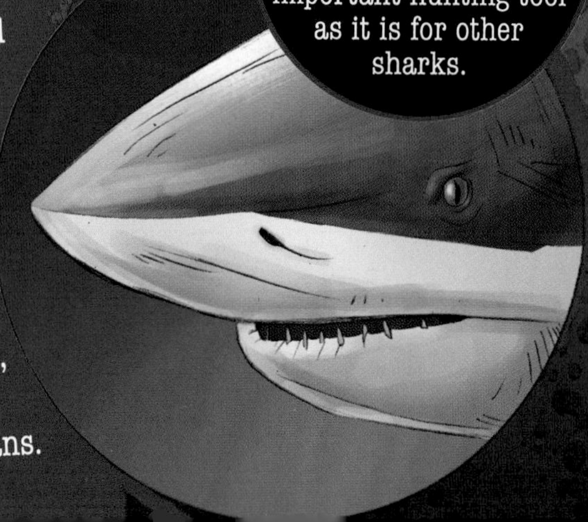

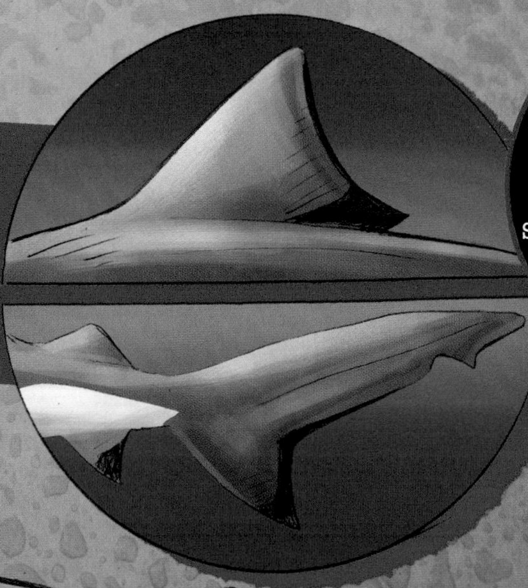

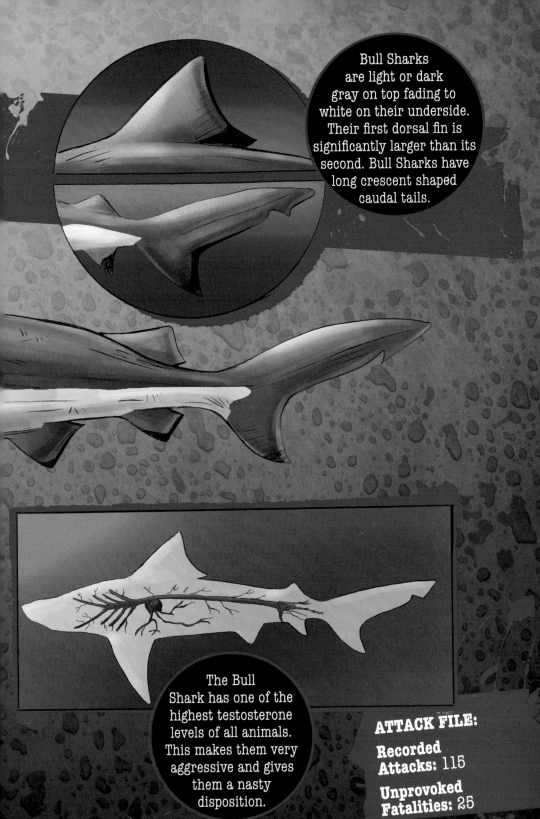

Bull Sharks are light or dark gray on top fading to white on their underside. Their first dorsal fin is significantly larger than its second. Bull Sharks have long crescent shaped caudal tails.

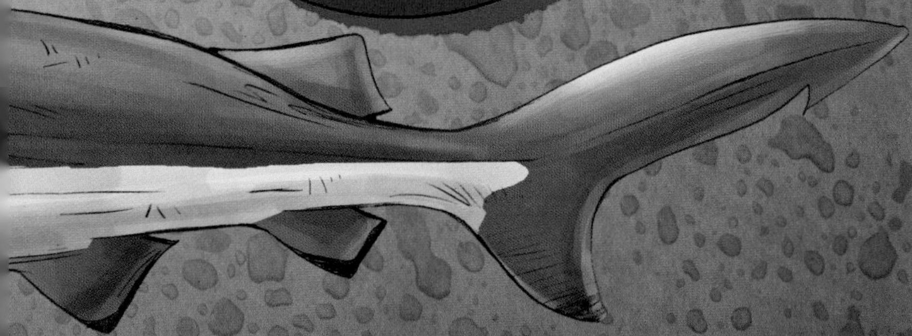

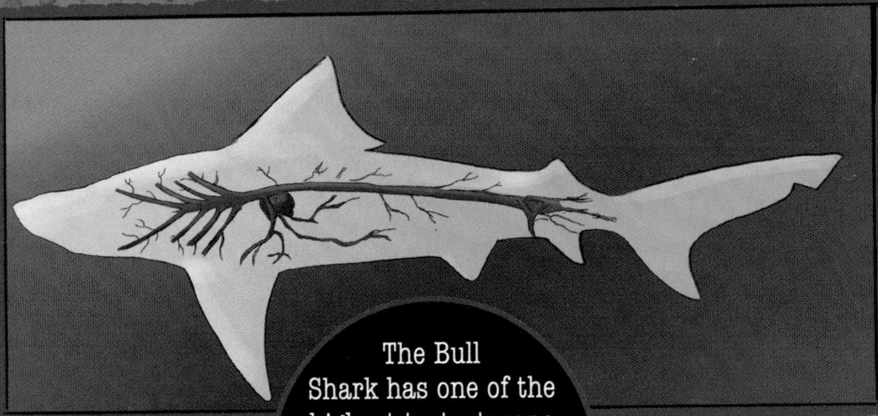

The Bull Shark has one of the highest testosterone levels of all animals. This makes them very aggressive and gives them a nasty disposition.

ATTACK FILE:

Recorded Attacks: 115

Unprovoked Fatalities: 25

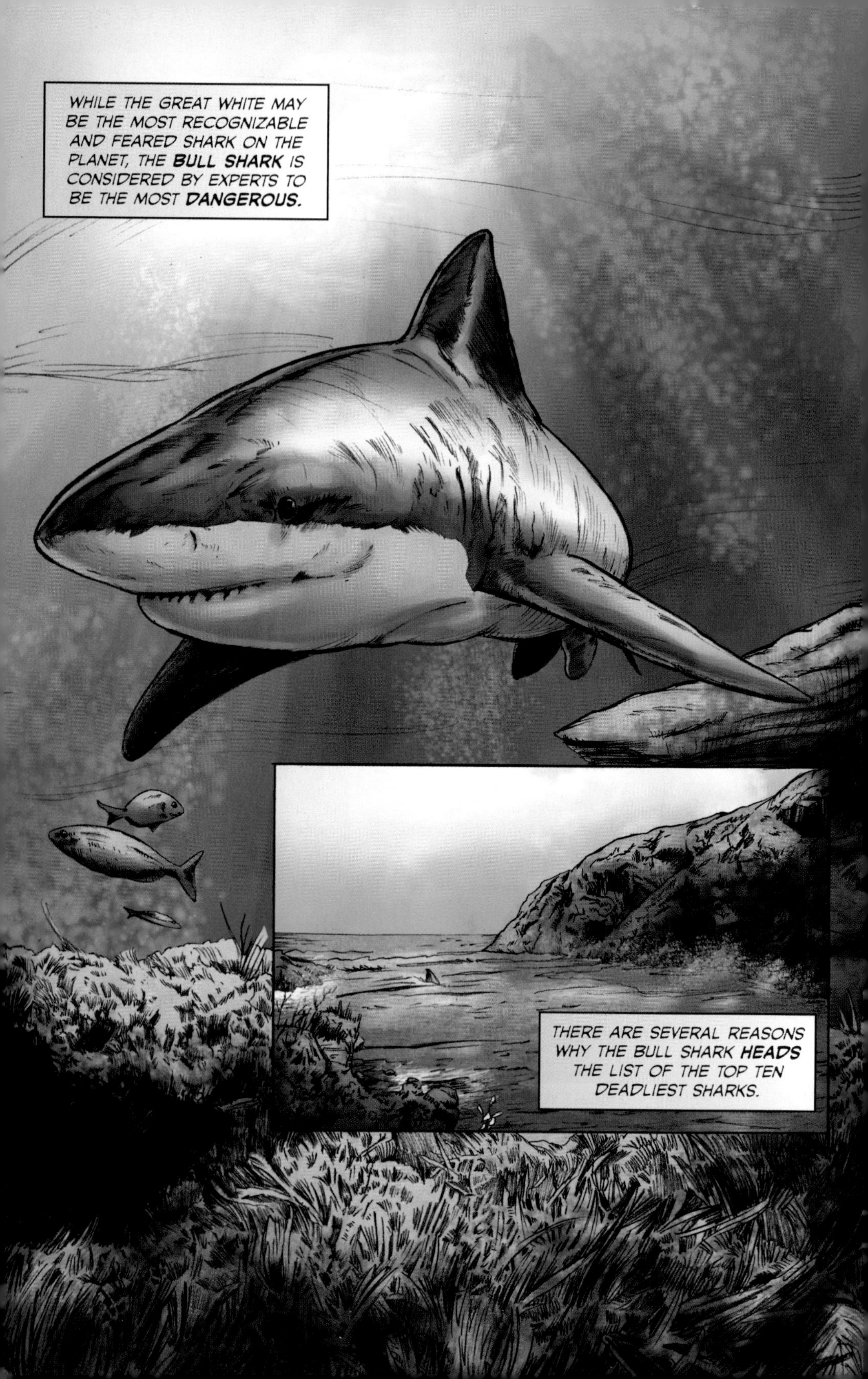
WHILE THE GREAT WHITE MAY BE THE MOST RECOGNIZABLE AND FEARED SHARK ON THE PLANET, THE **BULL SHARK** IS CONSIDERED BY EXPERTS TO BE THE MOST **DANGEROUS.**
THERE ARE SEVERAL REASONS WHY THE BULL SHARK **HEADS** THE LIST OF THE TOP TEN DEADLIEST SHARKS.

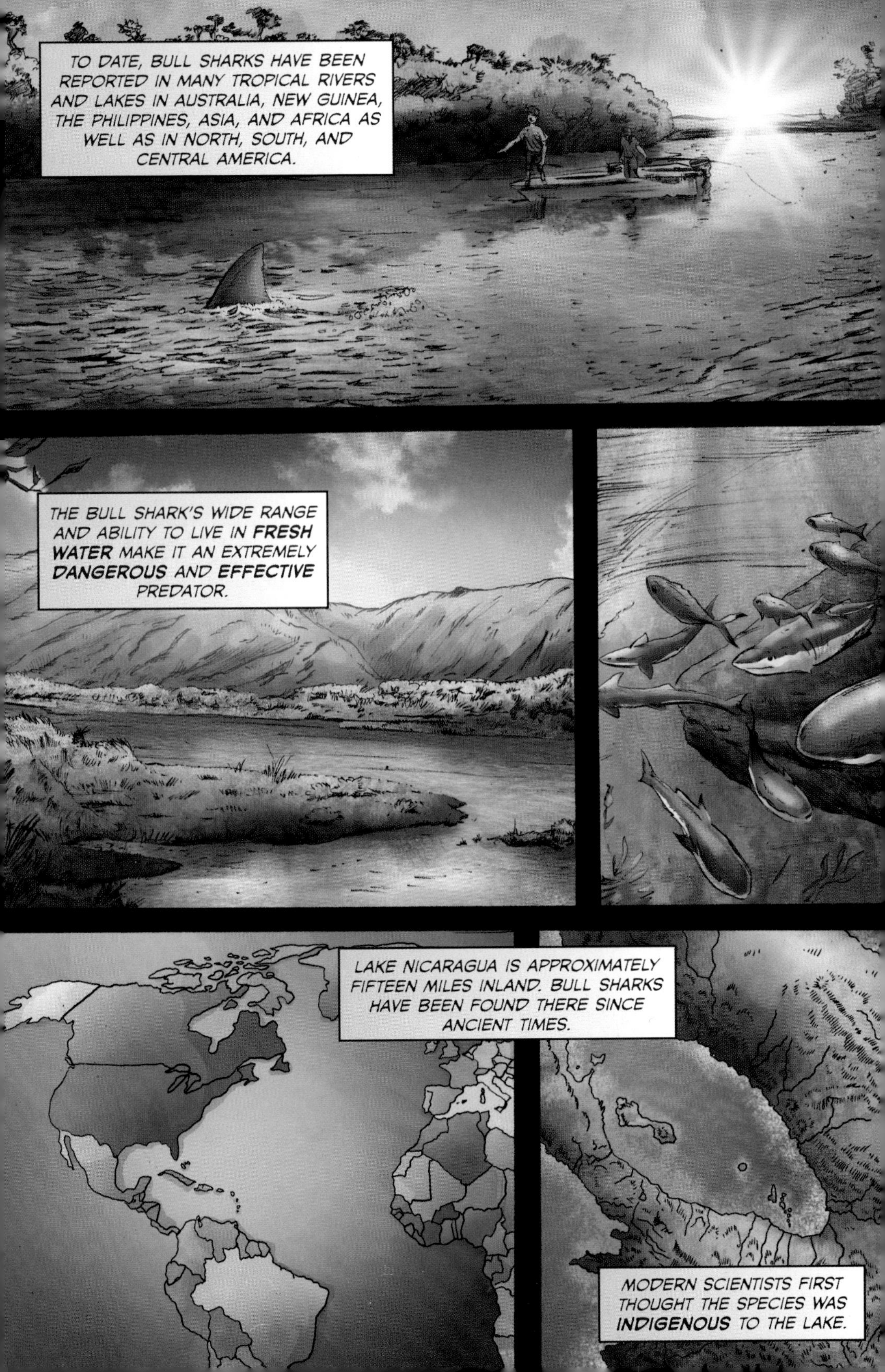
TO DATE, BULL SHARKS HAVE BEEN REPORTED IN MANY TROPICAL RIVERS AND LAKES IN AUSTRALIA, NEW GUINEA, THE PHILIPPINES, ASIA, AND AFRICA AS WELL AS IN NORTH, SOUTH, AND CENTRAL AMERICA.
THE BULL SHARK'S WIDE RANGE AND ABILITY TO LIVE IN **FRESH WATER** MAKE IT AN EXTREMELY **DANGEROUS** AND **EFFECTIVE** PREDATOR.
LAKE NICARAGUA IS APPROXIMATELY FIFTEEN MILES INLAND. BULL SHARKS HAVE BEEN FOUND THERE SINCE ANCIENT TIMES.
MODERN SCIENTISTS FIRST THOUGHT THE SPECIES WAS **INDIGENOUS** TO THE LAKE.

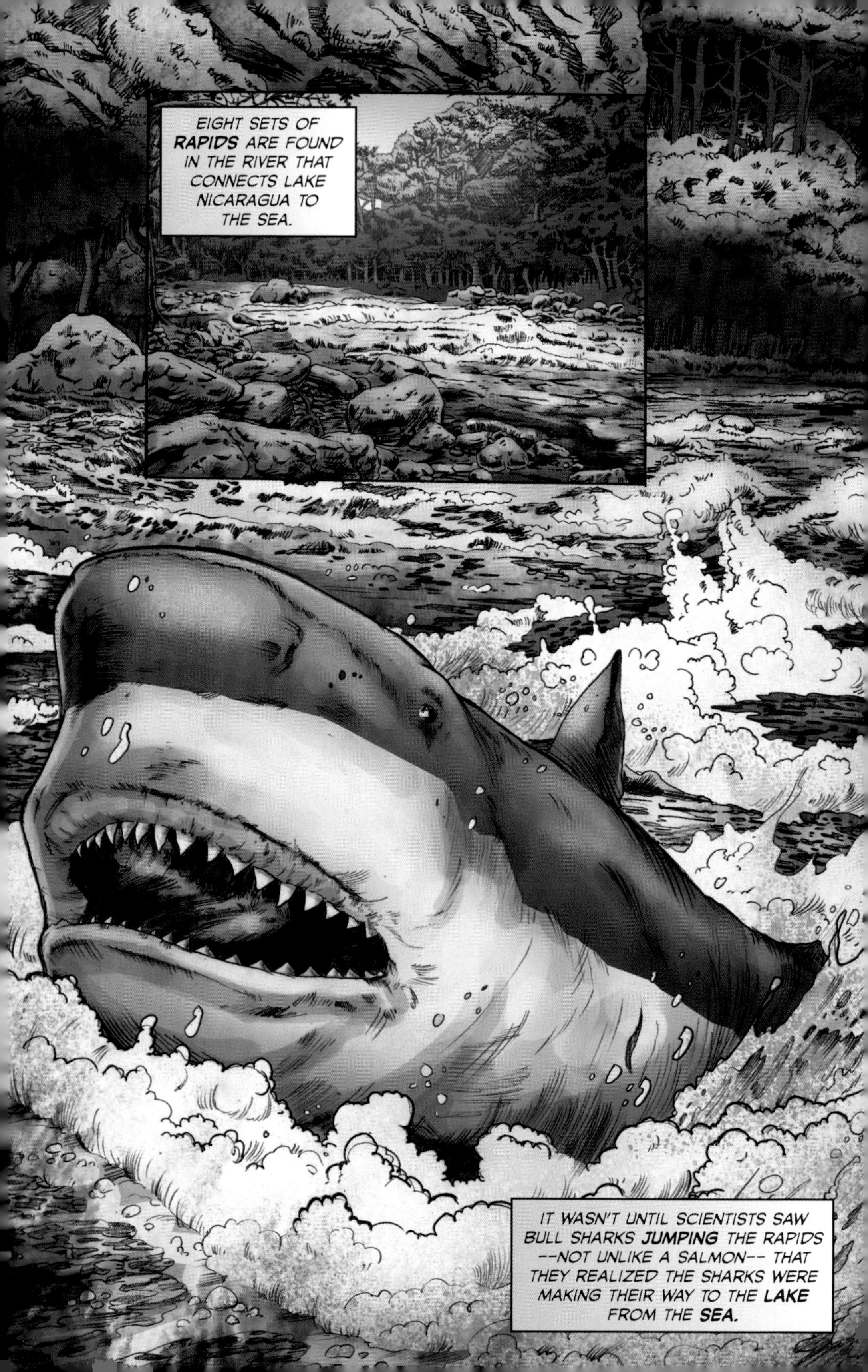
EIGHT SETS OF **RAPIDS** ARE FOUND IN THE RIVER THAT CONNECTS LAKE NICARAGUA TO THE SEA.
IT WASN'T UNTIL SCIENTISTS SAW BULL SHARKS **JUMPING** THE RAPIDS --NOT UNLIKE A SALMON-- THAT THEY REALIZED THE SHARKS WERE MAKING THEIR WAY TO THE **LAKE** FROM THE **SEA.**

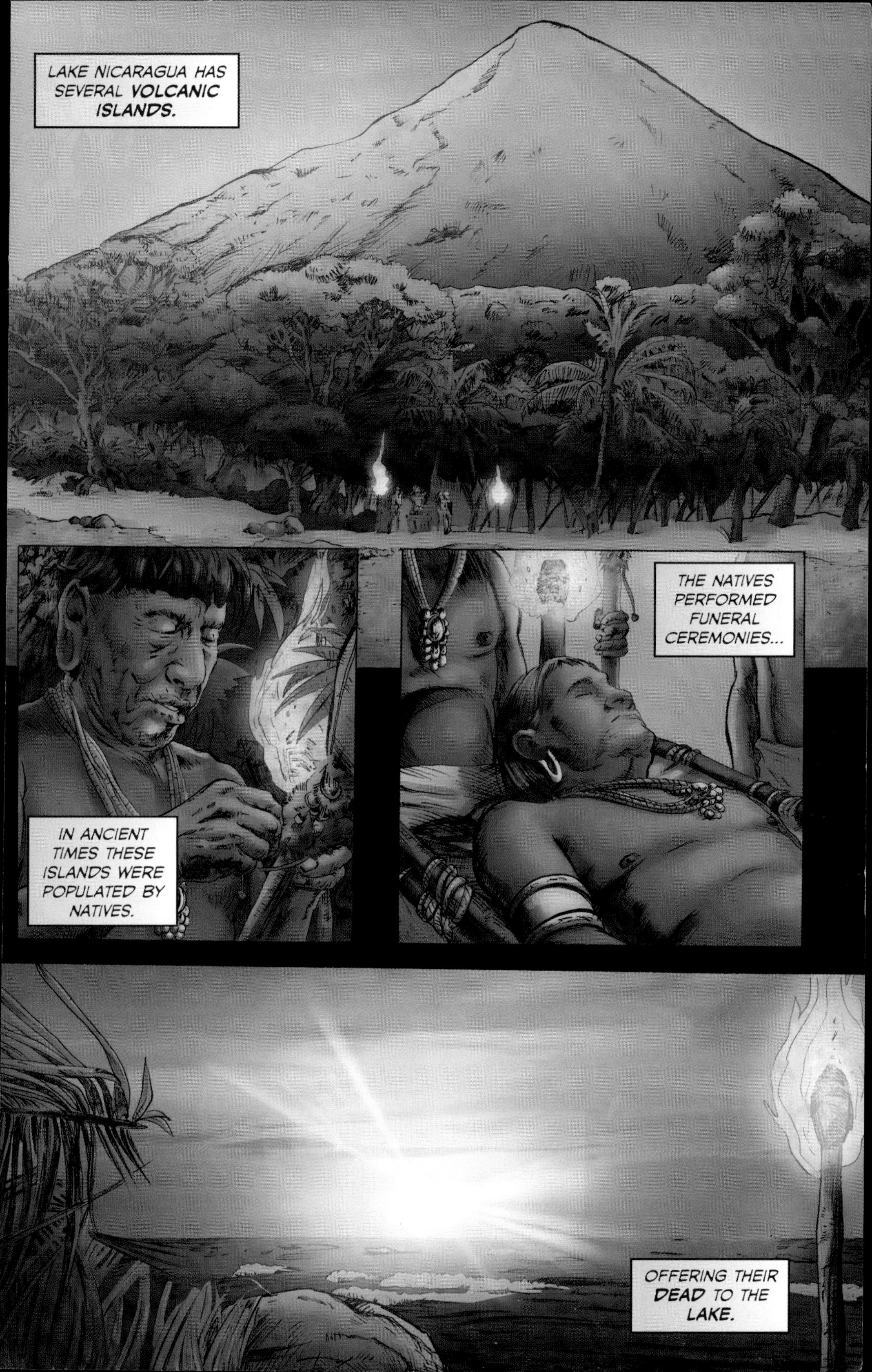
LAKE NICARAGUA HAS SEVERAL VOLCANIC ISLANDS.
IN ANCIENT TIMES THESE ISLANDS WERE POPULATED BY NATIVES.
THE NATIVES PERFORMED FUNERAL CEREMONIES...
OFFERING THEIR DEAD TO THE LAKE.

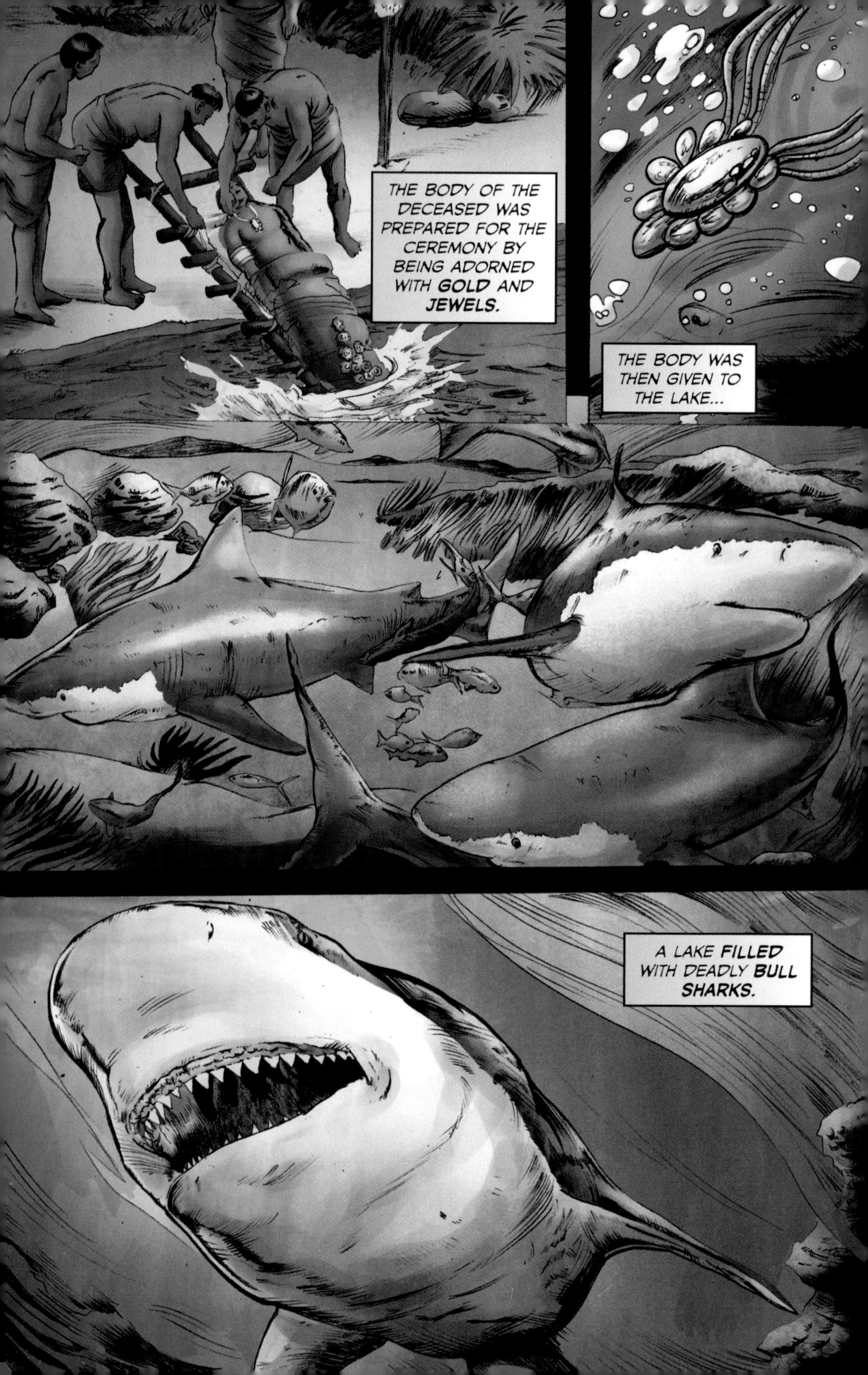
THE BODY OF THE DECEASED WAS PREPARED FOR THE CEREMONY BY BEING ADORNED WITH **GOLD** AND **JEWELS.**
THE BODY WAS THEN GIVEN TO THE LAKE...
A LAKE **FILLED** WITH DEADLY **BULL SHARKS.**

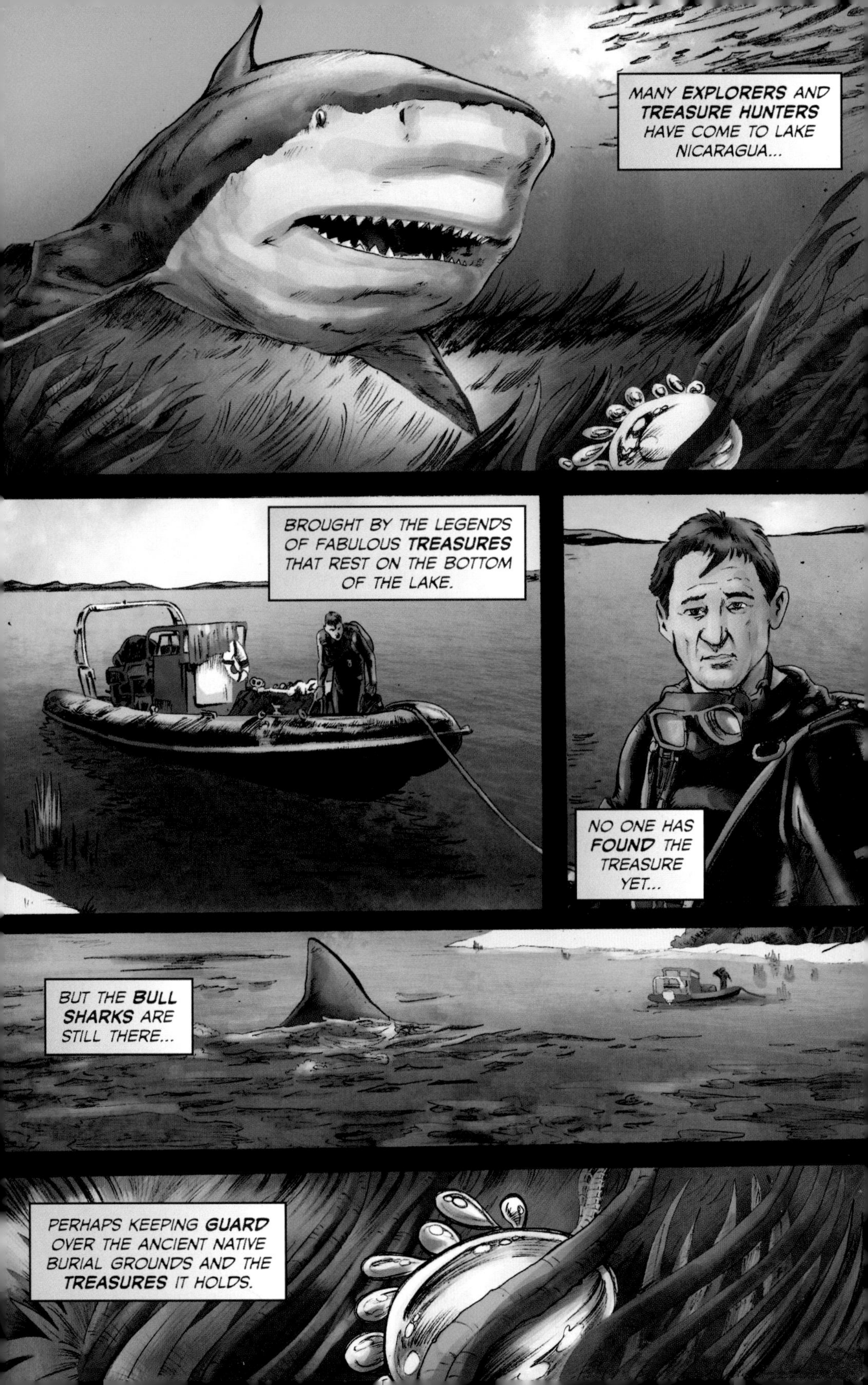
MANY EXPLORERS AND TREASURE HUNTERS HAVE COME TO LAKE NICARAGUA...
BROUGHT BY THE LEGENDS OF FABULOUS TREASURES THAT REST ON THE BOTTOM OF THE LAKE.
NO ONE HAS FOUND THE TREASURE YET...
BUT THE BULL SHARKS ARE STILL THERE...
PERHAPS KEEPING GUARD OVER THE ANCIENT NATIVE BURIAL GROUNDS AND THE TREASURES IT HOLDS.

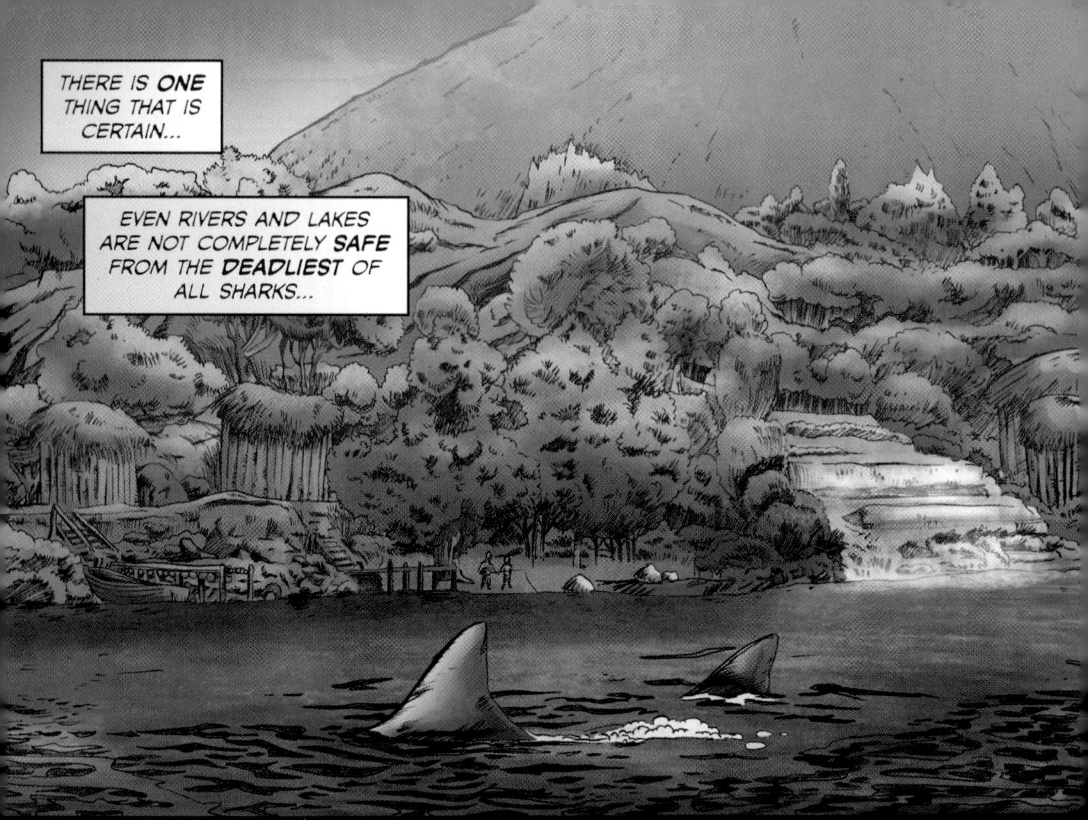
THERE IS **ONE** THING THAT IS CERTAIN...
EVEN RIVERS AND LAKES ARE NOT COMPLETELY **SAFE** FROM THE **DEADLIEST** OF ALL SHARKS...
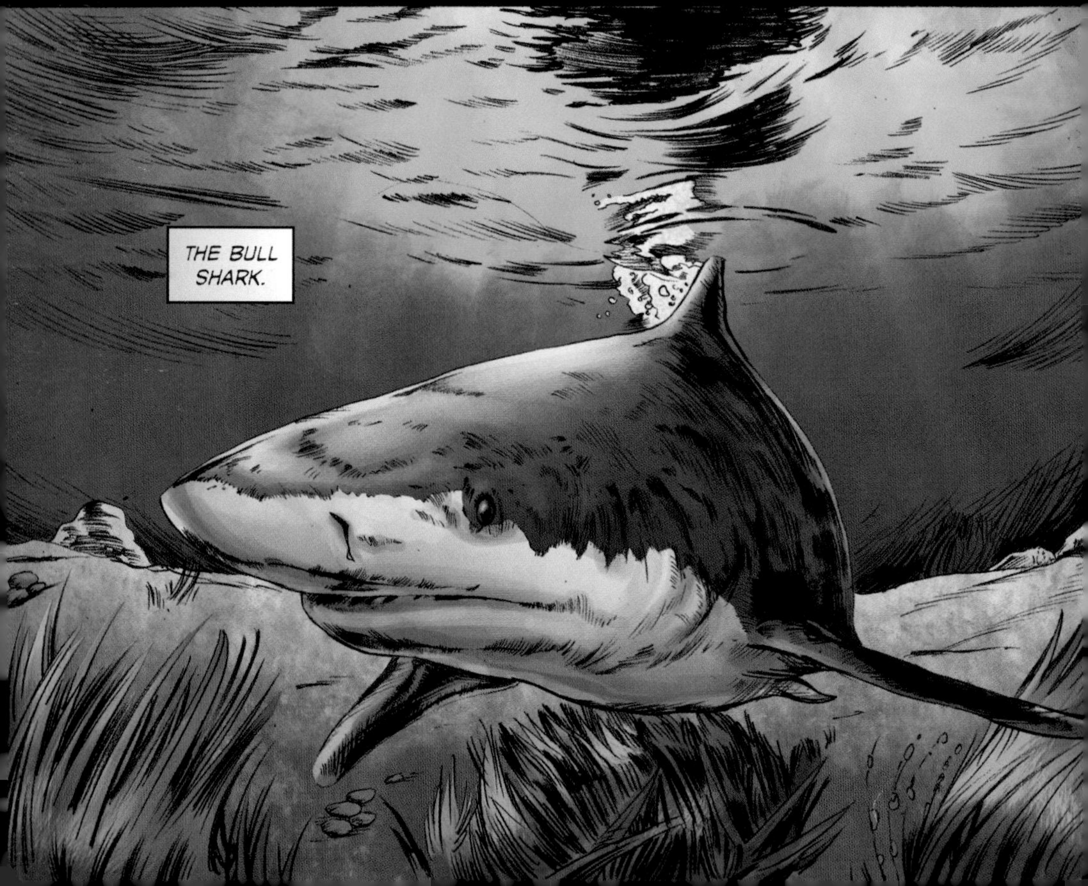
THE BULL SHARK.

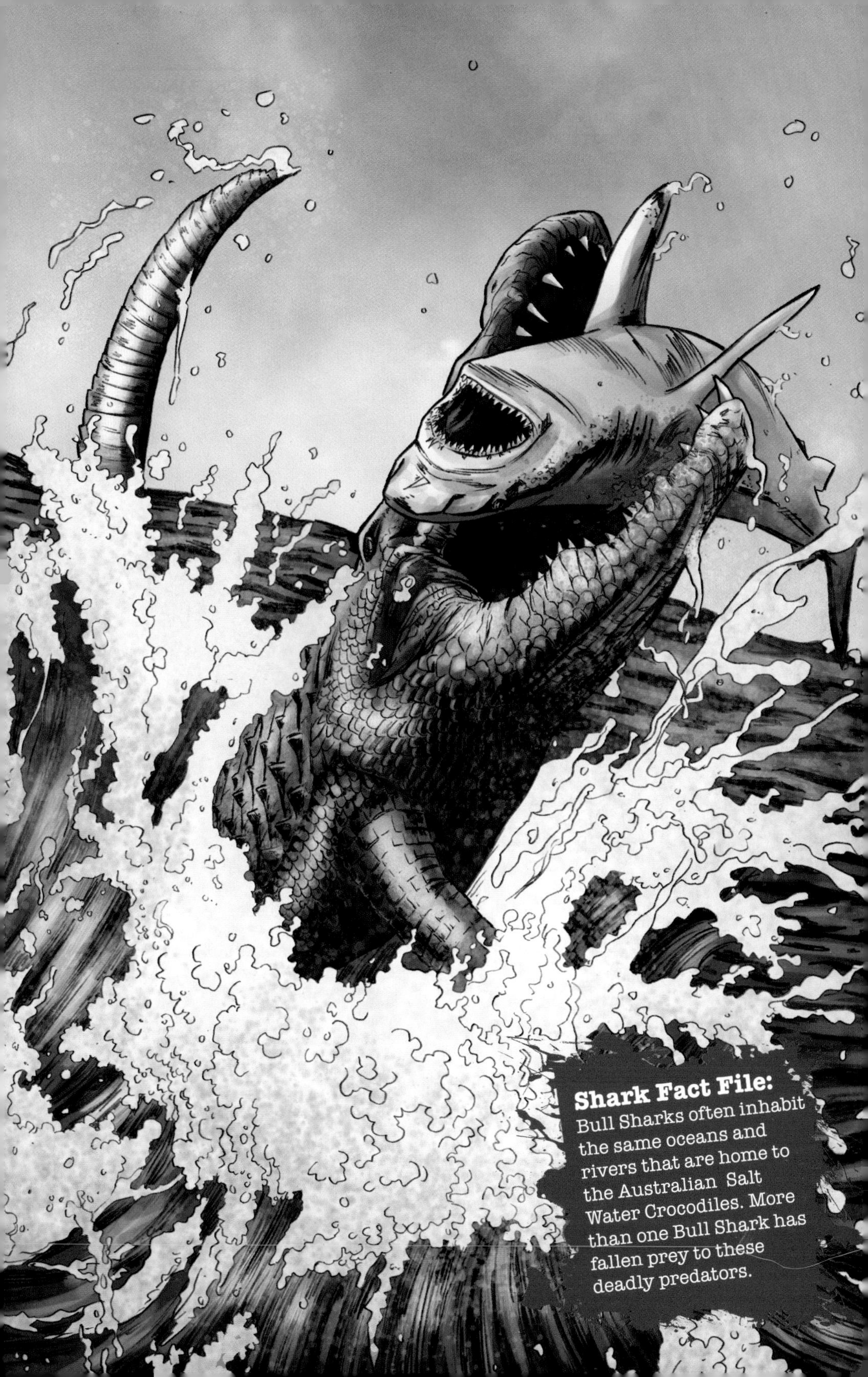
Shark Fact File:
Bull Sharks often inhabit the same oceans and rivers that are home to the Australian Salt Water Crocodiles. More than one Bull Shark has fallen prey to these deadly predators.

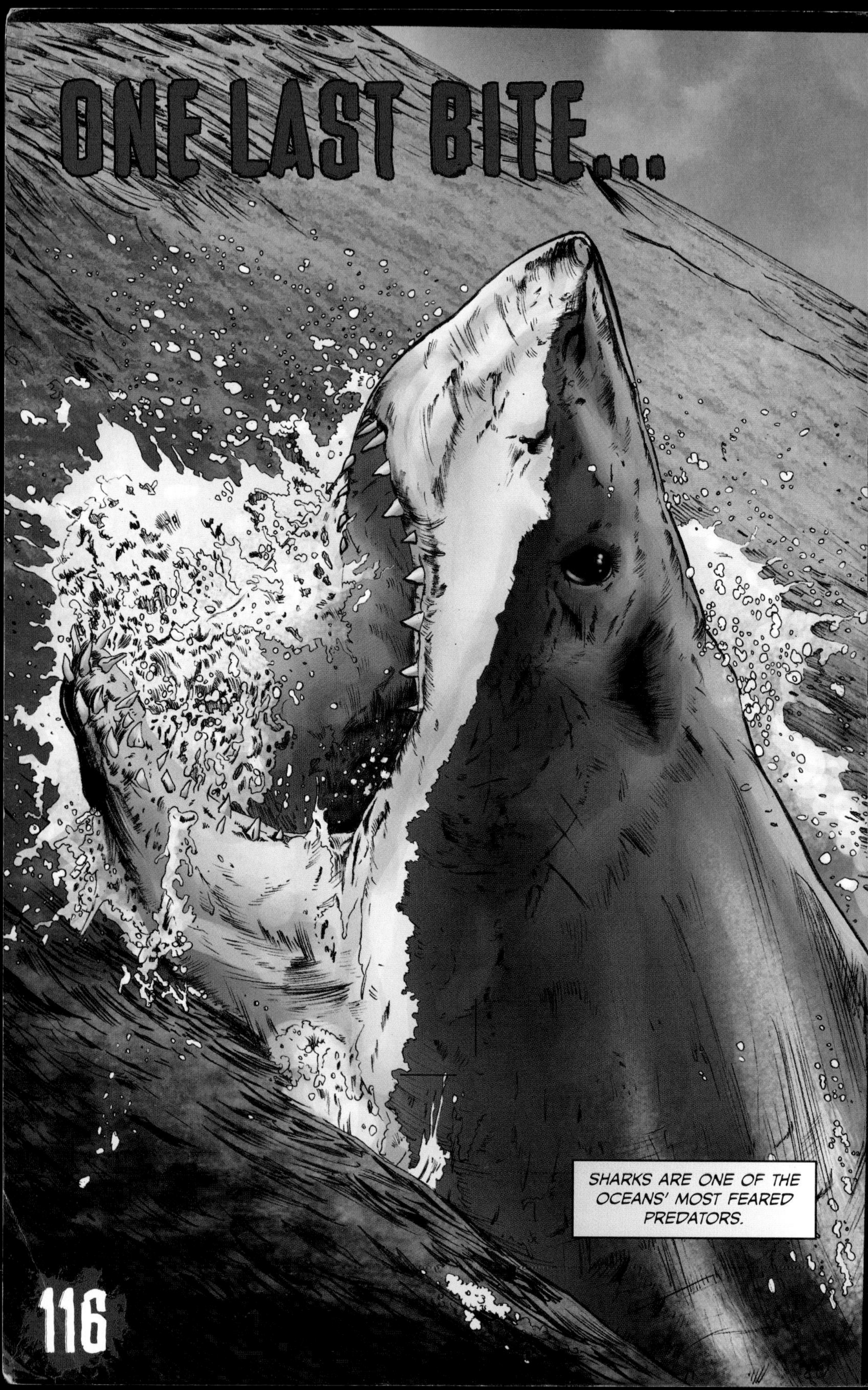
ONE LAST BITE...
SHARKS ARE ONE OF THE OCEANS' MOST FEARED PREDATORS.

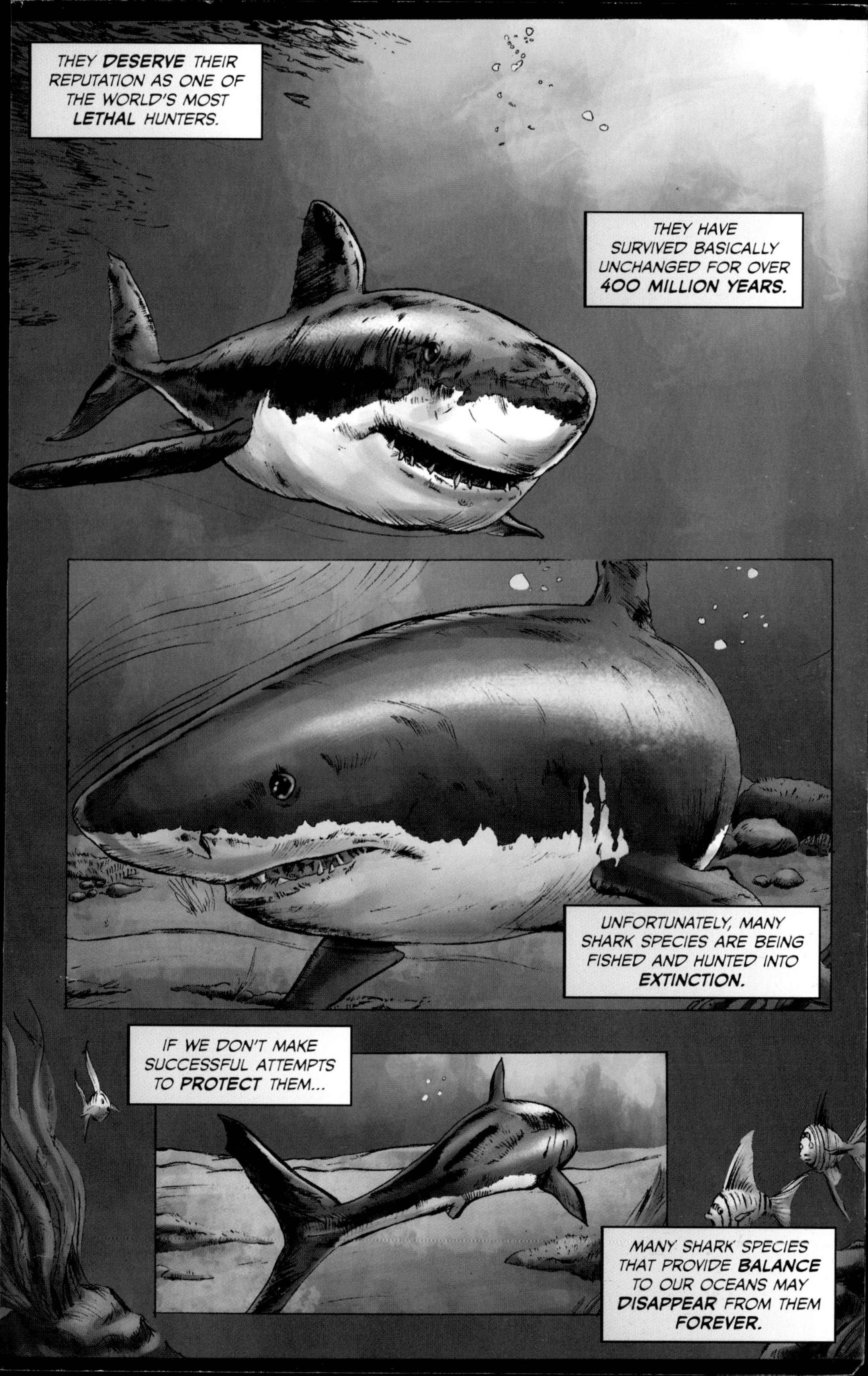
THEY DESERVE THEIR REPUTATION AS ONE OF THE WORLD'S MOST LETHAL HUNTERS.
THEY HAVE SURVIVED BASICALLY UNCHANGED FOR OVER 400 MILLION YEARS.
UNFORTUNATELY, MANY SHARK SPECIES ARE BEING FISHED AND HUNTED INTO EXTINCTION.
IF WE DON'T MAKE SUCCESSFUL ATTEMPTS TO PROTECT THEM...
MANY SHARK SPECIES THAT PROVIDE BALANCE TO OUR OCEANS MAY DISAPPEAR FROM THEM FOREVER.

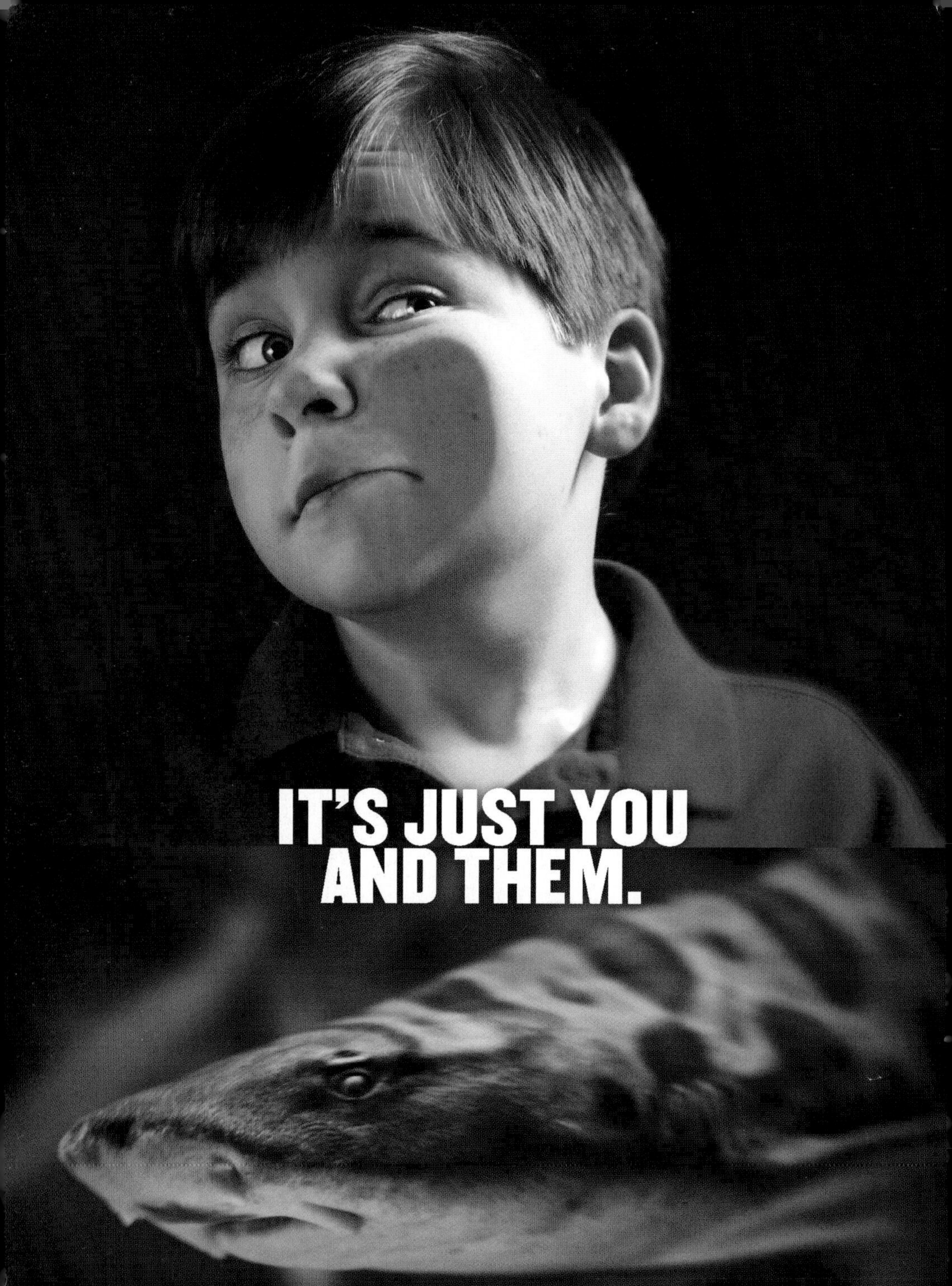
IT'S JUST YOU
AND THEM.

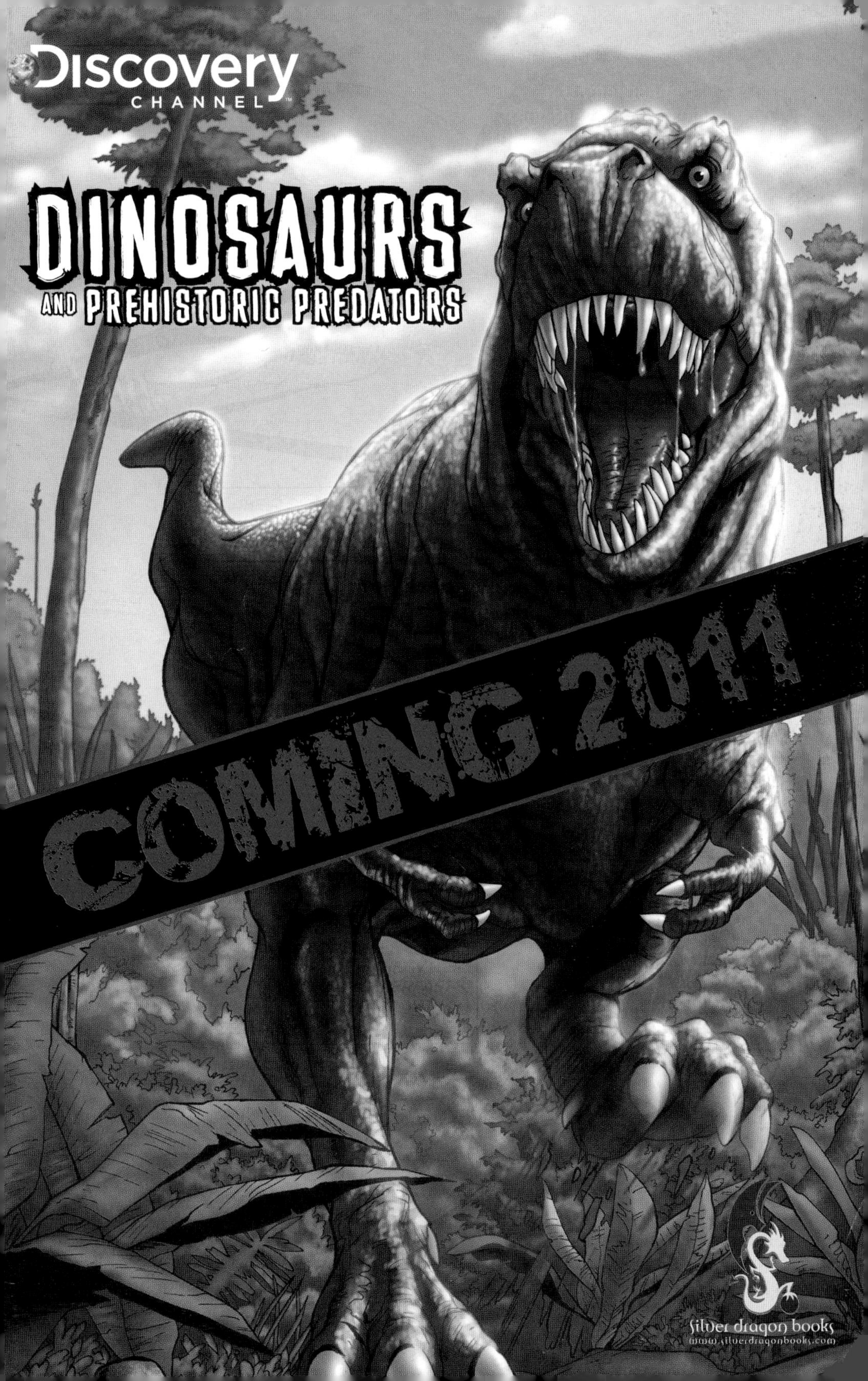
Discovery
CHANNEL
DINOSAURS
AND PREHISTORIC PREDATORS
COMING 2011
silver dragon books
www.silverdragonbooks.com

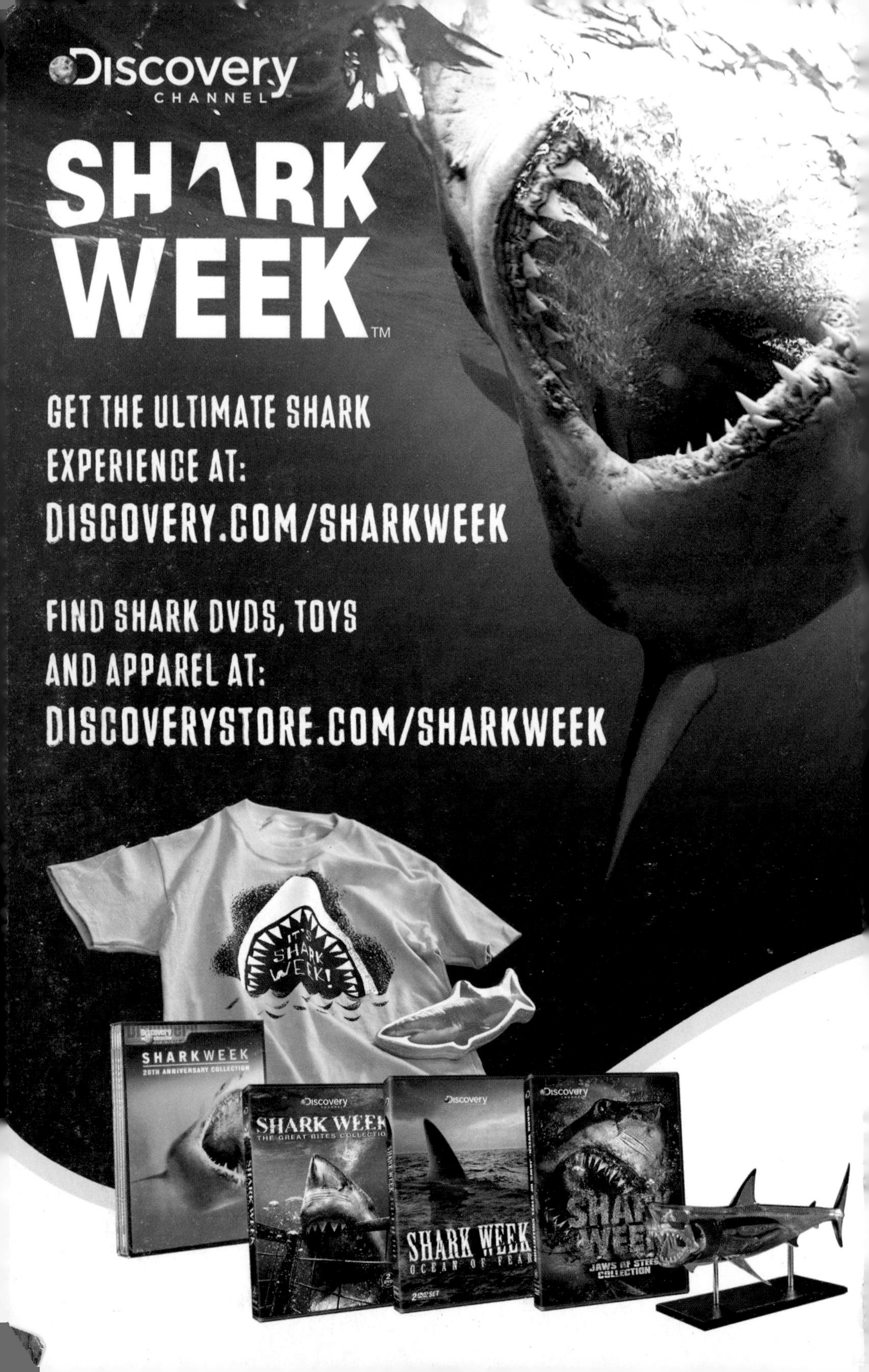

Discovery CHANNEL
SHARK WEEK
GET THE ULTIMATE SHARK EXPERIENCE AT:
DISCOVERY.COM/SHARKWEEK
FIND SHARK DVDS, TOYS AND APPAREL AT:
DISCOVERYSTORE.COM/SHARKWEEK
IT'S SHARK WEEK!
SHARKWEEK
20TH ANNIVERSARY COLLECTION
SHARK WEEK
THE GREAT BITES COLLECTION
SHARK WEEK
OCEAN OF FEAR
JAWS OF STEEL COLLECTION